ENGLAND'S GREATEST DEFENDER

ENGLAND'S GREATEST DEFENDER

THE UNTOLD STORY OF NEIL FRANKLIN

ALFIE POTTS HARMER

RedDoor

Published by RedDoor

www.reddoorpublishing.com

© 2019 Alfie Potts Harmer

The right of Alfie Potts Harmer to be identified as author of this
Work has been asserted by him in accordance with sections 77 and 78
of the Copyright, Designs and Patents Act 1988

ISBN 978-1-910453-79-7

A CIP catalogue record for this book is available from the British Library

Cover design: Rawshock Design

Typesetting: Westchester Publishing Services

Printed and bound in BZGraf S.A.

In loving memory of Charles Owen Potts

CONTENTS

PROLOGUE

Neil Who?

'The best defender I ever played with or against—yes, that good.'
Sir Tom Finney

In preparation for the 1970 World Cup finals in Mexico, reigning champions England flew out to South America two weeks before the tournament was scheduled to begin. Sir Alf Ramsey and his charges had made the early arrival to play two warm-up fixtures on the continent against Colombia and Ecuador in the hope of acclimatising to the high-altitude levels they would be met with in Guadalajara, the location of England's opening three games.

England were not alone in making such preparations. The Soviet national team made an early arrival to face Ecuadorian club side Liga Deportiva Universitaria, Sweden had played twice in Mexico during February and March, Bulgaria had played a couple of games in Peru, and even the South Americans of Brazil headed to Guanajuato in Mexico for their intense pre-tournament training, where the altitude is almost identical to that of Mexico City.

After an arduous journey, which involved a delay due to a blocked runway at El Dorado International Airport, the England team arrived at the Tequendama Hotel at around 6 p.m. Opened in 1953, the Tequendama is so typical of Bogotá—a lavish display of wealth and opulence plonked in the centre of extreme poverty and desperation. There seem to be only two classes of people in the Colombian capital, the super-rich and the utterly impoverished. It is a contrast which is impossible to ignore, and the England team were no exception. Upon their arrival, the England party was informed that there was a telegram waiting for them from back home, sent by a 46-year-old licensee who ran a pub in Lancashire. It was a good-luck message, assuring the players that they would have no problems with the altitude and wishing them all the best in the upcoming finals.

The man who sent the telegram was writing from experience. He had played his first game in South America after just five days in the city of Bogotá, and encountered no problems on the pitch. He also ought to have had experience playing for his country in a World Cup in South America, England's first in fact, but of his own volition in 1950 turned down the opportunity to do so as a sure-starter.

The man in question was Neil Franklin, quite probably England's greatest ever defender. Not just in terms of his ability—which was indeed exceptional—but also in terms of his style of play and the impression he left upon those who witnessed his talents. Franklin was, in many respects, the complete centre-half. Throughout much of his career, he was regarded as an oddity within the English game. A ball-playing centre-half during an era of stoppers who preferred to take a safety-first approach to the beautiful game.

Although he only stood at around 5 foot 10½ inches, markedly short for a centre-half in both the mid–early twentieth century and in the modern game, he was equally as proficient in the air as he was with his feet. The great Stanley Matthews described Franklin as being 'as dominant in the air as a Spitfire', before noting that whilst others would leave the pitch covered in mud, there would only be splashes on Neil, and the only real sign he'd been in a game of football at all would be the circle of mud hammered to his forehead.

When talking to some of the surviving players who played and trained with Neil Franklin, those last comments would come up time and time again. Last-ditch slide tackles which would often result in a mud bath at the time were not a common theme of Franklin's game, quite simply because they were rarely required. His ability to be in the 'right place at the right time', so to speak, was second to none; and as a consequence, he often made defending look effortlessly easy. These are comments we would later hear about the likes of Franco Baresi—but here was a boy from the Potteries earning the same plaudits half a century earlier.

The way Neil played the game was alien to some. Even whilst the national press printed page after page heaping praise upon him, he would still face criticism for his approach to the game from those around him, most notably from the uncompromising Glaswegian Bob McGrory, who managed Stoke City for some seventeen years. This criticism and the consequent feeling of being unappreciated at Stoke City was one of the key reasons for Franklin's ultimate departure from the Victoria Ground.

Much was made of Neil Franklin's departure from Stoke City for the Bogotá club of Independiente Santa Fe. When it happened, in May 1950, it sent shockwaves through the British game. Here was the nation's finest defender, a bonafide star of the country's national game, departing for the rogue (in a footballing sense at least) nation of Colombia. Neil was by no means the only British player to leave for Colombia: from England's First Division alone, he was joined by Stoke City teammate George Mountford, Manchester United star Charlie Mitten, and Billy Higgins of Everton. Mitten was an FA Cup winner and Mountford a very capable club winger, but neither garnered the same kind of press attention as Franklin, and understandably so.

The story was that Neil had suddenly upped sticks and vanished without a trace. He was labelled a mercenary and many other damning descriptions. The group of players themselves were often described as the 'Bogotá Bandits', as outlaws of the English game who had deserted their club and country in favour of the 'lawless' land of Colombia. Of course, the story told and the truth is not always the same thing. Neil's move to Colombia had not been sudden, or not in his head at least. It was a major decision and not one he took lightly.

It is a great shame that so few modern football fans have heard of Neil Franklin, and of those that have, the majority know about him solely because of the so-called 'Bogotá affair'. This ought not to be the case, and I hope to go some way towards rectifying that in this book.

Having said that, his ill-fated move to Colombia was a crucial, albeit brief, event in Neil's life. Tom Finney believed Neil was 'never quite the same' after the move, and certainly, his footballing career was irrevocably damaged by the whole episode. Yet, even upon his return, Neil's life was one full of colour. Reflecting on his playing career when it was drawing to a close, Neil said, 'It might be a subject for discussion as to whether my career has been successful or not, but whatever your conclusions on that score, you cannot deny that my career has been eventful.' Having spent hours upon hours charting the career of Neil Franklin, his ups and downs, from honours to tragedies, talking to those who knew him and even played with him . . . I can concur, one thing you could never level at Neil Franklin was that his career was dull.

Had his career not been blighted by his misbegotten move to Colombia, it is almost universally acknowledged that it would have been Franklin, not Billy Wright, who would have become the first England player to reach 100 caps, a sentiment later expressed by Wright himself. When Neil played his last-ever game for England against Scotland at Hampden Park, he had won a total of 27 caps, all of which were consecutive appearances, a record at the time, also eventually surpassed by Wright. If one also accounts for wartime internationals, Franklin made 39 consecutive full international appearances without once being dropped.

NEIL WHO?

Stanley Matthews, Tom Finney and Raich Carter, arguably the three finest English players of their era, all regarded Neil Franklin as the greatest defender they ever played with or against. There can be no higher praise of an English footballer in the 1940s and 50s.

The consensus may have been that Neil was shunned and disgraced following his return to England in 1950, and there is some truth to that, but he still managed to become the most expensive defender in world football when he joined Hull City in 1951. It speaks volumes that at the age of twenty-nine, following controversy and suspension, more than six months out of the game and being snubbed by all First Division sides, Neil Franklin—a centre-half, not a centre-forward, one ought not forget—came close to setting a world record transfer fee.

This, then, is the story of a rare talent. An untold story of England's greatest-ever defender, Neil Franklin.

CHAPTER 1

A Star is Born in Shelton

When Cornelius Franklin was born in Shelton, Staffordshire, the family he arrived in was already a large one, with one daughter and five sons. One more son soon joined the scene, so there were eight children all told, of which Neil was the second youngest. The family was somewhat split in two—the Franklins and the Plants. Neil's mother had all eight children, three with Neil's father and five with Mr Plant. On the Franklin side there was Neil, Reg and Harry, with Margaret, Cyril, Jack, Bill and Len on the Plant side.

Whilst it is true that a future star was born in Shelton on 24 January 1922, there were few indications of that upon Neil's birth. There was no footballing lineage in the Franklin family, nor was there a sporting one. Many footballers talk of being born with a football at their feet, but for Neil, whose father worked in the local gasworks, this wasn't the case. Even as a youngster, Neil Franklin played no more football and showed no greater enthusiasm for the game than your average schoolboy growing up in England at that time.

What's more, when Neil did play, whether that was with his friends in the local fields or at school in his early years, his ability drew little note. He himself conceded that at a young age, there was nothing extraordinary about his talents. This may come as a surprise to some. For those like Neil, a profoundly technical player, it is often felt that much of their ability is natural, but that was not so in this case at least.

A STAR IS BORN IN SHELTON

Neil Franklin's progress was largely down to hard work and graft, and as such, it was a very steady one. Whilst he would go on to be a rather short centre-half, as a schoolboy, Neil played as an inside-forward. As an early developer, Neil was very well built for his age. This is a huge plus in schoolboy football, even more so in the twentieth century, and although Neil never wanted to rely on his strength or physique, always striving to improve his technique and understanding of the game, it undoubtedly helped him at this stage of his life.

As the years passed by, Neil's game improved, and he began to set himself apart from the other boys. He first broke into his school team—Cannon Street School, in Hanley, and quickly found himself captaining the side.

A selection for the local Hanley Boys team followed, and having earned his stripes for Hanley in the inter-town competitions, it wasn't long until Neil was chosen for the Stoke Boys team. The Stoke Boys team was made up of the best young players from Stoke, Longton and Hanley, and they played annual games against Glasgow and Bradford. Following the trinity of school, local and regional team selection, Neil was asked to play in a schoolboys' international trial. It was the natural progression of a youngster who was now starting to become an increasingly assured schoolboy player, but it was here that Neil's progress would hit its first hurdle.

The fifteen-year-old was selected to play for a Midland team that faced the North at York. The youngster had played much of his recent football at centre-forward, but was told to play inside-right that day. Neil put in a solid if not spectacular performance, and could leave the field with his head held high, but he wasn't at all surprised to find out he had missed out on international schoolboy honours to the North's inside-right. His opposite number was the best player on the pitch, mesmerising the Midland team's defence, beating players at will and playing with an intelligence far beyond his years. Standing at just 4 foot 11, he was the smallest player on either side, but he was a wonderful technician, and went by the name of Leonard Shackleton.

Shack, as he was often known, went on to become one of the stars of the day. A footballing maverick nicknamed 'The Clown Prince of Soccer', he scored two goals from three caps for England Schoolboys, before becoming a full England international after the war. The Bradford-born forward scored a double hat-trick on his Newcastle United debut, going on to average a goal every other game for the Magpies, before setting a British record transfer fee when switching the black and white of Newcastle for the red and white of their North-East rivals Sunderland, where he spent the majority of his career.

Missing out on a schoolboy cap obviously came as a disappointment to Neil, but it may not have hit him as hard as it did others. The youngster who had considered himself no better than many of his peers just a few years earlier was now supremely confident in his own abilities. According to Neil, he had a feeling at the age of fifteen or sixteen that one day he would be pulling on the white of England and representing his country at full international level. By this point, he was being talked about as one of the finest, if not the finest, young player in the Potteries, and he could feel his game progressing nicely.

The progression of Neil's game is owed in no small part to the games master at Cannon Street School—Arthur Tams. Mr Tams, as he was known to Neil, showed great interest in the young player, and devoted much time to improving his game. The now defunct Cannon Street School in Hanley was one with a fine footballing reputation locally, and Arthur Tams coached both the school team and the Hanley Boys team that Neil represented. Neil described the extra training he did with Arthur as being hard and often rather tedious work, but whilst other schoolboy stars felt they knew it all in their mid-teens, Neil was happy to go over the basics time and time again, something he credited as hugely important in making the step up from schoolboy football to the professional game.

CHAPTER 2

From Setback to Success

More than just aiding Neil's abilities as a player, it was coach Arthur Tams who pointed the youngster in the direction of Stoke City once he left school. Arthur recommended that Neil should approach the club about getting a job on the ground staff at the Victoria Ground, the common route for a young player looking to make the grade in the 1930s. The ground-staff route into the game gave youngsters the opportunity to get in among the day-to-day running of a football club, see their local heroes at first hand and get a real thirst for the game.

Widely regarded as the best schoolboy footballer in the Potteries at this time, Neil felt confident Stoke would be all too happy to offer him a position, but was shocked when manager Bob McGrory informed him that Stoke City had already reached their maximum number of ground staff, and therefore couldn't offer him a position. It was the youngster's first exposure to the harshness of the game, but he took comfort in the fact that Stoke had turned him down as a ground staff worker, not as a player. The club were all too happy to offer him a deal as a player. There were, in those days, two options for a young player with aspirations of turning professional. Joining the club's ground staff, or signing amateur terms and finding work elsewhere to provide a regular income. Having had the first door shut on him, Neil quickly turned to the second, and it was Arthur Tams who helped him on this path once more.

Arthur was convinced that Neil was a future star of the game, and was determined to find work for him so he could continue to pursue a career within football. He approached Mr David Duddell, owner of 'D Duddell Ltd', a brickworks in Fenton, one and a half miles east of the Victoria Ground. Mr Duddell himself was a passionate Stoke City fan and a director at the club. This passion was in the blood, and his son would go on to serve as Stoke City chairman from 1953 to 1955, just a few years after Neil left the club. The Duddells' love of football meant Neil never really felt like he missed out on the footballing environment that being a ground staff worker would have presented. He loved working for Mr Duddell, and ultimately had no regrets about his earlier rejection at Stoke City. But as much as Franklin enjoyed working at the brickworks, he still craved training and playing football above all else.

During this time, from the age of fourteen up until his seventeenth birthday, Neil would train twice a week, every Tuesday and Thursday evening, playing a game every Saturday and sometimes an additional game midweek. Those training sessions were under the direction of Stoke City coaches Harry Cooper and Stan Clough, and Franklin enjoyed them immensely.

When it came to the weekend, Franklin would turn out for Stoke's third team, and—very occasionally, the club's reserve team. The third team played their games against other Football League third strings in the Midlands. At this point, it is worth talking a little bit about the Stoke City team of the late 1930s, and particularly their youth development.

The third team in which Neil Franklin played his football as a teenager was an exceptional one. During the immediate pre-war period, there was no finer youth team in the country than the one at the Victoria Ground. Alongside Neil were players such as Dennis Herod, John McCue, Frank Mountford, John Sellars and Frank Bowyer. Between them, those five would go on to make 1,866 league appearances for Stoke City. Then there were the likes of Bert Mitchell, Roy Brown and Bill Caton, all three of whom went on to have successful careers within the Football League away from Stoke.

Probably the least well known of those, Bill Caton, was captured and imprisoned by the Nazis in Italy during World War II, but managed to escape by hiding aboard a vehicle exiting the camp he was held in. Two years younger than Neil, Caton made only twenty-two league appearances for Stoke, later turning out for Carlisle and Crewe, but was remarkable for his long-throw, a tactic the Potters would become so synonymous with following Rory Delap's arrival at the club in 2007. Perhaps if Stoke had more Ryan Shawcrosses and Mamady Sidibes in those post-war years, Caton might have racked up a few more appearances.

In addition to the wealth of talent in Stoke's third team, former youth graduates such as Stanley Matthews and Freddie Steele were the stars of the Potters first team at this time. Simply put, Stoke City had the best youth recruitment in England at this time. It was often joked in the Potteries that if manager Bob McGrory saw a promising looking toddler or newborn, he would get an option to buy him there and then. The fierce competition at Stoke was both good and bad for Neil Franklin. It meant breaking into the first or reserve team was not going to come easily, but he also knew that should he work hard and progress well, this was a club all too happy to give their youngsters a chance.

In 1938, aged sixteen, Franklin made his reserve team debut for Stoke against Bury in the highly competitive Central League. Whilst it is not uncommon in the modern game for a very talented sixteen-year-old to break into a club's first team, in the late 1930s, a player under the age of eighteen was doing well to find themselves in the reserves. Reserve team football was not looked upon in the same way it is today. In the pre-substitution era, a first-team regular or even an international dropping down into the reserves was not unusual.

Even once Franklin had become a full England international,

he had no qualms about playing reserve team football had he been out of the team and his deputy impressed. He saw it as a challenge, and it was one he relished. But when he was just sixteen, it was as much an opportunity as a challenge. An opportunity to prove his ability at a technical and physical level above that of third-team football.

He put in a solid display in the reserves, but the following week he was back in the third team. This came as no great blow to Franklin, not least due to the praise he had received that day. Watching him in action against Bury had been Louis Rocca, one of the greatest talent spotters football has ever known. Rocca joined Manchester United (then known as Newton Heath) in the 1890s as a tea boy, but soon became a highly respected and consulted figure at the club. According to Rocca, it was he who suggested the name 'Manchester United' when Newton Heath came to rename themselves in 1902, but his influence stretched far beyond mere nomenclature. By the 1930s, Rocca had become assistant manager, and was tasked with finding the club a backer as their financial situation continued to deteriorate. He did so in the form of James W. Gibson, the man who would go on to own Manchester United from 1931 until his death some twenty years later.

Arguably Rocca's greatest legacy though, was the work he did as a scout. When the Manchester United Junior Athletic Club was founded, Rocca was made chief scout. He created an impressive scouting network, and brought in future United greats such as Johnny Carey, Stan Pearson and future fellow Bogotá Bandit Charlie Mitten.

What's more, in 1945, when former Liverpool right-half Matt Busby was offered the assistant manager's position at Anfield, Rocca acted quickly, convincing both Busby and Gibson that the inexperienced coach ought to take the top job at Old Trafford instead. It worked, and Busby became the Manchester United manager, holding that role for the next twenty-five years and winning thirteen trophies. Perhaps the greatest vindication of Rocca's genius came in the 1948 FA Cup final, when Manchester United won their first FA Cup for thirty-nine years and only the second in their history. Seven of United's starting XI that day had been brought to the club by Louis Rocca and the scouting network he had implemented.

Upon seeing Franklin play for Stoke's reserves, Rocca predicted a great future for the sixteen-year-old. This was a big deal for the teenager, and although he quickly found himself back in the third team, he took a lot of confidence from Rocca's assessment of his ability.

One should note that by this stage, Neil Franklin was a centre-half and only a centre-half. Whilst he had played near to all of his schoolboy football as either an inside or centre-forward, upon his arrival at Stoke City, he was immediately identified as a centre-half. Whether this was due to his strength, aerial prowess or any other reason is not known, or at least not to Neil Franklin. This was a decision made by the coaches at the Victoria Ground, and although he didn't have a say, he didn't have any complaints. Franklin was just happy to be playing football.

On 24 January 1939, Neil's 17th birthday, he was called into the office of manager Bob McGrory and offered professional terms. The teenager was delighted, and made that clear to McGrory, but asked if he could become a part-time professional instead, so as to stay on at Mr Duddell's brickworks. That is a mark of how much Neil enjoyed working for Mr Duddell but, unsurprisingly, McGrory rejected the proposition, stating, 'We want you to become a professional player, and as far as we are concerned, it's full time or nothing.' Franklin obliged, and as much as Duddell and Franklin were disappointed to be parting company, both knew it was for the best.

CHAPTER 3

Hitler Robs England and Stoke

When history reflects on the crimes of Adolf Hitler, his waging a war of aggression and crimes against humanity will understandably take precedent over his disruptions to the Football League and international football in Europe between 1939 and 1945, but the lack of competitive football over this period was a great shame for the club and country of Neil Franklin.

England's feeling of superiority in the years prior to their 1950 World Cup failure, and humbling at the hands of Hungary in 1953, may now be dismissed as folly and arrogance, but that ought not be the case. As much as football's founding nation went on to become complacent whilst their rivals overtook them, for much of the 1930s and 40s, it is not unreasonable to suggest England were the best team in Europe and quite possibly the world. In November 1934, for example, when England faced Italy at Highbury, the game was billed as 'the real World Cup final' by the press. This was due to Italy's victory at the 1934 World Cup, which had seen them crowned the competition's second champions just five months earlier. The Italian team boasted the likes of Giuseppe Meazza, Giovanni Ferrari and even the great Argentine Luis Monti, and they later went on to prove their class by winning the 1938 World Cup in less controversial fashion than their success on home soil, yet they were well beaten by the English.

Although England only won the game 3-2, they held a 3-0 lead at half-time, and much of the Italians second-half improvement was put down to their aggressive approach to the game which saw four English players badly hurt, with injuries ranging from a broken nose to a fractured arm.

Italy's reign as world champions officially spanned from 1934 to 1950, and in that time, they played England three times, drawing once and losing twice. During those immediate post-war years, England faced the best that Europe had to offer, and rarely did they come unstuck. A 4-0 win over Italy, an 8-2 win over the Netherlands and a 10-0 win over Portugal. Those were just a few of England's results between 1946 and 1948, and reflect why a feeling of superiority among the England camp was far from arrogance alone. The fact that England didn't play in their first World Cup until 1950 then, is a real shame, as there could certainly have been a couple more stars on the current England shirt had the Three Lions competed in those three 1930s tournaments, or indeed if there had been any tournaments to compete in during the 1940s.

Similarly, Stoke City's greatest-ever team was undoubtedly between 1939 and 1946. During those wartime years, Stoke City could have fielded a team including the likes of Neil Franklin, Stanley Matthews, Freddie Steele, Frank Soo, George Mountford, Frank Mountford, Frank Bowyer, Syd Peppitt, Tommy Sale and Billy Mould. When the war did finally come to a halt, it could be seen in just one season what that team would have been capable of over those years.

Neil Franklin was just seventeen when the Nazi's invaded Poland and the war began. His career had scarcely had a chance to begin when it was put, indefinitely, on hold. For more than a year, the youngster would understandably be ruing his misfortune and feeling somewhat sorry for himself, up until around September 1940 when the Blitz began and Franklin quickly realised there were more important matters at hand than football.

Neil, like all professional footballers, had his contract suspended during the war. As he was too young to join the Services when war broke out, Franklin continued to play football every

Saturday. Wartime football was a world away from the Football League though. In the first wartime season, 1939–40, Stoke City won their regional league, the West Regional Championship, ahead of the likes of Manchester United and Liverpool, but Franklin made just one appearance. He would make more than thirty appearances for the Potters in each of the wartime seasons that followed, but the standard of football was a long way shy of what the youngster had been looking forward to. To give an example, when Stoke played a friendly against Nottingham Forest towards the back end of that first war league season, they faced an opposition defence made up entirely of their own players, namely—Doug Westland, Jack Challinor and Tom Brawley.

In 1941, then of required age, Franklin joined the Royal Air Force. His first posting was to the seaside town of Blackpool. Pre-war form went out the window during those war years, as 'guest appearances' were allowed, to give footballers in the services a semi-regular fix. This meant the great military areas tended to produce the greatest wartime teams, and nowhere in Britain was more of a hotbed of footballing talent between 1939 and 1945 than Blackpool, as the young Franklin would soon discover. So high was the standard at Blackpool, the senior side would only look at you if you had at least a handful of international caps to your name. Neil did not, and as such, it was the Blackpool Services side for him. The Services side was essentially a Blackpool second team, but it was a still strong one, featuring the likes of Harry McShane, Dave Russell and a future England teammate of Neil's, Stan Mortensen. The Blackpool Services XI competed in the Lancashire Combination division, which they won two out of the three seasons in which it ran.

Just how little pre-war form meant during the wartime regional leagues and competitions is best exhibited by the likes of Blackpool and Aldershot. The Tangerines had finished just six points above the First Division relegation zone in 1938–39, the last full Football

League season, whilst Aldershot had finished mid-table in the old Third Division South. During the war though, Blackpool won three consecutive North First Championship titles and one Football League War Cup trophy, whilst Aldershot regularly competed towards the top end of the London League, mixing with the likes of Arsenal and West Ham.

It was Willie MacFadyen who had first approached Neil about playing football in Blackpool. MacFadyen, a sergeant during the war, had been one of Scotland's most prolific pre-war forwards with Motherwell, before joining Huddersfield Town, where he helped the Terriers reach an FA Cup final at Wembley in 1938. The sharp-shooting Scot was in his late thirties by this point, but still managed to guest for Blackpool. He ordered Franklin to get his boots from Stoke and get into training.

Training in Blackpool and training in Stoke would be very different, Neil quickly found out, with that in Blackpool being led by the flyweight boxer Tiny Bostock. The aptly named 'crooning boxer', Tiny was a teetotal non-smoker from Leek, who had been encouraged to get into boxing by a clergyman. A former choirboy, Bostock sang solo at churches and other venues during his boxing career. He fought his first bout in 1932 and his last in 1945, hanging up his gloves with a record of 120 bouts, 92 wins, 22 losses and 6 draws, a highly creditable record in something of a golden era for the flyweight division. His most famous victories came against Filipino boxer Small Montana and European champion Valentin Angelmann. Bostock served as both an instructor and as a sergeant during the war.

After five months in Blackpool, Franklin moved on to Hereford, where he was to train as a physical training instructor (PTI), a common role for footballers during the war. Another five months passed and Franklin moved on once more, this time to Weston-super-Mare to take a flight mechanics' course, where his football was put on hold briefly. In Hereford, Neil had been able to turn out fairly regularly for Stoke, but in Weston-super-Mare, his only football was a handful of appearances for Aberavon in the south of Wales.

As well as the wartime football he played for Stoke City, Blackpool Services and Aberavon, Franklin also made guest appearances for Lincoln City, Wolverhampton Wanderers and Gainsborough Trinity. Throughout all this time, Neil was working hard on his game, and his ability was not going unnoticed. He came onto the radar of the RAF selectors and soon began turning out for the Service representative sides. Wartime football was an incredibly ersatz version of the real thing, but if there was one benefit, it was for young players like Neil. At both club and Services level, Franklin was now playing against senior players, something he would have been unlikely to be doing at this stage in the Football League. Once more, it was a challenge the youngster relished. Neil once stated, 'You get nowhere in football if you confine your playing activities to a class inferior to your ability. You don't learn anything by playing with or against poorer players. It is the better players who teach you the arts and crafts of the game, always providing, of course, that you are willing to learn.'

As Franklin turned out more and more in representative and club games, the press started to notice him as a player of considerable talent and potential. By 1944, he was being suggested for the England team. On 18 November 1944, following a local tie between Stoke City and Port Vale, Arthur Shrive of the *News Chronicle* wrote: 'Franklin is undoubtedly the finest young centre-half-back in the country, and it cannot be long before the FA selectors recognize his merit'. Neil read these comments and numerous similar ones, then restricted to small sections of the newspapers' back pages, but couldn't see it himself. Wolverhampton Wanderers stalwart Stan Cullis was England's centre-half. Six years Franklin's senior and as assured as they come, Cullis was a top centre-half, and Neil couldn't see himself dislodging the Wolves star anytime soon.

Less than a month later, he would be proved wrong, and Mr Shrive would be proved right. When Stoke City arrived at Highfield Road to play Coventry City on 2 December 1944, manager Bob McGrory received a telegram from the FA informing him that Neil Franklin had been selected to play for an FA XI at Bradford the following Saturday.

Stan Cullis had been posted overseas, and as a result, the FA needed to identify some alternatives for the centre-half position. However, in his first international honour, just weeks shy of his 23rd birthday, Franklin was not selected at centre-half. Huddersfield Town's Alan Brown, who never won an official peacetime cap, played there, whilst Neil came in at right-half as a last-minute replacement for his Stoke teammate Frank Soo. The game, between the Army and the FA, took place at Park Avenue stadium in Bradford on 9 December 1944. The teams that day read:

FA XI: Bert Williams (Walsall), Laurie Scott (Arsenal), George Hardwick (Middlesbrough), Neil Franklin (Stoke City), Alan Brown (Huddersfield Town), Syd Foss (Chelsea), Frank Broome (Aston Villa), Len Shackleton (Bradford), Willie Price (Huddersfield Town), Stanley Mortensen (Blackpool), Les Smith (Brentford).

The Army: Frank Swift (Manchester City), Bert Sproston (Manchester City), Walley Barnes (Arsenal), Matt Busby (Liverpool), George Smith (Charlton Athletic), Joe Mercer (Everton), Billy Elliott (West Bromwich Albion), Archie Macaulay (West Ham United), Don Welsh (Charlton Athletic), Maurice Edelston (Reading), Johnny Deakin (St. Mirren).

It was two star-studded XIs, and you may have noticed the name Len Shackleton in the FA XI. The man who deprived Neil of a schoolboy cap all those years before was now his teammate.

HITLER ROBS ENGLAND AND STOKE

Stanley Mortensen was another player Neil already knew well, having played alongside him for Blackpool Services a few years earlier. Both XIs were blessed with great talent, but on a freezing cold night in West Yorkshire, played on more ice than grass, a scarce amount of that talent and quality was on show. The game ended in a 1-1 draw, but in spite of his own dissatisfaction with his performance, Franklin received largely positive comments from the press following the match.

Two weeks later, Neil received his second international honour, this time at Highfield Road, where he had learned of his first selection only three weeks earlier. His second outing for the FA XI came against the RAF. Stanley Mortensen would be playing for the opposition on this occasion, as would Stoke City teammates Stanley Matthews and Frank Soo. On Franklin's team were Len Shackleton once more and the great Tommy Lawton. In an open game, the RAF ran out 6-4 winners, Franklin scoring once for the FA, whilst Mortensen bagged a hat-trick for the RAF.

The now 23-year-old had obviously done enough to convince the FA selectors, as just a fortnight later he made his England debut at Villa Park against Scotland. Whilst it was his first England appearance, Franklin still didn't pick up his first cap, as wartime fixtures were not met with such honours. This didn't lessen the experience for Neil though, whose pride in representing his country is perhaps best shown by the fact that he cried before that game against Scotland when the national anthems were played. The teams that day read:

England: Frank Swift (Manchester City), George Hardwick (Middlesbrough), Laurie Scott (Arsenal), Neil Franklin (Stoke City), Joe Mercer (Everton), Frank Soo (Stoke City), Les Smith (Brentford), Tommy Lawton (Everton), Stan Matthews (Stoke City), Stan Mortensen (Blackpool), Sailor Brown (Charlton Athletic).

ENGLAND'S GREATEST DEFENDER

Scotland: Bobby Brown (Queen's Park), Jimmy Stephen (Bradford), Bob Thyne (Darlington), Jim Harley (Liverpool), Matt Busby (Liverpool), Archie Macaulay (West Ham United), Jimmy Delaney (Celtic), Billy Liddell (Liverpool), Andy Black (Heart of Midlothian), Willie Fagan (Liverpool), Jock Dodds (Blackpool).

One thing you may notice looking at those lineups is the number of Stoke City players in the England XI—three, with Everton the only other team to have more than one representative. To this day, young players called up to the national team talk of the importance of having a familiar face or someone to take them under their wing when first selected. Neil was lucky enough to have a few, and who finer than Stanley Matthews to take you under their wing. The England team were staying at the Grand Hotel in Birmingham, where Matthews and Soo helped Neil settle in, before Matthews went one step further, taking him across the street to meet the Scotland side staying at another hotel.

Both on and off the pitch, Neil Franklin was supremely calm. From the highest of highs to the lowest of lows, Neil simply wasn't one to lose his cool, and you will see throughout this book that you can comfortably count on one hand the times in which he did so. Despite this, in the build-up to his England debut, there were some nerves. England won the game 3-2 in front of an impressive crowd of 65,780 at Villa Park, with Mortensen bagging a brace. Although England had won the game, Franklin was disappointed. He feared he had not done himself justice, and left the field wondering whether he would ever turn out for England again. The comments in the press the next day then, came as some surprise. 'Franklin, Brown and Mortensen, England's newcomers, played themselves into the national side for Hampden', wrote Frank Coles of the *Daily Telegraph*, whilst the *Daily Mail* commented that he did 'a difficult job with success'.

HITLER ROBS ENGLAND AND STOKE

The national press weren't yet gushing about Franklin, but it was far from the scathing accounts he expected to read of himself. And true enough, two months later Franklin was back playing for England in their next game, against Scotland again. The tie was played at Hampden Park in front of a typical packed house of 133,000 spectators, and England won even more emphatically, 6-1 on this occasion. The game took place just two days after the passing of Franklin D. Roosevelt and began with an impeccably observed minute's silence before that famous Hampden roar rained down onto the pitch.

Even though only three weeks passed, an awful lot had happened by the time Franklin next pulled on an England shirt for a game against Wales. The Soviet Union had launched the Battle of Berlin, during which time Adolf Hitler committed suicide and was replaced by Karl Dönitz. The war was drawing to an end, for Britain at least, and just two days after the Wales game, Dönitz would sign the act of military surrender.

There was a feeling of celebration throughout Britain then, when, on 5 May 1945, England faced Wales at Ninian Park. A crowd of 25,000 witnessed a Raich Carter masterclass. Aged thirty-two, the man they called the 'Silver Fox' was as scintillating as ever. A virtuoso display was capped off by a great hat-trick in a 3-2 win. That performance meant Carter couldn't be dropped for England's next game, a Victory International at Wembley Stadium on 26 May. The FA had tried to organise a game against a Russian representative side, but the difficulties of travelling in Europe meant that was not possible, so France were selected as the opposition instead. The game would be best remembered for the performance of French goalkeeper Julien Darui. Later named France's 'Goalkeeper of the Century' by *L'Équipe*, Darui saved one shot after another, most notably a Leslie Smith penalty, and the match finished 2-2.

Less than a month later, Franklin was running out for England once more, the FA having agreed to play two games in Switzerland as the Swiss Football Federation celebrated their 50th anniversary. The first game would take place in Bern and the second in Zurich. The Swiss kindly sent their own plane to pick up the England team, and it became the first Swiss aircraft to land in Britain since the war had started six years earlier. The England team stepped off the plane and into the scorching summer heat of Bern in 1945 to rapturous applause from thousands of Swiss citizens. As well as playing in both games, Franklin enjoyed seeing the sites of Switzerland with his tour partner Micky Fenton, the great Middlesbrough striker who averaged better than a goal every other game over the course of his career. Fenton was the oldest player in the England camp, and despite now being a regular fixture, Franklin was the youngest. Together, the duo saw great Swiss runners and world record-breakers Gunder Hägg and Arne Andersson in action, as well as travelling on Europe's highest railway, the Jungfraubahn.

The first of the two games on that tour is perhaps best remembered as being Tom Finney's first in an England shirt. Other than that, it was a rather forgettable occasion for the England boys. The searing heat proved a challenge, and the Swiss were helped by the unorthodox tactics of coach Karl Rappan that were implemented for the first time in this game, and also the excellent performance of left-back Willi Steffen, who would join Chelsea the following year. Switzerland won the game 3-1, and England's unbeaten run, which stretched almost three years, was over. The second game, against a strong Swiss 'B' XI in Zurich, saw a much-improved performance, with Finney, Watson and Fenton among the goals in a 3-0 win.

England played six more wartime internationals after their trip to Switzerland before official peacetime internationals returned and caps were rewarded once more. A 1-0 win over Northern Ireland, a 1-0 defeat to Wales, a 2-0 win over Belgium, a 1-0 defeat to Scotland, a 4-1 victory over Switzerland and a 2-1 defeat to France made up those last six wartime games, all of which Franklin featured in.

In total, Neil appeared in 12 wartime and victory internationals for England, as well as a number of representative and inter-league games. None of those 12 appearances were met with official caps, and in them, England had a record of 7 wins, 1 draw and 4 defeats. For Stoke City, he made 194 appearances between the Football League being suspended in 1939 and resuming in 1946, in which he scored 3 goals.

CHAPTER 4

Pipped to the Title by Liverpool

The 1946–47 season, the first post-war campaign, has to go down as one of the most epic and entertaining in the long history of the Football League; and for no team is that more decidedly the case than Stoke City, who experienced ecstasy and agony on their way to ultimate final-day heartbreak.

Before we get into the season itself though, we must look at the Stoke City squad of 1946—an exceptional group of players and the finest ever assembled in the Potteries. In the mid–late 1940s, when the England team was incredibly strong, having a sole representative in the national side was a source of great pride for a club and its local area. Whilst in recent times it has become not uncommon for a club such as Manchester United or Tottenham Hotspur to have a handful of players start for the national team, this was highly irregular during Neil's time with England.

Stoke City then, were very much the exception, having Neil Franklin, Stanley Matthews, Frank Soo and Freddie Steele all gaining international honours. Whilst much of Stoke's success in the 1946–47 season must be attributed to fine team play and partnerships across the field, it is with three of those four players that we shall begin, as one—Soo—departed for Leicester City before the 1946–47 season began. An obvious starting point would be Stanley Matthews. Still regarded by many as the finest footballer England has ever produced, Stan was a phenomenon, and arguably the first truly global star of the beautiful game.

PIPPED TO THE TITLE BY LIVERPOOL

Pelé described him as the man who 'taught us the way football should be played', and Franklin was equally quick to praise his long-time teammate. When Neil made a guest appearance at a Sunday league tournament years after his retirement, he was approached by a Stoke City fan who told him he was the club's greatest ever player, greater even than Matthews. Neil took the praise with the same awkward appreciation that he always displayed when showered with superlatives. It wasn't a sentiment he could agree with though. 'The greatest player I have ever played with, against or seen in action', that is how Neil Franklin summed up his former England and Stoke City teammate.

Matthews was a magnificent student of the game. Neil did not believe a second could pass in which Stan did not think about football. His diet and exercise regimes were so far ahead of their time that they raised more than one or two eyebrows. Having made his Stoke City debut in 1932, aged seventeen, he shot to national stardom in 1937, aged twenty-two, when he scored a hat-trick for England against Czechoslovakia at White Hart Lane. Ironically, whilst it was that feat which propelled Stan into the national consciousness, goal scoring was never a notable aspect of his game. Modern football fans assessing the career of Sir Stanley Matthews might be quick to spot his goal-scoring record and question his status as an all-time great, especially those born into the disparate Messi-Ronaldo era, but to do so would be to misunderstand his role on a football pitch.

As a winger in the W-M formation (see chapter six), Matthews had three main duties: to stay out wide, beat his full-back and deliver pinpoint balls into the box. In respect of those three tasks, Matthews was without peer. Despite his professional career spanning thirty-three years, full-backs the nation over still never fully found a way to deal with the 'Wizard of the Dribble'. Stan's era is littered with players who could score over 30 or even 40 goals a season, but none who could dominate a full-back and create chances for others as routinely and consistently as he could.

Hearing a former teammate of Matthews talk is somewhat reminiscent of how Cristiano Ronaldo's former Manchester United teammates describe the Portuguese star. Both may have been wingers and Ballon d'Or winners, but more pertinently, both trained harder and longer than anyone else, and whilst their games differed greatly, both were obsessed with becoming (and later remaining) the best player they could possibly be. The one criticism of Matthews, and funnily enough it is the same one often levelled against Ronaldo, is that he could be big-headed or arrogant.

This was an accusation Franklin staunchly disagreed with. Matthews could be shy, quiet and reserved, and that could sometimes be misconstrued. Certainly he knew he was a star and a crowd drawer—he was, and pretending otherwise would simply have been false modesty.

During his time at Stoke, Matthews would have three major disagreements with the club, the last of which would lead to his departure for Blackpool. The transfer would ultimately see Stoke City's greatest-ever campaign come crashing down, and we shall deal with how it arose later on in this chapter, but first we ought to move on to Freddie Steele.

Every great team needs a great centre-forward, it could be suggested, although Vicente Del Bosque may argue otherwise, and Stoke City's centre-forward was something special. I have been told that Stanley Matthews considered Freddie Steele to be a finer centre-forward than England great Tommy Lawton, but whilst Franklin never quite went that far in his praise, Steele certainly merits his place among the pantheon of great English centre-forwards of his generation.

In February 1937, aged twenty, Steele scored five goals in a 10-3 destruction of West Bromwich Albion. He went on to score

36 goals for Stoke that season (1936–37), still the most goals scored by a Stoke player in a single season, and 33 of those coming in the league made him the First Division top scorer for the campaign. Unsurprisingly, Steele's fine form led to an England call-up. His entire international career spanned only seven months, but in that time, he scored eight goals from just six caps, averaging a goal every sixty-eight minutes. Steele scored against Scotland, Norway (x2), Finland (x2) and Sweden (x3).

Just as 1937 looked to be the perfect year for Freddie Steele, it ended with a serious knee injury. Although he returned to football and was as prolific as ever, Steele shocked the English game by announcing his intentions to retire at the tender age of twenty-three, having suffered depression following the injury. A psychiatrist eventually motivated him sufficiently to change his mind, but before Steele could announce his return, World War II broke out.

By the wars end, Steele was thirty, but he still spearheaded Stoke City's attack in the 1946–47 campaign, bagging 29 league goals. Remarkably two-footed, quick, strong and a force to be reckoned with in the air, Steele scored a total of 159 goals in 251 games for Stoke, excluding his wartime exploits. At the time of writing, he still holds the record for the most goals scored for Stoke City in a single season (33), the most league goals for Stoke (140), and the most FA Cup goals for the club (19), all in spite of his struggles with injuries, depression and losing his best years to the war.

And so we come to Neil, who was twenty-three when the war drew to a close. Whilst he had obviously lost a sizeable chunk of his career, Franklin had not lost his prime years, and still had an awful lot of football ahead of him in only his early–mid twenties, unlike so many of his wartime England teammates. He may only have officially made his Stoke City debut on the 5 January 1946 in a 3-1 FA Cup victory over Burnley, having been seventeen when the Football League was suspended, but upon its return he was an England international, arguably the first name on the team sheet and a bonafide star in the Potteries.

On 31 August 1946, the Football League returned after a seven-year absence, and Stoke City kicked off their campaign with a 2-2 draw against Charlton Athletic. A crowd of 32,335 flocked to the Victoria Ground that day, as clubs around the country experienced bumper crowds for the return of peacetime football. The season began under a dreary backdrop. A markedly hot July had led to water shortages, until torrential rain and thunderstorms broke out across Britain on the 26th and 27th days of the month.

The flooding ruined Britain's wheat crop, rationing had to be introduced on bread, and it wouldn't come off ration until 1948. The country was facing a bleak and destitute outlook, so it was no wonder that the returning escapism football presented proved such a lure.

Stoke City themselves faced a conflicting situation. Supporters were frustrated with the lack of investment in the playing squad and perceived lack of ambition, but manager Bob McGrory was quietly confident. Whilst a number of First Division clubs returned to the Football League with a blend of ageing and inexperienced players, many of his star players were in their prime: Neil Franklin was 23, Stanley Matthews was 31, Freddie Steele was 30, Alec Ormston was 27, Frank Mountford was 23 and George Mountford was 25.

The entire backbone of McGrory's side were neither too young nor over the hill. Franklin and Matthews were starring for England, and Freddie Steele had scored 36 goals in 37 games in the final War League. Despite this, the club made a dreadful start to the season. Goals by Ormston and Steele saw a point picked up on the opening day, but Stoke lost their next three, losing twice to Bolton and once to Middlesbrough. Stoke had been beaten 5-4 at Ayresome Park, but whilst the game had yielded no points, it did see a much-improved performance by the boys from the Potteries.

PIPPED TO THE TITLE BY LIVERPOOL

They finally got their first win of the season in mid-September, as Derby County were beaten 3-2 at the Victoria Ground, with 35,218 in attendance. The win kick-started a good run for Stoke, who won their next five games, which included inflicting a first defeat of the season on Manchester United. The run took the Potters into the upper reaches of the First Division table, but external factors threatened to halt their impressive form. Prior to a 5-2 win over Chelsea, the Players' Union (the precursor to the PFA) were threatening strike action. The post-war attendance boom was seeing a lot of money pour into the game, and the players wanted their share.

Ultimately, the government stepped in, managing to appease both the Football League and the Players' Union, for the time being at least. But whilst that crisis was averted, another was lurking around the corner for Stoke City and Bob McGrory. The Potters had been without their star man Stanley Matthews for all but one of their six consecutive wins through injury, as had England for their last two outings, and the results suggested neither club nor country had missed their famous right winger. In the Stoke team, Matthews had been replaced by George Mountford (no relation to his namesake Frank), a fine club winger who had joined Stoke during the war from Kidderminster Harriers, aged twenty-one.

Mountford had established himself in the Stoke side during the war, whilst Matthews guested predominantly for Blackpool. No one was surprised to see the number-seven shirt return to Matthews once league football returned though, least of all George himself. Two injuries to Stan early in the season had seen Mountford return to the team, and he didn't disappoint. The uncapped wide man was naturally less skilful than Matthews, but he brought a directness and an exceptional work rate to McGrory's side, as well as averaging a goal every four or five games during his first spell with Stoke.

In the England side, Matthews had been replaced by Tom

Finney, the Preston winger who was six years his junior and a remarkable talent. The Lancashire-born star had made wartime appearances for England on the left wing, but in Matthews' absence his full international debut came in his preferred role on the right. In the two games Stan missed, England beat Northern Ireland 7-2 and Eire (Ireland) 1-0, with Finney scoring in both games.

Matthews had a point to prove then, upon his return to fitness in mid-October. He made himself available for selection on 15 October, with the Potters set for a trip to Highbury in four days' time. Bob McGrory was faced with a dilemma which has troubled managers since they first came into being in the nineteenth century, and still does right up to the present day. Stick with a winning team, or bring a star player back into your starting XI?

His response was to suggest that Matthews have a run-out in the reserves whilst Stoke travelled to Arsenal, so as to ensure he was fully fit. Stan did not take too kindly to the suggestion. As much as the idea of playing in the reserves seemed to offend him, so too did McGrory's insistence that it was only a suggestion. A rarely enraged Matthews told McGrory, 'You're the manager of this club, so manage it.' McGrory didn't turn his suggestion into a demand, and Matthews didn't turn out for the reserves. Instead, the 31-year-old returned to Blackpool, leaving increased speculation behind in Stoke, which quickly spread across the country.

The newspapers reported that Matthews had refused to play in the reserves, and were quick to accuse the winger of being arrogant. In truth, Stan hadn't actually disobeyed any club orders, but it was clear what the manager's preferences were, and Stan had chosen to go against that.

Franklin came down firmly on the side of his teammate in the dispute, claiming that, 'If he said he was fit, he was fit, because Matthews will never lay claims to fitness unless he is absolutely

100 per cent. So a fit Matthews is a first team player.' Of course, Neil had his own disagreements with McGrory, and was a close friend of Stan's, so his views should perhaps come as little surprise. It would also seem to be rather at odds with Neil's own stance on reserve team football, given that he himself, now the Stoke captain, and an England international, saw no insult in dropping into the reserves.

The rumour mill was in full swing in Staffordshire at this time, with new Matthews-related stories bandied about every day, many of which were untrue. One such story stated that the Stoke City players had approached McGrory and demanded that Matthews not be immediately reinstated to the team, but rather earn his spot in the side like anyone else, with some even going so far as to suggest his teammates told the manager that they flat out didn't want Stan in the side.

This seemed entirely at odds with Franklin's own view, and as club captain, he suspected he would be aware of any such occurrence—but fearing Stan might hear the story and believe it, Neil called a team meeting, and asked if anyone had approached McGrory or didn't want to play alongside Matthews. Upon assurances from every member of the club's playing staff that no element of the story was true, Neil wrote to Stan to tell him that no one had spoken to Mr McGrory and that they were all too pleased to play alongside him. Franklin also released the statement to the public, in the hope of alleviating some of the ill feeling towards Stan in Stoke, and to ensure the falsehood didn't snowball any further.

There was, at that time, divided opinion in Stoke regarding Matthews. He was, and remains to this day, the region's greatest gift to the world of football, but at thirty-one, it was considered to be obvious that his best days were behind him. A fee of £20,000 was being suggested, at a time when £14,500 was the British record transfer fee. For an ageing winger whose game was heavily reliant on pace, deemed by some to be becoming big-headed and happy to pick and choose the games he wanted to play in, there were advocates for letting the man who had been with Stoke City since the age of fifteen go.

Unlike during Stan's first dispute with the club over the amount of his loyalty bonus in 1938—which had seen the city of Stoke unite and publicly cry out, 'Matthews must not go!'—this time there was a pro-Matthews and an anti-Matthews camp, although those in favour of letting the wide man go were still in a minority. The dispute was settled on Tuesday, 22 October, three days after Stoke had been beaten 1-0 by Arsenal, with Matthews' deputy George Mountford missing an open goal, whilst Stan posed for photos at Bloomfield Road, the home of Blackpool FC. The club agreed to let Matthews do most of his training in Blackpool, provided he attend any 'special' training sessions in Stoke, and gave him a week's holiday. Whilst he was away, Stoke lost again, this time to pre-season favourites Wolves, who inflicted a 3-0 defeat on the Matthews-less Potters in front of the Victoria Ground's biggest crowd of the season.

Mountford was injured in that defeat, paving the way for a seamless return to the outside right position for Stan as Stoke travelled to Sunderland. Both home and away fans eagerly anticipated the return of a national star, and Roker Park saw Sunderland set their record attendance for the season (57,290). With all eyes on Stan, he didn't disappoint. Left-back Jack Jones was humiliated and beaten with ease time and time again, as Matthews made a mockery of both the Sunderland defence and those who had suggested his best days were behind him. Frank Baker scored the only goal of the game to give Stoke a historic first win at Roker Park.

He may have been back in the Stoke City side and back beating full-backs at whim, but all was not right with Matthews and

McGrory. Following Franklin's letter, Stan now believed McGrory to have been the source of the rumours that the players themselves had asked for him to be left out of the side, in order to justify his decision in light of criticism from supporters should it backfire. Neil's close friend and goalkeeper Dennis Herod's comments suggested this was more than just paranoia on the part of Matthews, stating, 'McGrory was a crafty man. It would be just like him to do something like that, but we didn't know for sure.'

The rumours surrounding Stan, whilst not wholly positive, only served to add to his celebrity. He was a household name in Britain. With such fame comes both positives and negatives. At the peak of his renown, Stan's return to the Potters side coincided with 'Rag Week', and students from Sunderland Technical College (now the University of Sunderland) saw an opportunity to make a few quid. They headed to the hotel in which the Stoke City squad were based on the day of their match against the Wearsiders in the hope of kidnapping Matthews. Whilst the Stoke City star's name was almost universally known, in the days before the regular broadcasting of games, his face was not. The cunning students were not that easily defeated though, and set about pretending to be autograph hunters and asking passers-by to point out Matthews. Unfortunately for Neil, he was pointed to, supposedly by a troublesome teammate.

Franklin was called to the telephone, but before he could get there, a crowd of students grabbed him, carrying him out of the hotel and onto a tram. Despite Neil's pleading, the students were unmoved. Eventually, they allowed the England international to call Mr McGrory, who by this stage had already phoned the police. The Stoke City boss was not the type to be overly amused by such pranks, especially not within hours of a match. The police warned the students against holding Franklin any longer, and he was soon returned to the Stoke City party, but not before parading through the streets to help the students reach their £400 target. Despite taking it in good spirit, Neil did describe the incident as 'one of my most alarming experiences'.

Confidence was high following the Sunderland win, and the club went on another good run, suffering just one defeat from their next nine games, which naturally came against bottom-of-the-table side Huddersfield Town. Franklin had to feel some responsibility for Stoke's slip-up at Leeds Road, having lost the ball whilst striding out of defence in the build-up to Huddersfield's winner and the only goal of the game. Such instances are always likely to be occupational hazards for defenders who are so comfortable on the ball, and McGrory often urged Neil to take a more safety-first approach, but it just wasn't in his nature. Lesser players may have lost confidence from such an incident, but Franklin had faith in his own game. He had been a colossus in the early stages of the season, imposing himself on games through his reading of the game and providing quick, incisive passes to the Potters wide men and forwards. And sure enough, the following week he was at it again, not giving his old pal Stan Mortensen a sniff as Stoke overcame high-flying Blackpool by four goals to one.

A victory over rather more a modest opposition in the form of Brentford by the same scoreline the following week propelled Stoke into the First Division's top four. The good people of Staffordshire hadn't yet begun putting the baubles on their Christmas trees, but talk of the championship was rife. Stoke's best previous performance in the First Division had come shortly before the war in the 1935–36 season, when the club finished fourth. That had been manager Bob McGrory's first in charge of Stoke, but whilst their fourth placed finish was impressive, they did trail runaway winners Sunderland by nine points, a sizeable gap in the two points for a win era.

There was a different feel about the 1946–47 season. None of the pre-season favourites had pulled away, and despite their dreadful start to the campaign, the Potters were within touching distance of the top of the division. What's more, they were playing a brilliant brand of football. McGrory may have been a strict disciplinarian, but his football didn't reflect that. He favoured attack over defence, and both Stoke's goals for and against columns reflected that.

Work had been done on the defence, however; Billy Mould, whose place at centre-half Franklin had taken after the war, moved to full-back, where he proved highly effective. Mould was a fine player, although he was the antithesis of Neil, a stopper pure and simple. Frank Mountford and Jock Kirton, the latter the only non-Englishman in the Stoke squad, operated as very capable midfield destroyers. Matthews, George Mountford, Baker and Ormston gave Stoke serious depth and attacking intent on the wings, whilst centre-forward Freddie Steele continued to find the back of the net, and—crucially—avoid injury.

There seemed to be no attempts to curb such title talk by McGrory, who stated after the Potters' fortuitous victory over Everton courtesy of a George Antonio handball in November, 'Wouldn't it be a strange thing if that late goal won us the championship.' By that time, it looked as though any team who finished above Liverpool would be in with a good shout of winning the league, so the festive period presented both a huge opportunity and a huge challenge for the Stoke City side, as they came up against the Merseysiders twice in two days.

The two ties, which took place on Christmas Day and Boxing Day, would give a good indication of Stoke's title credentials, and they came slap bang in the middle of a hectic festive schedule which saw them play four games in seven days. The Christmas Day game would see Stoke entertain the Anfield boys, but they were in no mood for handing out gifts to their opponents. The Potters put on a show, much to the delight of the home crowd. A fine performance resulted in a 2-1 win, courtesy of two goals by Freddie Steele, both assisted by Matthews. The scoreline flattered Liverpool, with goalkeeper Ray Minshull impressing in a rare outing for the Reds. A day later the two sides met again, this time at Anfield. Despite the catastrophic conditions as a historic winter began to brew, both teams played good football, but carved out little in front of goal. The deadlock was finally broken by veteran South African winger Berry Nieuwenhuys, in what would be his last season with Liverpool, before Albert Stubbins put the game beyond doubt late on with a classy strike.

A win and a loss against their title rivals would have looked like a reasonable return, but both Matthews and Ormston picked up knocks in the second match against Liverpool, and Stoke lost 1-0 away at lowly Charlton Athletic the following week. Matthews returned the week after and the Potters got back to winning ways, although it was Ormston's deputy Bert Mitchell who stole the show on the left flank, scoring twice in a 3-1 win over Middlesbrough. It would be two weeks before Stoke played their next league game, with the second week of January bringing the FA Cup Third Round, the stage in which Stoke entered the competition. It's easy to forget that at this time the FA Cup was still seen as the pinnacle of the English game, and whilst Stoke may have been in a title race, the league would take no focus away from the cup.

McGrory's men were drawn away to Second Division Tottenham in the Third Round, and a crowd of 65,681 turned out at White Hart Lane, roughly twice Tottenham's average for the 1946–47 season, evidence of both the appeal of the FA Cup and the lure of seeing Stanley Matthews in the flesh. Stoke started brightly against their lower league opposition, and took a two-goal lead into the break, but Spurs fought back in the second half, earning themselves a 2-2 draw to force a midweek replay at the Vic. The second tie between the two teams was decided by the brilliance of Stanley Matthews. He beat Tottenham defenders at will, scoring the game's only goal after twenty-nine minutes and sending

Stoke into the Fourth Round draw, where they considered themselves somewhat fortuitous to be drawn against Third Division North side Chester City.

Just one league game would come between Stoke's FA Cup ties with Tottenham and their trip to Chester, and that was a disappointing 3-0 defeat away to Derby County. Stoke continued in their FA Cup tie at Sealand Road as they had left off in their league game against Derby, and a packed crowd watched the Third Division North side more than match their First Division opponents, ultimately feeling somewhat disheartened at only forcing a replay. The replay, which came just four days later, was played under treacherous conditions at the Victoria Ground. The pitch at the Vic was far from renowned for its durability; even in the mildest of years it would descend into a mud-bath by mid-October, so a harsh winter rendered it virtually unplayable.

The winter of 1946–47 was one of the harshest ever experienced in the British Isles. It began in late January, caused by an anticyclone which sat over Scandinavia, resulting in strong winds, temperatures as low as -21°C and several inches of snow falling across the country. It was in the days between Stoke's first game with Chester and the replay that the worst of this weather began, but Britain would have to contend with extreme conditions for the next two months. February continued as January had ended, bitterly cold and with heavy snow. The highest temperature recorded in the whole of Britain in the February of 1947 was 5°C. Most of the country only went without snow for a few days all month, and it was taking a serious toll. The ferry service across the English Channel was suspended due to pack ice and entire villages were cut off, with the RAF having to deliver ration packs to them. As the situation worsened, roads became cut off, coal was stuck at the pits and the country began a devastating fuel shortage which hit industries so hard that four million people soon found themselves claiming unemployment benefits.

The winter saw food rations cut to levels lower than at any stage during the war. By late February, even Buckingham Palace, the Houses of Parliament and, ironically, London's Central Electricity Board had been forced to work by candlelight. Some of the heaviest snow came in the first week of March, seeing record blizzards and a record 83 inches of lying snow being measured in County Durham. When temperatures did finally begin to rise in mid-March, the situation didn't get any better. Rapid thawing of the snow combined with heavy rainfall led to the major rivers across Britain bursting their banks. Over 100,000 properties were affected, and the Thames experienced its worst flooding of the twentieth century.

The consequences of January to March 1947 were enormous. The floods alone caused around £320 million worth of damage (equivalent to over £11 billion in 2019), the nation's overall industrial output was down 10 per cent for the year, and the farming industry was in ruins. Coming so soon after the Second World War, at a time when the Labour Party was still spending enormous amounts on the armed forces and the soon to be born NHS, it led to a huge loss of confidence domestically in Clement Attlee and his government, and internationally in both Britain and the pound. The exchange rate dropped from $4.03 to $2.80, and it proved the death knell for any aspirations Britain may have had of remaining a world superpower. Further consequences, of course, were the postponement of many football matches, and it saw the longest Football League season in history, with the season dragging on five weeks longer than planned.

The FA Cup Fourth Round replay between Stoke City and Chester City would not be postponed though, and despite the conditions, both teams put on a fine show in front of a 22,663-strong crowd in much need of cheering up. Freddie Steele bagged a brace, an Ormston miss-kick somehow found the back of the net and Matthews missed a penalty in a 3-2 win.

Stoke drew Sheffield United in the next round of the cup, but had league ties with Preston and Manchester United to contend with first. In one of their most accomplished performances of the season, Stoke humiliated Preston 5-0 at the Victoria Ground, with Matthews running riot as his heavily billed 'rival' Tom Finney was kept quiet. Only 8,456 braved the harsh weather to witness the Potters take on Manchester United next at Maine Road, in a game that finished as a 1-1 draw, with both teams scoring once from the penalty spot.

The FA Cup returned three days later, and the visit of Sheffield United was greeted with such anticipation that the authorities felt it best to make this the first all-ticket match in Stoke City history. As the great freeze gripped Staffordshire and the rest of Britain, 39,688 still found their way to the Vic. On a surface woefully unfit for football and highly dangerous, Stoke had the better of the chances, but crashed out 1-0 due to a freak goal by Harold Brook. The cup might have been the Holy Grail, but the pain of that Sheffield United defeat was certainly eased somewhat the following Saturday, as Stoke thrashed Chelsea. Franklin and his teammates were 6-1 up before the half-hour mark in a staggering game, although no goals were scored in the hour of football which followed. The result meant Stoke had done the double over the London side, scoring 11 goals in the process.

Another London side were relatively easily dispatched the following week at the Vic, Arsenal this time, in a win which left Stoke just three points off top spot with two games in hand. The Potters were coming into form at just the right time, especially since their next game was against the league leaders Wolves. The side from Wolverhampton were in shaky form, and Stoke travelled to Molineux with much confidence, but it would prove to be a long afternoon for Stoke and Franklin. A 3-0 defeat marked the beginning of a dreadful March for Stoke. Normally so assured, Neil wasn't his usual self in the game, and was at fault for two of Wolves' three goals. As the country suffered heavy flooding, Stoke's title hopes were in danger of sinking.

They didn't finish a game for three weeks following defeat to Wolves, with the club's next game at Aston Villa being abandoned at 2-2 in the second half, before back-to-back draws against Portsmouth and Everton once football finally resumed. Stoke ended March winless, but all was not lost. Blackpool, who had ended March top of the league, lost two, won two and drew one in April. Wolves also won only twice in March, and were reserving their full wobble for April. For Stoke, meanwhile, April would be as busy as it was brilliant. McGrory's men played six games in twenty-two days, and won every one of them.

The Potters began the month by thrashing Grimsby Town, before exacting revenge on Huddersfield Town with a 3-0 win the following day. Two days later, Stoke played their third game in four days, beating Grimsby once more, completing a rather rapid double over the Mariners. Five days later they travelled to Bloomfield Road, where they ended any lingering title hopes Blackpool may have had with a confident 2-0 win. The month was rounded off nicely with comfortable wins over the lowly duo of Blackburn Rovers and Brentford.

All may have looked rosy in Staffordshire in terms of results during April, but despite the six consecutive wins which soon became seven, there was another storm brewing, although not one of a literal sense on this occasion. Stanley Matthews was set for his third major conflict with Bob McGrory and the Stoke City board, and this one would prove to be his last. Stan reportedly told Stoke he would be unable to play in the away game at Grimsby in the first week of April due to a rush of bookings at the hotel he owned in Blackpool. However, Matthews later claimed his reasoning for asking not to be involved in the game at Blundell Park was entirely a footballing one. He was due to appear for England against

Scotland on 12 April, and felt four important games in eight days would prove too great a strain on his body.

Whichever account you choose to believe, on this occasion at least, McGrory's ire was at least somewhat understandable. Franklin was typically the first to stick up for Stan, but it's hard to make a case for him here. Even if his withdrawal from the squad was due to England's game against Scotland, Neil too would be involved, and he never voiced any concerns about contending with the exact same schedule. That being said, if the account Matthews gives in his autobiography is accurate, McGrory did actually agree to rest Stan for the Grimsby game, and the real altercation came five days later when Stoke headed to Blackpool. The convincing manner of Stoke's 3-0 win over Grimsby had left Matthews half-expecting to be left out for the game against Blackpool, but he was pleased to be informed by McGrory that he was back in the team. Half an hour before kick-off though, kit donned and ready to come up against the players he trained alongside day to day, McGrory popped his head around the door to tell Stan he had changed his mind, and he was out the side.

It's fair to say Stan wasn't best pleased, and matters were only made worse a week later when Stoke played Brentford. McGory told Matthews that he was recalling him as his outside-right. After the game, Stan discovered the only reason he had been recalled was due to an injury to Bert Mitchell, a fact confirmed to him by Franklin, but denied by the Stoke board. It was at that moment, according to Stan, that he knew his time at Stoke City had come to an end. The relationship between McGrory and Matthews had been strained at the best of times. Stan felt the Scot still held a grudge from their time playing together in the early 1930s, when Matthews had dislodged McGrory's friend and fellow Scot Bobby Liddle from the Stoke side at the age of seventeen. Others felt he was jealous of Matthews and the limelight which followed him, whilst some thought he had a legitimate case for selling the now 32-year-old England international.

Once the board had been persuaded by player and manager, it was decided Stan would be allowed to leave Stoke City after seventeen years with the club. He was asked where his destination of choice would be and he naturally replied Blackpool. After prolonged negotiations, with the deal seemingly off more than once, Stoke finally decided to accept Blackpool's offer of £11,500, and the deal was sealed whilst Matthews was in Glasgow representing a Great Britain XI in a 6-1 win over a Rest of Europe XI. The impact of Matthews' departure and the decision to sell him would be debated in the Potteries for decades to come.

Franklin didn't sit on the fence when asked about Stan's sale a few years later, stating, 'If he [Matthews] had not been sold to Blackpool in 1947, I am sure Stoke would have won the First Division Championship.' Dennis Herod was even more damning in his assessment of the sale: 'Bob McGrory's jealousy of Stan's fame cost Stoke their best chance of the First Division title. Before our last game at Sheffield United, he sold a world-class player and we lost that match without him. I am not taking anything away from McGrory who did a great deal for Stoke City. But he wanted the limelight himself and was jealous of players like Stan and Neil Franklin.'

Matthews may have gone but there was no time for grieving, as Stoke had three games remaining in the fight for the title. Without Matthews (sold) and Franklin (international duty), the Potters slumped to a 0-0 draw with mid-table Sunderland at the Victoria Ground, but they followed that up with a huge win away at Aston Villa. By this point, we are well into the additional time which had to be added to the season due to the terrible weather endured months earlier. Going down to the wire, four teams were still battling it out for the title: Wolverhampton Wanderers, Manchester United, Stoke City and Liverpool. Manchester United ended their season first, playing their final game on 26 May, a highly impressive 6-2 win over one-time title challengers Sheffield United.

The victory put them second, level on points with Wolves but behind on goal average and one point above both Liverpool and Stoke, all of whom had a game to play, with Wolves crucially facing Liverpool on the final day. When the two title challengers faced off at Molineux on 31 May, anything but a Wolves win would keep Stoke in it, and they got their wish, with an away win for the boys from Anfield. The Merseysiders went to the top of the table on 57 points, two points ahead of Stoke, but the Potters had a far superior goal average. All this meant that Stoke City went into their final game away at Sheffield United knowing a win would see them crowned champions of England for the first time in the club's history.

They would have to wait more than two weeks before the biggest game of their lives. The winter postponements meant Sheffield United still had two more games to play, and they ended a run of three straight defeats with victory over Arsenal in the penultimate game of their season. In an effort to maintain fitness levels and keep team spirit high, the Stoke players went on a tour of Ireland over this break. The tour was not exactly a roaring success. Franklin forgot his passport, meaning he had to return to Stoke and the squad missed their ferry. Once finally aboard, the tumultuous journey resulted in numerous players suffering chronic sea-sickness. The Potters played two games, winning one, losing one and losing Alec Ormston to a ligament strain.

All in all, it was a nightmarish trip, but there could be no excuses come 14 June. Whatever problems Stoke may have been having, Sheffield United had them five-fold. The team from the Steel City were without a handful of regular starters, most notably their brilliant inside-forward Jimmy Hagan. In his place was Jack Pickering. A player of some pedigree, Pickering had spent his entire career with the Blades and he had been capped once by England in 1933. However, that was fourteen years earlier, and now Pickering was a 38-year-old veteran on the verge of retirement, making his first appearance of the season in the final game of the campaign.

Naturally then, it was Pickering who gave Sheffield United the lead after three minutes, and it looked as though the Yorkshiremen could break Stoke's FA Cup and league dreams all in one season. Just over sixty seconds later though, Ormston—who had managed to return from his injury—met a George Mountford cross with a fierce strike to level the scores. It was a hard slog in the pouring rain all afternoon for Stoke, and in truth, the hosts were the better· team. After a horrible mistake which led to United's opener, Dennis Herod saved shot after shot in the Stoke goal. In the torrid conditions, John McCue lost his footing early in the second half, Pickering stole in and squared the ball to Walter Rickett who restored Sheffield United's lead.

Stoke desperately needed some inspiration or a piece of magic, but their magician had departed for Blackpool. Sheffield United hung on for a 2-1 win, and Liverpool were crowned champions of England for the first time since 1923. It would be a defining moment in the history of Stoke City Football Club, and not just because it denied them of their first piece of silverware. Bob McGrory's pursuit of England stars Tommy Lawton and Wilf Mannion would both prove fruitless in the summer that followed. Instead, Stoke's two big money signings, Tommy Kiernan and Jimmy McAlinden, both missed large chunks of the next season through injury and failed to make the desired impact when fit. A serious injury to Freddie Steele saw him miss over half of the campaign, and a particularly dreadful September set the tone for the season, as overnight Stoke went from title challengers to serious relegation candidates.

McGrory's men didn't get relegated in the 1947–48 season, finishing the campaign 15th and six points above the drop, but they would never challenge at the top end of the division again. McGrory resigned in May 1952 and Stoke were eventually relegated to the Second Division in April 1953, a week before Stanley Matthews lifted the FA Cup with Blackpool in what would go on to be known as the 'Matthews Final'.

CHAPTER 5

The Art of Defending

'A centre-half is a member of a football team and he should, therefore, be as good a footballer as anyone else in the team.'

Neil Franklin

Neil Franklin was a supremely intelligent footballer. His reading of the game and positional awareness was second to none. He dispossessed opponents with scrupulous nous and precision, was exceptional in the air, and possessed great strength and speed over short distances. A footballing polymath, despite his many attributes, the one aspect of his game which managers, players, fans and newspaper columnists always zeroed in on was his ball-playing abilities.

The quote that opens this chapter, made by Neil himself, largely sums up his attitude towards defending and defenders, although it is perhaps the most politely he ever put it. Franklin went as far as stating that anyone who was unable to pass a ball swiftly and accurately wasn't in fact a footballer at all. He wrote in his autobiography, 'Any lout can knock a man off a ball, but it takes a footballer to take a ball off an opponent and then beat others, either by dribbling or by passing the ball correctly.' Like so many of the great sides that we have seen in the early part of the twenty-first century, Franklin was a staunch believer in the opinion that possession was king, and surrendering it was one of the greatest crimes a footballer could commit.

He believed centre-halves should never resort to the great

aimless hoofing of a ball downfield. They ought to look first to make a swift pass to a teammate. If one was not available, then they should hold onto the ball until one became available. If no player made themselves available, then Franklin believed a pass back to the goalkeeper was the best course of action, even if it did lead to jeers from the crowd. Then, and only then, in the remarkable circumstance that no teammate made themselves available to you, a pass to the goalkeeper was not viable and the opportunity cost of taking on an opposition player was too great, Neil felt a kick into touch was still of greater help to your team than a boot downfield, for an opposition throw-in presents you with an immediate opportunity to regain possession of the ball, something a hoof downfield may not.

Neil's views may seem extreme, even to a modern reader, never mind one in the 1940s, 50s or 60s, but he makes a compelling case for them. Of course, the criticism of such a standpoint is that Franklin talks from an extremely rare position, as one of the finest ball-playing defenders the game has ever seen. And even then, 'with all the guile and intelligence of the most cerebral of inside-forwards', as Stanley Matthews put it, Neil still endured plenty of criticism and boundless scrutiny for his approach to the game. Ultimately though, it made him the finest centre-half in Europe, and as such, he speaks as a man with considerable authority when it comes to the art of defending.

The position of centre-half that Neil played was already undergoing a transitional phase towards the tail end of his career. It had been created in the mid-1920s, when the 2-3-5, or 'Pyramid' formation was largely phased out and replaced in England by the W-M formation. Modern football fans are unlikely to be familiar with the W-M formation, the creation of which is often attributed to former Huddersfield Town and Arsenal manager Herbert Chapman. In truth, Chapman was almost certainly not the first man to employ the W-M, but he was undoubtedly its most successful exponent.

The W-M came into prominence during the 1925–26 season, after the offside laws had been altered during the summer of 1925. It took teams some time to adapt, but the W-M (which would probably be described as a 3-2-2-3 or 3-2-4-1 in modern terms) was soon adopted by the vast majority of Football League teams, as well as the English national team. Below is an example of what the W-M formation looked like:

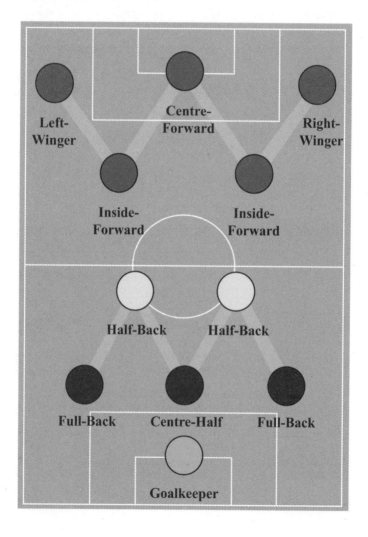

THE ART OF DEFENDING

Since the W-M replaced the Pyramid formation, the centre-half position was created by a midfielder (a half-back, or more specifically, a centre-half-back) dropping into the defence. As such, it was perhaps only natural that the centre-half-back that had become the centre-half should be more of a ball-playing defender.

The W-M would remain as the approach of choice for football teams in England for around thirty years, until Hungary brutally exposed its rigidity and defensive flaws with a 6-3 win against England at Wembley in 1953, and a 7-1 win in the less-remembered return fixture in Budapest. The brilliance of the Magical Magyars was largely responsible for the change in formations that followed in England, and as such, the changing nature of the centre-half throughout much of the 1950s. Today, the position is more commonly referred to as centre-back, a term that sprung up on the continent before Franklin had even hung up his boots, and teams now tend to play two or even three of them.

Whilst Neil appreciated the honesty of such terms as 'centre-back' or 'stopper', rather than centre-half, he loathed the connotations they suggested. In the early 1950s, Franklin bemoaned how full-backs, half-backs and even centre-forwards were transitioning into centre-halves in the twilight of their careers. 'At one time you chose a tip-top centre-half and built a team [a]round him. Today, you do just the opposite. You build a team and then choose a centre-half. Why the position has even become the last haven of rest for players who are nearing the end of their careers. It has also become the position anyone can fill.' As the footballing centre-half made way for the no-nonsense centre-back, Franklin was far more suited to playing in defensive midfield. So it should come as no surprise that in the swansong of his career, he did the opposite of so many fellow ageing pros, occasionally moving away from the role of centre-half and operating instead as a defensive midfielder.

The overall quality of the English game, and without doubt the quality of the English national team, was considered to have deteriorated in the 1950s, and Neil Franklin had a number of theories as to why this was, but perhaps chief among them was the 'death', as he put it, of the ball-playing centre-half.

The reason centre-half became the position of choice for ageing stars in the 1950s, was because it had become an incredibly static position. The classical centre-half was much more closely aligned to what we might call a sweeper than he was to a modern centre-back. A centre-half in the Neil Franklin or Stan Cullis mould was expected to roam around the defence, always looking to get in a position to intercept the ball, sniff out opposition attacks and then—crucially—carry his team forward. Whether it be carrying the ball forward or switching it out to the flank, the centre-half (or at least the good centre-half) ought to be intelligent, mobile and a capable ball player. In the 1950s, however, the centre-back's job would come to be defined by the centre-forward. He would become a purely counter-active player, whose sole task was to restrict the effectiveness of the opposition's centre-forward.

What we may call 'man marking', Neil called 'following the centre-forward like a lapdog'. He believed the forward's ability to then drag you around wherever he wanted and open up gaps for his teammates meant the centre-half was no longer doing his job, something that was very apparent when England were humbled at the hands of the Hungarians. Franklin branded this 'destructive' football, and he saw it as the major factor as to why the continentals surpassed England in the time between his starring in England's great side of the late 1940s and the superiority of others which was already pronounced by the early–mid 1950s. Whilst the rest of Europe focused on ball retention, through their control and passing ability, the English were fixated with size, power and speed. 'While we were cheering the hefty brutes who could kick a ball from one goalmouth to the other without stopping to think whether they would gain advantage by so doing, the continentals worked on the system that to play football you must have the ball.' The views expressed here by Neil were far from exclusive to him, although it is fair to describe him as a footballing purist towards the extreme end of the scale. One might suggest, though, that there was scant change in the English approach to the game for over half a century after he expressed those views, and they have now become borderline cliché.

At this point, it's probably worth talking a little bit more about Neil Franklin as a footballer, his ability, and his standing in the history of the game. The title of this book makes a rather bold claim, and it would seem improper to not make at least some attempt to justify it. If you look back even to the earliest stars of the game—at home or abroad—say Steve Bloomer or Arthur Friedenreich, the most highly regarded players of every generation are almost always forwards or midfielders, and there are a few reasons for this. One is that genius in forwards and highly offensive players is easy to recognise, not least simply by noting the number of goals they score. The ability to beat a man and create chances for your teammates, too, is eminently noticeable. With midfielders, even those of a less attacking persuasion, most keen football fans can recognise when a midfield player controls a game. But a defender? It is far more difficult to spot genius in a defender, especially a central defender. How many defenders go down as having been so brilliant that they are considered on a par with or superior to the finest midfielders and forwards of their generation? Franz Beckenbauer would certainly meet the criteria, providing one classifies him as a defender. As good as Franco Baresi was, few would put him on a par with Diego Maradona. England's own Bobby Moore is a player held in extremely high regard in England, but you will seldom find a football fan who considered him the equal or better of Pelé, and rightly so.

It is fair to say history has not been as kind to Neil Franklin as it has to any of the aforementioned defenders, and there are obvious reasons for that, with a lack of footage and silverware chief among them. Yet almost all who witnessed his talents had no hesitation in putting Neil on the same pedestal as Stanley Matthews, Tommy Lawton or Tom Finney, the equivalent stars of the day. That does not necessarily 'prove' anything, but it should be noted how few central defenders earn that kind of universal acclaim.

The title of England's greatest defender is the one bestowed upon Franklin in the title of this book. Bobby Moore is probably the man most familiar with that tag, and for good reason too. He captained England to glory at a World Cup, won more than 100 caps for his country and was still a top-level player and full international in his early thirties, unlike Franklin. Moore shared a number of attributes with Neil: he too was comfortable on the ball and capable of spraying accurate passes out of defence. Peter Coates drew comparisons between the pair in February 2017, stating, 'My memory at Stoke just about stretches back to Neil Franklin, an exceptional player, one regarded by his generation in the same way that Bobby Moore was a generation later.'

The Stoke City chairman is one of a diminishing number of people to have watched both players up close. I am yet to talk to anyone of sufficient vintage to have seen Franklin play who doesn't consider him the finest centre-half England have ever produced. When Tom Finney picked his 'Best Ever England XI' in 1989, he described Bobby Moore as 'the perfect centre half and role model skipper', yet he put England's World Cup winner at half-back in his selection, reserving the centre-half spot for his ex-England teammate Franklin, who he described as simply 'the best England defender of all'.

David Miller, the former chief sports correspondent for *The Times*, and David Lacey, the *Guardian*'s football correspondent for thirty-eight years prior to 2002, both picked Franklin alongside Moore in a back four in their England dream teams. So too did Norman Giller, the writer and historian who spent ten years as the chief football reporter for the *Daily Express* and has authored more than a hundred books. Billy Wright also put Franklin at centre-half in his 'England Dream Team', humbly moving himself to his original position of half-back to make way for the man who preceded him at centre-half for England.

In fact, all but one 'all-time', 'greatest' or 'dream' England XI I have come across which has been written by anyone who saw Neil Franklin play, places him at the heart of their defence (the exception being Tommy Lawton's *'The Lawton XI'*). Of course, most also feature Bobby Moore, and who was the superior of the two is frankly unimportant. What it shows is that Neil Franklin is a grossly underrated and forgotten star of the game.

CHAPTER 6

The Burnden Park Disaster

Although the end to the 1946–47 season had been a tragedy for Stoke City in a footballing sense, Neil Franklin and his teammates had been involved in a genuine tragedy fifteen months earlier.

The 1945–46 season was a transitional one. The war had finished, but the timing of its conclusion—twinned with the nationwide upheaval of the immediate post-war period—meant the Football League couldn't fully reinstate the league system. Instead, league football would persevere with a regional format for a further season, in the form of a makeshift Football League North and South. But whilst the Football League would take another year to make a full return, it was decided that the FA Cup should be immediately reinstated.

In the absence of a proper league format, the importance of the FA Cup—making its return after six years away—grew further. This was particularly evident at the Victoria Ground, where Bob McGrory began resting his star men in league games to ensure their freshness and fitness for the cup. Confidence was high among the Stoke City group, with wins against the North League table-toppers Sheffield United, their Steel City neighbours Sheffield Wednesday, and Burnley securing their route into the quarter-finals.

The Potters hadn't reached the semi-finals since 1899, and there was a feel-good factor around Staffordshire when the club got a relatively favourable draw in the form of Bolton Wanderers. The Victoria Ground had been expected to set its record attendance for the visit of the Lancashire club, but a bitterly cold Saturday afternoon saw them fall just short of the record, as 50,735 crammed into the Vic. The game was won by the brilliance of two Bolton players: namely Stan Hanson and his heroics in goal, and the genius of former England international inside-forward Ray Westwood, who scored one in each half to secure a 2-0 win for the visitors.

For this season only, the FA had introduced a two-legged system for every round of the cup, in order to increase club revenues. Despite the healthy lead Bolton took back to Burnden Park, spirits within the Stoke City camp remained high, and they believed they could turn the tie around. Upon arrival in Lancashire, the Stoke players discovered that their supporters felt the same way. Fans had made the journey from Staffordshire in their thousands, and this gave the players a further confidence boost.

Bolton fans too had flocked to the ground in unprecedented numbers. The club's record crowd at that time was 69,912, which had been set in 1933, and this game was sure to smash that record. By 2 p.m., the Railway Embankment End was full, with enough supporters outside the ground to fill it once more. To make matters worse, one of the club's stands, the Burnden Stand, was still closed. That end of the ground, which held just shy of 3,000 fans, had been appropriated by the Ministry of Food as a store during the war, and was yet to be returned to the club for their use.

The attractions of the game were plentiful. Not only was it the latter stages of the FA Cup in the post-war attendance boom, with both team's supporters fancying their chances, there was also the added appeal of Ray Westwood and Stanley Matthews. Westwood was a wonderful and prolific inside-forward born in the Black Country, and he had lit up the first leg. The indomitable Matthews was, of course, the country's greatest footballing star whose presence alone added thousands to any gate. Westwood, who spent nineteen years with Bolton, was the uncle of future Manchester

United and England wing-half Duncan Edwards. Westwood and Edwards both shared a rare genius on the pitch, but they would sadly both also be involved in two of the game's greatest tragedies. Matthews and Westwood taking part in a game of such magnitude made it as attractive an occasion for the neutral as it was to the fans of the two sides from Bolton and Stoke.

The final ingredient in what ultimately proved to be a devastating cocktail of appeal in this match was the weather. Whilst the first leg had been a bitterly cold affair at the Victoria Ground, the game at Burnden Park would be played under excellent conditions, with the sunshine of 9 March convincing those fair-weather fans that a trip to the football would be the best use of their Saturday.

With stands already heaving with supporters, enormous numbers gathered outside as queues continued to grow. Within forty five minutes of kick-off, it began to dawn on those outside the ground that they weren't going to make it inside the stadium, or not in time for kick-off at least. Some began taking matters into their own hands, and with the number of supporters in the stadium evidently at breaking point, the turnstiles were shut at 2:40 p.m. Fans jumped over turnstiles and pressure was building around the railway line, where inadequate fencing was unable to prevent people from gaining access. The Railway Embankment End in general was a very rudimentary stand: basic terracing made up of little more than mud, bricks and steel barriers dotted around after every five sets of steps. What's more, during the war, these steel barriers had been replaced in certain places by wooden ones.

With the Burnden Stand out of action, so too were its turnstiles, and that meant congestion began to build up around the Manchester Road End, where fans with tickets for the Railway Embankment End and the Burnden Paddock had to enter the ground. As a result, a number of police officers had been tasked with directing supporters towards the correct turnstiles. This was problematic, as the sixty police officers on duty at Burnden Park that day would become incredibly strained as the day went on. Of those sixty, just fourteen were patrolling the Railway Embankment End, where the tragedy itself took place.

Roughly fifteen minutes prior to kick-off, a frightened twelve-year-old boy convinced his father that they ought to leave the ground. As tens of thousands tried to get in, they attempted to get out. The boy's father, Norman Crook, eventually found a route out, picking the lock of an exit gate using one of his own screw keys. Unfortunately, whilst the son and father had managed to escape the chaos, the gate was subsequently used as a way in, as some fans continued to force entry.

People were fainting up to an hour before the game had even kicked off, such was the strain in certain areas of the ground, and this continued as the players entered the field. Men, women and children were being passed down the stands to the relative comfort of pitchside. A ball had not yet been kicked but paramedics were already struggling to cope with the number of people needing help. Once the players did enter the field, they could see that the ground was incredibly full, but the alarm bells were not yet ringing.

The sight of packed out crowds, children on the tracks and swooning supporters being passed down the stands on people's shoulders, whilst never a happy sight, was far from an uncommon one for the players on either side. Indeed, the first leg only a week earlier had seen similar scenes, with the *Sentinel* reporting, 'Boys were passed down to the front to sit around the edge of the track as a crush is relieved'. Similarly, to supporters not in close proximity to the most strained areas, it merely looked like a very well-attended cup tie.

Suggestions that this was more than just congested terraces surfaced quickly though, as fans spilled onto the pitch in the opening moments of the game. After roughly five minutes of play, the referee, Mr George Dutton, brought the game to a halt. Once the pitch had been cleared, play resumed, but not for long. A second stint of five minutes was played before Mr Dutton had no option but to halt proceedings once more. This time a much larger invasion onto the pitch had taken place by the corner flag at the Railway Embankment End. The police horses were of little use now, as people continued to tumble onto the field. The game could not continue, and Mr Dutton called over the two captains, Neil Franklin and Harry Hubbick, to inform them that there would be a stoppage.

'He told us that some people had been injured and suggested that we leave the field until some sort of order had been restored. Both Harry Hubbick and I thought it was a sensible idea, so Mr Dutton, his two linesmen and the twenty-two players walked off the pitch and into the dressing room.' That was Neil Franklin's recollection of the conversation, but there appears to have been some discord between different players' accounts of what had happened at that point in time. Neil wrote, 'As far as I could see, the railway embankment was uncomfortably full of people, and there was the usual depressing sight of the fainting and the fainted being passed over the heads of the crowd, and the whole mass of spectators swaying in a most alarming manner. But as far as we players could see, nothing untoward had happened.'

Neil's close friend and Stoke City's goalkeeper Dennis Herod saw it slightly differently, later stating, 'I'd served in North Africa, Italy and Normandy and I'd seen plenty of dead people. I knew those people hadn't fainted. I knew they were dead.' Bolton's Nat Lofthouse also recalled being aware of casualties, having overheard a policeman telling the referee, 'I believe those people are dead', whilst pointing to bodies strewn by the side of the pitch.

Whilst it seems there was a difference of understanding in the seriousness of what had happened, even those who knew there had been fatalities were wholly unaware of the extent at this stage. When the players left the field at 3:12 p.m., doctors had already put the estimated death toll at twenty-eight. Those Stoke City players, like Neil, who were unaware of any deaths at all, became aware of them moments after returning to the dressing room. Reserve players George Mountford, Billy Mould and Alex Ormston entered pale-faced and bearing the news that they had heard of 'two or three' deaths. It would be twenty minutes before Mr Dutton re-entered the Stoke City dressing room to tell the players that Bolton's chief constable had ordered that the game be continued.

It was a controversial decision and an unpopular one with many people. Stanley Matthews later said he was 'sickened' that the game was allowed to continue, and certainly none of the twenty-two players involved that day were any longer concerned about the outcome of the match. However, the decision made by William Howard was far from an easy one. There was no PA (Public Address) system in place at Burnden Park at the time, and as such, no way of communicating with supporters the severity of the situation. It was feared that an abandonment of the game after just ten minutes could lead to unrest, disgruntled supporters and potentially further incidents and deaths. These fears were substantiated by the widespread boos that rang out around the ground when the players first left the field. It was an awful decision to have to make, but ultimately if it saved lives and prevented injuries, it was surely the correct one. Neil shared his thoughts on those who criticised the chief constable's decision to resume the game in his autobiography.

'It is easy to say that, but we must remember that in those days hardly any clubs possessed a public-address system. The disaster was confined to one small corner of the ground, and fewer than 10 per cent of the huge crowd which assembled for that ill-fated Cup-tie knew that people had been killed. It is not certain how they would have reacted to an announcement sent round on a board to the effect that the match had been abandoned. To me, it just doesn't seem practicable that someone could chalk on a board: "People have been killed. The match is abandoned." Some people said that it was ghoulish to continue the game after people had lost their lives, but I feel I am speaking for all the players when I say that we were only too pleased to get it over. It would have been much more terrible to replay the game on the same ground.'

In the twenty minutes plus that the two sets of players had been waiting in their dressing rooms, much had happened on the field and in the stands. A mass pitch invasion had taken place shortly after the players left the field, whilst others had sought refuge in the closed Burnden Stand. Mounted police cleared the fans from the field of play so the players could return, but the pitch bore the marks—quite literally—of the disaster that had just taken place. As well as being terribly churned up by the thousands who had spilled onto it, it was also a great deal smaller. With the dead and injured still being cleared away and roughly a thousand fans spread around the touchlines, sawdust was used as makeshift line markings.

Those supporters who remained unaware of the tragedy that took place that day right up until the final whistle must have been bemused at both team's performances. There was a distinct and obviously understandable lack of intensity and attacking intent from both sides. Frank Baker struck the crossbar for Stoke in a rare sighting of goal, whilst Nat Lofthouse saw a shot of his fail to find the back of the net having got stuck in the mud on Dennis Herod's goal line. There was no half-time break; the players simply switched ends and play was resumed. Franklin later reflected on returning to the pitch that day and the emotions going through the players' heads.

'And so, at long last, we got the order to go back on to the field, but as soon as we left the dressing-room the full force of what had happened hit us. When you leave the visitors' dressing room at Burnden Park, you walk along a corridor, past the home team's dressing-room, and then turn right into the tunnel leading to the ground.

'Usually the corridor is clear, but on this occasion it was full of bodies. We saw the victims laid out there and suddenly realized that they were dead. How many were dead we didn't know, but we knew that it was a frightening number, and as soon as that realization hit us, all thoughts of football left us.

'No longer was this a Cup-tie in which Stoke City had to battle against a two-goal deficit. It was now just a mere formality that we completed ninety minutes and to hell with the result. No one wanted to score, let alone win.

'True, the sections of the crowd which were not aware of the disaster cheered and egged on their favourites, but their favourites knew what had happened and felt sick. We just went through the motions on a pitch that was now ankle deep in mud, and it was a blessed relief when Mr Dutton blew the final whistle.'

The crush itself had occurred in a tiny pocket of the ground just by the corner flag at the Railway Embankment End. When supporters who had been locked out broke down a sleeper fence from the railway and surged into that end of the ground, it had severe consequences for those in front of them. Eyewitness Bill Cheeseman recalled, 'All of a sudden, those that were in front of us seemed to go—all falling down like a pack of cards.'

Thirty-three people died. Over five hundred were injured. It was the deadliest accident at a sporting event in British history, and would remain so until 1971, when exactly twice as many people were killed in the second Ibrox disaster. The star factor draw of Matthews and Westwood was evidenced by where the deceased had travelled from, with only seven of the thirty-three who lost their lives being from Bolton. The rest had travelled from the likes of Wigan, Heywood, Stockport and across the north-west.

Excluding active servicemen and women, more people died at Burnden Park that day than had died in Bolton during the war.

A handful of those killed had fought in the war. One such fan was Frank Jubb of Rochdale. Only recently demobbed, Frank had served as a Royal Artillery gunner and spent three years as PoW during the war. The cruelty of being a survivor of the deadliest conflict in human history only to be killed at a football match was not lost on anyone. Stanley Matthews wrote in his autobiography, 'To survive a war, only to die at a football match sent a shiver running down the spine of nearly every one of us.'

The disaster left an indelible mark on everyone who was at Burnden Park that day. Matthews, a man with a training regime that would make an SAS soldier blink twice, was unable to train for days. He spoke candidly about the scarring effects of the tragedy in his book, writing, 'For several days, I could not bring myself to train. In my mind I kept seeing the body bags and was too distressed to even think about football. [. . .] The disaster left me dazed. Even now it's hard to write about the day because such was the enormity of the tragedy that whatever words you summon seem trite and irrelevant.'

Neil's son, Gary, told me that his father rarely spoke about that fateful day. Neil wrote in his book that the disaster, 'still haunts me and all those who were connected with it', as well as describing it as his 'greatest football nightmare'.

Welsh lawyer and two-time MP Moelwyn Hughes was tasked with leading an official enquiry into the disaster. He concluded that all stands/enclosures ought to require a safety certificate, which would only be granted once the ground had been deemed safe by an expert panel. The criteria for being deemed safe would include scientific calculation of the maximum number of people allowed entry, mechanical counting of the number of people entering at each turnstile, with a central coordination of the system and a general inspection of all enclosures to ensure they were safe to house vast numbers of supporters.

Hughes' report, which was published four months after the disaster, was critical of the Football Association. The last report of its ilk, which had been written in 1924, laid the responsibility of crowd safety at the door of football's governing body. Hughes wanted to hand this responsibility over to the local authorities. Hughes' reforms and recommendations seemed largely common sense, but they fell on deaf ears. The closing stages of his report possibly anticipated this, stating, 'Compliance with the recommendations of this Report will cost money. They will involve grounds in a loss of gate money on popular days . . . The insurance for greater safety for the public demands a premium.'

Not everyone agreed. Neither the FA, the government or club chairmen acted strongly. Crowd limits were introduced at large grounds, minor improvements were made to some barriers and enclosures, and a good number of teams did bring in automatic machines to help them know when a certain enclosure was full. This was a woefully insufficient response to a serious tragedy. Grounds up and down the country continued to pack out rudimentary enclosures such as the one at the Railway Embankment End, as public safety took a back seat in favour of penny-pinching.

The cheaper alternative of all-ticket matches was preferred to the genuine stadium upgrades and improvements that were required. Some who risked fronting the costs of such improvements, along with many in the media, simply pointed fingers at supporters, or 'hooligans', foreshadowing the narrative that would surround Hillsborough forty-three years later. The *Manchester Evening News* posited, 'perhaps the war has left people with less respect for the law than they used to have', whilst the Chelsea manager Billy Birrell declared, 'war has made everyone more aggressive'. In truth, there were fans who had gained illegal entry, whether that was jumping over turnstiles, access through the gate picked by Mr Crook or the route in via the broken-down sleeper fence by the railway; but to lay the blame at those people solely would be not just simplistic, but dishonest.

The FA and Bolton Wanderers have to take responsibility for a hefty portion of the blame. The enclosure where the crush took place, and many, many more just like it across the United Kingdom, were not fit for purpose. In his report, Hughes found that one of the collapsed barriers was rusty and in a state of disrepair. Furthermore, Bolton Wanderers had created a recipe for disaster in many respects. Despite the game having all the hallmarks of a blockbuster sell-out, Bolton reportedly expected a crowd of just 50,000. The fact that all the seats in the Manchester Road Stand (sometimes referred to as the Main Stand) had sold out didn't seem to dissuade them from this belief, with the *Bolton Evening Standard* declaring that there would be, 'plenty of room for spectators without tickets'. An estimated 85,000 attended the match, at a time when Burnden Park had a supposed capacity of 60,000.

Whether the war really had made people more aggressive, one can draw their own conclusions, but there seems to be a stronger case for attitudes towards death having changed. Almost 500,000 men, women and children from the United Kingdom lost their lives during World War II, just shy of 1 per cent of the country's overall population. Had people become slightly more emotionally hardened to bereavement? Bolton's club historian Simon Marland suggested as much, saying, death was 'something that had happened in a lot of families, to a lot of people, obviously, not just overseas but actually in their own backyard'.

The lack of recognition at the time for those who lost their lives was perhaps a reflection of that fact. Whilst a Disaster Fund was set up, which raised £50,936, it is a sign of the times that there was nothing at Burnden Park to honour or pay homage to the dead up until 1992, when a memorial plaque was added to the ground. When Bolton moved to the Reebok Stadium (now the University of Bolton Stadium) in 1997, the plaque remained, being unveiled by club legend and president Nat Lofthouse in 2000 at the Asda supermarket which occupied the site. In 2016, a permanent memorial plaque in memory of the dead was unveiled at the University of Bolton Stadium, with a representative of the club saying that it was 'no longer the forgotten disaster'.

CHAPTER 7

England's First Choice

*'To field an England team without including him
was basically unthinkable.'*

Tom Finney

Between 1946 and 1950, Neil Franklin won twenty-seven consecutive full international caps for England. In doing so, he broke a record set by Ernie Blenkinsop which had stood for seventeen years. Franklin could accurately be described as the first name on the England team sheet over those four years, in what was almost certainly the finest group of players the nation has ever assembled.

If one accounts for wartime internationals as well, Neil made thirty-nine appearances for England, never being dropped. His peacetime England debut, and as such his first official cap, came against Ireland at Windsor Park in Belfast. The tie, which took place on 28 September 1946, was the first match of the 1946–47 British Home Championship. Franklin was played in his preferred role of centre-half-back, and England ran out comfortable 7-2 victors.

Two days later he won his second cap, against Eire in Dublin. Neil described the crowd at Dalymount Park that day as the most vocal he ever experienced, writing, 'Never have I met such enthusiasm—no, not even at Hampden Park.' England had expected to record a rout similar to the one in Belfast, but found their opponents in a resilient mood. They avoided a shock though, winning

1-0 thanks to an 82nd minute goal by Tom Finney. It is worth taking a look at England's starting XI that day:

> Frank Swift, Laurie Scott, George Hardwick, Billy Wright, Neil Franklin, Henry Cockburn, Tom Finney, Raich Carter, Tommy Lawton, Wilf Mannion, Bobby Langton.

Despite the notable omissions of Stanley Matthews and Stan Mortensen, it was a star-studded lineup and a reflection of England's quality at the time. At least eight of those players are among the finest England have ever produced in their positions. The England players that day were just happy to come away with a win though, and Neil was no exception, having faced a tough battle with Eire's centre-forward, Mick O'Flanagan. 'My vivid memories of that game remind me of the great struggle I had in my personal duels with Michael O'Flanagan, the Eire centre-forward. I was certainly glad to see them back of him, and of his brother, Dr Kevin O'Flanagan, who played outside-right.'

Outstanding sportsmen, the O'Flanagans remain to this day as the only Irish brothers to have both won international caps in rugby and football. Mick O'Flanagan's battles with Neil that day came in the only game he ever played for Ireland, having been called up due to an injury to first-choice forward Davy Walsh. The brothers played together for six years at Bohemians, where they had a penchant for alternating flanks in an attempt to bamboozle defenders. By 1946 though, Kevin had left Bohemians to join Arsenal.

Franklin and his teammates made light work of their next two international opponents, beating Wales 3-0 at Maine Road and the Netherlands 8-2 at Leeds Road. That emphatic victory over the Dutch, in which Tommy Lawton scored four goals, came just eight months after the Burnden Park Disaster. The terrace of the Dalton Bank End at Leeds Road was just as shoddy as the Railway

Embankment End at Burnden Park, and the FA's decision to have the national team play there so soon after the tragedy at Bolton rather made a mockery of their claims that public safety had always been 'uppermost in the minds of those responsible for football crowds.'

England's next match, which came against Scotland, was the final game of the 1946–47 British Home Championships, and they dropped points for the first time, drawing 1-1 at Wembley with just shy of 100,000 spectators in attendance. England still topped the group, whilst the Scots came last. By now, Franklin was an assured international footballer earning widespread acclaim. Norman Giller wrote of England's draw with Scotland, 'Wright and Franklin were developing into the Britton and Cullis of peacetime football. There could be no higher praise.'

Having lost one and drawn one in their two wartime games against France due to the brilliance of Julien Darui, England beat the French 3-0 at Highbury in May 1947, in what would be their last outing before going on an overseas tour of Switzerland and Portugal. Both destinations would prove to be memorable for Neil, although for very different reasons. The Swiss were something of a bogey team for the English. They had beaten England 2-1 shortly before the outbreak of World War II, and went one better with a 3-1 win during the only wartime meeting of the two sides.

They proved to be tricky opposition once more in 1947, taking the lead after twenty-seven minutes before shutting up shop. The attacking talents of Matthews, Carter, Lawton and Mannion struggled to break down the Swiss, and on the one occasion in which they did, the referee Victor Sedz ruled Lawton's goal to have been offside. In Raich Carter's final appearance in an England shirt, England lost in a peacetime match for the first time since May 1939. It was a sad end for one of the most gifted players to have ever turned out for the country.

Three days later though, Franklin was back in action, in

ENGLAND'S FIRST CHOICE

England's first ever 'B' team international. England flew from Zurich to Geneva to face a Swiss 'B' team. Three decades before England under-21s came into existence, Walter Winterbottom was an advocate of having an England second string, keen to use it as a way of blooding players into the national team. Billy Wright wrote in his autobiography that the England team was intended to be an 'FA XI', but the Swiss billed it as 'Switzerland B vs England B' in an attempt to draw a larger crowd. The England side borrowed their kits from the RAF, but whatever their intentions, it has gone down as the first official fixture played by an England B team.

Six of England's starting XI that had been beaten in Zurich started the game in Geneva, and Franklin was one of them. The game passed without a goal, but certainly not without incident. Neil was a very calm operator. Despite being no stranger to conflict both within and outside of the game during his life, he was always one to steer well clear of any fracas or violence. Over his entire career, he was never sent off, and having retired before yellow cards were introduced, he was never even cautioned.

Neil frowned upon violent and dirty players, stating:

'I took up professional football as a job. I regarded myself purely and simply as a public entertainer, a professional sportsman who got paid for his job. My colleagues and opponents were in the same class. Therefore, I have never been able to understand why I should be expected to hurt a fellow player. After all, a window-cleaner doesn't go around pushing his fellow window-cleaners off their ladders, does he? So why should sportsmen be expected to hurt their fellow sportsmen and do them out of jobs?

'To me, football is a game to be played with the head and the feet, and when I say the head, I also include the grey matter which we are all supposed to have inside our heads. If you have nothing more than physical strength then you can never hope to be a success at soccer. Any lout can knock a man off a ball, but it takes a footballer to take a ball off an opponent and then beat others, either by dribbling or by passing the ball correctly.

'However, despite my dislike for physical violence on the football field, I was involved in one regrettable incident—in May 1947.'

The incident Neil is referring to took place in that game between England B and Switzerland B in Geneva. An England team that contained the likes of Finney, Mortensen, Mannion, and only one player who never won a full cap for England, outclassed a Swiss second string, but found themselves on the receiving end of a number of forceful challenges. As the game approached its final stages, Hans Siegenthaler broke away. A pacy wide forward who represented Switzerland once at the 1950 World Cup, Siegenthaler was popular with the home crowd, given that he played for Zurich-based side SC Young Fellows Juventus. Typically alert, Franklin moved across and tackled Siegenthaler, before passing the ball downfield.

Neil tended to be reluctant to praise himself, but he did describe the tackle as being timed perfectly. He was shocked then, when the referee blew his whistle and awarded the Swiss a free kick. 'I was amazed to hear the referee whistle, and when I turned round, Hiegenthaler [Neil misspelt his name] was writhing in agony.' The popular local forward's seeming injury angered the crowd, who began invading the pitch and making their way towards Neil. Before he knew it, objects were being launched in his direction. Neil recalled, 'As I went up to the player and was helping him to his feet, I suddenly saw that the crowd was in a whale of a temper. Some of them had left their forms and were advancing on to the field, and two empty beer bottles and an umbrella were winging towards me.'

A quick-thinking Frank Swift rushed to Neil's aid, picking up the umbrella in question and using it to ward off fans and usher them back towards their seats. The England goalkeeper was not a small man, and his threats of, 'Now get back before I have to do something with this' proved more effective than the police's attempts to force fans back into their seats. Reflecting on the debacle, Neil wrote, 'Looking back on the incident, I can laugh, but I assure you it was far from pleasant. My knees felt like unset jellies, and I cannot imagine what I would have done if the crowd had got hold of me.'

The second leg of the overseas tour saw England fly from Zurich to Lisbon, where they were to face Portugal at the Estádio Nacional. It was the second time Neil had played at the ground, having done so once with the RAF during the war, and it was a stadium he afforded greater praise than any other. Talking of his first experience playing there, he wrote, 'We were honoured to be allowed to play on the now famous Estádio Nacional, one of the greatest of all the sports stadiums in the world. Every spectator sits down to watch the game in comfort, and the whole thing is the last word in luxury. They tell me it cost more than half a million pounds.' The stadium has since become famous in Britain for playing host to the 1967 European Cup final, which Celtic won, with the team becoming known as 'the Lisbon Lions'. The stadium remains virtually unchanged from how it was when Neil played there in the 1940s, but it is now almost inoperative, restricted to hosting the final of the Taça de Portugal and not much else.

Portugal would prove the perfect tonic for the defeat and panic of Switzerland though, and England ran out 10-0 winners. Tommy Lawton and Stan Mortensen both scored four, whilst Finney and Matthews notched once each. Lawton's opener came after just seventeen seconds, which remains the fastest goal ever scored by an England player, and the Three Lions were two goals up a minute later. Mortensen's quadruple came in his England debut, introducing himself in some style. Neil called the game 'the easiest walkover in which I have ever played'.

The Portuguese made tactical substitutions without consulting the referee and even switched the ball for a smaller one in an attempt to get a foothold in the game, but it proved futile. Neil marked one of the most prolific forwards the game has ever known that day, one Fernando Peyroteo. A big, strong poacher of a forward who was a real threat in the air, Peyroteo scored 544 goals in 334 games for Sporting Clube de Portugal, his only club, and 15 goals in 20 games for Portugal. He was unable to pose any kind of threat that day though, as England left Portugal humiliated, with Neil describing it as, 'a massacre more than a football match,' adding, 'I would have roared with laughter on that May 25th, 1947, if anyone had told me that within eight years Portugal would beat England 3-1 in an International.'

One man who may have had less fond memories of England's demolition of Portugal is Dicky Robinson. A promising young centre-half who had broken into the Middlesbrough side at the end of the war, Robinson had been called up as a reserve for the games in Switzerland and Portugal, aged only twenty. With Neil carrying a knock, he was expected to start the game in Lisbon as a stand-in for England's regular centre-half. However, just thirty minutes before kick-off, Franklin declared himself fit, and was reinstated to the side. Robinson gained honours representing the Football League, and was called up again as a reserve, but he never won a full cap for England.

It would be four months before England next took to the field, overseas once more in Belgium this time. England took an early lead through Tommy Lawton after thirty-five seconds, and were 3-0 up with just a quarter of an hour played. The game ended in a 5-2 win for England, with Stanley Matthews receiving a standing ovation from the home supporters. There had yet again been suggestions that Matthews was finished, and boy did he prove the sceptics wrong. If Stan had made a pound every time someone incorrectly predicted that he was finished, it probably would have equated to more money than he made in his entire 33-year career. The 'Wizard of the Dribble' put in a five-star performance, assisting every one of England's five goals in Belgium, with some labelling it his finest display to date.

The Belgian press were full of praise, not just for Matthews but for the entire England team. One newspaper stated, 'The Englishmen played a game which has no equal.' A month later, England were 3-0 up inside fifteen minutes once more, this time against Wales. Astonishingly, Matthews set up every single one of those goals as well. Eight assists in two England internationals should give some insight into what a special player he was. In the 1946–47 season, Stan played 23 games for Stoke. In those 23 games, the Potters notched some 41 goals. Records from the time suggest that Stan played a direct role in 30 of those 41. Such statistics rather contradict those who claimed he wasn't a 'team player'.

Anyhow, England didn't add to their tally and ran out 3-0 winners against the Welsh in Cardiff. Two weeks later, the Three Lions played their first game on home soil in over six months, playing host to Ireland. There would aptly be fireworks in the game, which took place on Guy Fawkes Night at Goodison Park. Three goals in the last eight minutes saw the game end 2-2, the Belfast-based Ireland side avoiding defeat against England for the first time in thirteen meetings. It was a shock result, but England had the chance to make amends two weeks later in a friendly against Sweden at Highbury. They did so, winning 4-2, but Franklin was unable to shut out Sweden's Gunnar Nordahl.

Possibly the finest footballer Sweden have ever produced, Nordahl would transfer to Italy just a couple of years after this game against England. To this day, he sits comfortably at the top of AC Milan's all-time leading scorer charts, despite spending just six years at the San Siro. In total, Nordahl scored 442 goals in 504 games in his career, and 43 goals from 33 caps for Sweden. Franklin had befriended the 1948 Olympic Gold medallist a year earlier whilst representing the RAF in Stockholm, and later described him as, 'just about the best centre-forward I have met'. Nordahl scored once, but England got the win they so desperately needed going into a crucial game against Scotland.

In the final tie of the 1947–48 British Home Championship, 135,375 spectators turned up at Hampden Park to watch Scotland entertain England. The Scots were playing for pride, having already lost to both Ireland and Wales, but they couldn't restore any against England, who won 2-0 to retain their crown. Scotland had started the game brightly, and Neil had been key in preventing them from scoring and giving England a foothold in the game. Rave reviews came his way in the morning papers. 'Lack of penetrative power at inside forward, plus a brilliant display by Neil Franklin, Stoke City centre half, prevented a Scottish victory,' said the Aberdeen *Press and Journal.*

The last game on England's 1947–48 season calendar was quite probably the most significant international Neil ever played in. To celebrate fifty years of the FIGC, the governing body of Italian football, Italy were to host England on 16 May 1948. Italy had been world champions in 1934 and 1938, and with the World Cup having been put on hold during the war, they were still the holders of the World Cup when they met England in 1948. As much as their team had changed since those two conquests, they were still regarded as the best Europe had to offer. Right across the continent, the press were taking enormous interest in the tie.

The England team felt like the underdogs in Turin. The baking heat was sure to favour the locals, and Neil stated that, 'most people in Europe were looking towards Turin and expecting us to be beaten.' At a time when the majority of the England team were earning around £10 a week, the Italian players had been offered the equivalent of a £100 bonus each should they emerge victorious, a sign of their thirst to record a first win over England. Of Italy's starting XI, seven played for Torino, and would be playing at their club's home ground. Among them was Valentino Mazzola, regarded by some as the greatest Italian footballer of them all. All seven would be killed almost exactly a year on from this game in the Superga air disaster. It is no wonder Grande Torino players dominated the Italian national team: they had won five consecutive Serie A titles prior to the disaster, with a 70 per cent win percentage over those five campaigns.

England were not disappointed by the standard of their Italian counterparts, in fact, they were very impressed. Italy dominated the early exchanges, as England struggled to adapt to the heat and keep their opposition at bay. Tommy Lawton conceded, 'Probably on sheer football alone, the Italians had the edge on us', whilst Tom Finney described them as 'a wonder team packed with talent.' England went 1-0 up inside five minutes courtesy of a driven shot by Stan Mortensen from a tight angle, but make no mistake, the Italians were on top. They put England under severe pressure in the first twenty minutes, with Wright and Franklin both impressing, and Frank Swift making three smart saves in his first international game as captain.

AC Milan forward Riccardo Carapellese was causing particular headaches for England's backline with his running in behind. Neil described him as being 'like half a dozen greyhounds rolled into one'. In the 23rd minute, England doubled their lead entirely against the run of play. Franklin brought the ball out of defence, playing a through-ball into the feet of Mortensen who crossed for Tommy Lawton. Between England's first and second goals, Torino's Romeo Menti had two goals chalked off for offside by the Spanish referee, and unrest was beginning to fester within the Italian ranks.

From that point on, England put in a very assured display. Tom Finney made sure of victory with two goals in two second-half minutes. The 4-0 margin certainly wasn't a fair reflection of the game, but it was an enormous compliment to the spirit and talent of the England team. It was a monumental achievement for all involved. Tom Finney wrote in his autobiography, 'aside from the 1966 World Cup victory, it had a very good claim to be the highpoint of the English game.' Neil wasn't one to downplay it either, writing, 'Certainly this was the most dramatic game I have ever played, and when I am old and grey I shall look back to that day in Turin in 1948 when we beat the mighty Italians by 4-0 after looking as if we were booked for a hefty defeat.'

A four-month break from international football followed, before England were back in action with a trip to Copenhagen. The King and Queen of Denmark were in attendance as England dominated the Danish but were toothless up front. The Denmark team was made up entirely of amateurs, but they were a talented bunch. They had come third in that summer's Olympics in London, defeating Great Britain's amateurs 5-3 in the Bronze medal match. Their team boasted three outstanding forwards: John Hansen, Karl Aage Hansen and Karl Aage Praest. All three would leave Denmark and turn professional within a year of this match, becoming famous and successful players in Italy's Serie A, most notably with Juventus.

Also in the Denmark side that day was Viggo Jensen, a tireless and talented left-sided player who would go on to become a teammate of Franklin's at Hull City. Neil's old schoolboy opponent and occasional wartime teammate Len Shackleton made his England debut, and should have opened the scoring, but after rounding the goalkeeper his shot got stuck in a mound of mud as the rain poured down in the Danish capital. Ultimately, England's forwards put in a poor showing, and England recorded their first goalless draw since the end of the war. Of England's five forwards that day, only Stanley Matthews would retain his place for the next international, and it would be Tommy Lawton's final cap as an England international.

That next international came just a couple of weeks later with the return of the British Home Championships. The shake-up to the forward line worked, as England put six past Ireland at Windsor Park. A forgettable 1-0 win against Wales followed, forgettable for the spectators at least: Neil's performance earned distinction, along with Billy Wright's. England's final game of 1948 was a bit more like it, as Switzerland were put to the sword at Highbury. An unfamiliar looking lineup featuring a number of debutants exacted some revenge on the nation's bogey side, scoring six goals without reply. England played just six games in the calendar year of 1948, winning five, drawing one, scoring nineteen and conceding two. A very good case could be made for England having assembled their strongest-ever team in 1948.

Neil was involved in two further matches with England in 1948 though, both 'B' team games. Curiously, England's first three 'B' team matches were all played in Switzerland, and Neil featured in all three. The second and third of these encounters came on 19 and 22 May 1948 in an end of season tour of Switzerland. The small southern city of Bellinzona played host to the first tie, as England 'B' took on Switzerland, winning 5-1. Three days later, they travelled 150 miles north to the historic town of Schaffhausen, in what Neil described as a 'nice, easy jaunt'. There, they were to meet local side FC Schaffhausen, or a Swiss representative side, or possibly a mix of the two, to celebrate the opening of the club's new ground, Stadion Breite.

England 'B' won 6-0, but for those precious few who were present that day, the game would be remembered for the performance of Stanley Matthews. Neil reflected fondly on the trip in his autobiography: 'One of the journalists who were on tour with us had written in his newspaper that Stanley Matthews was finished—oh, how many times has that been said! Stan took a poor view of this report and said so. Then he proceeded to make the critic eat his words in the best possible way—by giving a great performance on the field at Schaffhausen. I have seen Stan many times, but I don't think I have ever seen him in more brilliant fettle.

'But then, how many times has that been said? The trouble with Matthews is that he should, by all rules and regulations, be finished, but he goes gaily on. It is incredible to me that he can still remain on top, and yet every time I see him he looks as good as, if not better than, ever.

'But still people go on saying that he is finished. Maybe that is why he still goes on proving that he is the greatest footballer the game has ever seen. Certainly he is for my money.'

The first game of 1949 didn't arrive until April for England, and when it did, they recorded their first defeat in twenty-three months at the hands of Scotland. They lost again a month later, suffering consecutive defeats for the first time in almost thirteen years. The second defeat came at the hands of Sweden in Stockholm. The Swedes were a strong outfit, led by Englishman George Raynor. Yorkshire-born, Raynor had taken the reigns with Sweden after brief spells with an Iraq XI and Aldershot Reserves, but he proved himself to be a talented coach in Scandinavia. Under his steward-ship, Sweden won gold at the London Olympics in 1948, came third at the 1950 World Cup, won Bronze at the 1952 Olympics and reached the final of the 1958 World Cup. Raynor returned to England in 1958 with dreams of managing the English national team, but found his overseas achievements overlooked. Sometimes referred to as the greatest manager England never had, the only domestic role he ended up landing in 1958 was one at Skegness Town. For the only time in Franklin's career, when playing against Sweden, England were genuinely outclassed by the opposition. Neil reflected on the match in his book, writing, 'so superior were the Swedes that they had a three-goal lead at half-time. None of us could do anything right. Certainly I couldn't, and I think we were all glad to get to Oslo.'

England restored some pride later that month, with 4-1 and 3-1 away wins against Norway and France respectively. They were back to losing ways in the first game of the 1949–50 campaign though, when they lost to the Republic of Ireland at Goodison Park in September 1949. Three players made their England debuts that day, and one of them slotted in next to Franklin in England's backline. His name was Bert Mozley, and he was donning the famous white of England for the first time just two days prior to his 26th birthday. It would be a debut and birthday to forget though, as he gave away a penalty and England lost at home to a team from outside the Home Nations for the first time ever.

Mozley, who is now ninety-five, is the second-oldest living England international, and the only living man to have played alongside Franklin in the England national team following the death of Roy Bentley. A really colourful character, he was kind enough to talk to me about his career at Derby, his three England caps and what it was like to play alongside Neil Franklin. It is almost seventy years since his disappointing international debut, but the incident which marred the tie, from Bert's perspective at least, lives long in the memory. The nonagenarian wasted no time in telling me that it was never a penalty, and that Middlesbrough forward Peter Desmond had taken a dive. The referee, John Mowat, didn't agree, and he pointed to the spot.

Fortunately, Mozley won a couple more caps in the England side, winning both games, before Alf Ramsey made the right-back berth his own. When I asked Bert what he thought of Neil as a player and whether he shared the likes of Matthews' and Finney's rating of him as the finest centre-half they played alongside, Bert told me, 'I agree, he was a tremendous centre-half.' In response to the question of what made him such a special player, Bert replied, 'It was his ability to be in the right place at the right time . . . He made everything look easy.' A one-club man who spent his entire career at Derby County, Mozley almost followed Franklin to Colombia in the 1950s, but for a FIFA intervention. Sixty-two years on from his retirement from football, Mozley now resides in British Columbia, Canada. He said he was glad he never made the move to South America, despite joking about the paltry £20 loyalty bonus he received upon retirement for his ten years of service to Derby County.

As mentioned, England won their next two games, which came against Wales and Ireland. England's forward line were firing on all cylinders as they put four past the Welsh and nine past the Irish. These were the opening two ties of the 1949–50 British Home Championships. It was the last Home Championship that Neil would be involved in, and also the most significant. The 1950 World Cup was the first edition of the tournament that British teams had agreed to enter. There was a rather convoluted and rudimentary qualification process for the finals in Brazil, but FIFA decided that the two highest placed nations out of the four represented in the British Home Championships would qualify automatically for the first World Cup in twelve years.

However, Sir George Graham, the Scottish FA's chief executive, declared that Scotland would only accept FIFA's invite if they were crowned British champions. It was an unpopular decision at the time and one which seems even more astonishing today. Although England had won their first two games against Wales and Ireland very convincingly, so too had Scotland, beating Ireland 8-2 and Wales 2-0. That set up a fascinating final game between England and Scotland at Hampden Park. England had already booked their place at the finals, as they were assured of at least finishing as runners-up, and had accepted FIFA's offer whether they finished first or second. Despite having a superior goal difference, that was not a decisive factor in the championships, so even a draw for Scotland would see them head to Brazil as joint British champions.

Before that game though, there was the small matter of Neil Franklin's penultimate England appearance; and it was a friendly against the might of Italy once more. Having beaten the Italians in the heat of Turin, they were now hosting the continent's most feared side on a chilly November afternoon at White Hart Lane. Both Alf Ramsey and Willie Watson were making only their second outings for England, and Walter Winterbottom's side looked

disjointed in defence. In what was far from Neil's most assured performance, a powerful Italian forward line was giving England
some headaches. Carapellese who had earned Neil's praise during
the game in Turin was now captaining Italy, whilst Inter Milan forward Benito Lorenzi was proving a real handful.

Argentine-born number ten Rinaldo Martino came agonisingly
close to breaking the deadlock. A championship winner in Italy,
Argentina and Uruguay, Martino scored 15 goals from 20 caps for
Argentina, but this was the only game he ever played for Italy.
He would be denied of a goal in his solitary cap with the Azzurri
by the brilliance of Wolverhampton Wanderers goalkeeper Bert
Williams. Nicknamed 'The Cat', for obvious reasons, Williams had
the game of his life, making excellent stops to keep out efforts by
Martino, Lorenzi and Carapellese.

The Italians must have felt cursed against the English, as having dominated much of proceedings, they found themselves behind
less than fifteen minutes from time. A fierce shot by Jack Rowley
beat Giuseppe Moro, and the ball was in the back of the Torino
goalkeeper's net once more five minutes later, courtesy of a fluke
lob by Billy Wright. It was another cruel scoreline that didn't reflect
the quality of the Italians' play, and they emerged with a great deal
of credit having had their team decimated by the Superga disaster
just six months earlier.

England would have to wait five months before taking to the
field once more for that crucial game with the Scots. Whilst
England had nothing to play for in terms of qualification for the
World Cup, they were still keen to win back the British title and
silence the Hampden crowd. More than 133,000 spectators are
believed to have crammed into Scotland's home stadium that day,
and there were some unusual decisions made by the Scottish FA's
Selection Committee. In a starting XI dominated by Rangers players, three players were handed their debuts, one of whom the
panel had reportedly never seen play. That man was Willie Moir,

who had been the top scorer in England's top flight the previous season with twenty-five league goals from the inside-right position for Bolton Wanderers. He would later captain Bolton in the famous 'Matthews Cup final', but this would prove his only cap for Scotland.

In what was a closely fought match, Williams was in fine form in the England goal once more, and Roy Bentley proved a constant thorn in the Scots side in only his second international. It would be Bentley, Chelsea's star forward, who won the game for England, scoring the only goal just past the hour mark after bursting into the box and shooting past Cowan. Franklin was England's defensive linchpin as was so often the case, and no one on either side could have known that he was wearing the white of England for the last time that day, on 15 April 1950. Yet, aged twenty-eight, Neil knew that it would be the last time he turned out for his country, or at least that it would be his final game for some time.

The victory saw Scotland miss out on the World Cup, although England were humiliated anyway. In truth, the England team had been in a decline of sorts immediately following their 4-0 win in Turin. Just six months after that famous victory, all but three players (Neil Franklin, Billy Wright and Stanley Matthews) had been axed from the side, as Walter Winterbottom began to exercise his increased control over selection. By the time the 1950 World Cup arrived, great players like Tommy Lawton, Frank Swift, Raich Carter and George Hardwick had all played their last games for England, and a 35-year-old Stanley Matthews had been overlooked for the last 11 games, spanning some 15 months.

Franklin, an absolute constant and class act in England's defence since the end of World War II, ruling himself out of the finals in Brazil, was like a knife to the heart of the FA then. Author Norman Giller wrote, 'Now England had lost their lynchpin with the World Cup just weeks away. It put the England selectors in a dither as to whom to play in the vital centre-half role, this in an era before the two central backs system. Everything at the back revolved around the pivotal position of the man in the number-five shirt, and Neil Franklin was the best by a country mile. England had lost their anchor, and would soon be all at sea.'

This was no exaggeration. Between Neil's last game for England against Scotland in 1950 and their humiliation at the hands of Hungary just three years later, they tried out ten different players in the role of centre-half. Clearly, Franklin could not be replaced, and in the half decade that followed Neil's last appearance, a leaky England defence crashed out of two World Cups, conceded thirteen goals in just two games against Hungary and were beaten by a Portugal side they had annihilated 10-0 in 1947. It is impossible to say how different results would have been if Neil Franklin had remained a part of the England team throughout this period, but his omission was evidently an enormous blow.

It ended where it had begun for Franklin, with victory over the Scots. His first wartime England appearance had come against Scotland, and so too had his final peacetime one. In total, Neil won 27 official caps for England, never being dropped. Accounting for wartime appearances, that figure becomes 39—again, never being dropped. In his 27 peacetime outings, England won 20, drew 3 and lost 4, scoring 92 goals and conceding 28. A win percentage of 75 shows that Neil was part of a successful England side, and one suspects you would do well to find an England international with as impressive a record over such a number of games.

CHAPTER 8

Tensions Building

'As we were lining up before the game, we had to wait until the marching bands cleared the pitch. Neil was standing alongside me, somewhat pre-occupied. "See that lot, Tom," he said, indicating the band. "They're probably on more money than us." I looked at him and laughed, but he wasn't laughing.'

The above extract is taken from Tom Finney's autobiography, and the game he was referring to was Neil's last England appearance at Hampden Park against Scotland. Incredibly, there was some truth to Neil's claims. In the FA Cup final, for example, £280 was the amount shared between the winning side, with a maximum of £20 per player, whilst the losers received no bonuses at all. The marching band that played at half-time, meanwhile, were paid £350 in total.

Neil Franklin's decision to leave Stoke City, his boyhood club, and turn his back on the England national team, despite being the first name on the team sheet, was an enormous one. The move caused a media frenzy at the time, and it was always assumed that it had been purely financially motivated. The economics of the transfer certainly had a lot to do with it, and we shall come to that, but money was not the only reason that Neil Franklin swapped Staffordshire for Bogotá in 1950.

Dennis Herod described Bob McGrory as being 'jealous' of his two star players, Stanley Matthews and Neil Franklin, and both had fractured relationships with the oft-abrasive Scot. Matthews had sought a move away from Stoke on multiple occasions, and as we know, he finally got his wish when he joined Blackpool in 1947. Stan's departure was the beginning of the end in terms of Stoke City as a side that challenged for titles or honours. Neil's relationship with McGrory only worsened following the exit of his international teammate, and at the start of the 1948–49 season, he handed in a transfer request.

Neil loved playing for Stoke City. Tom Finney, probably Neil's closest friend in football outside of those he played alongside at club level, described him as, 'a Potteries boy and proud of it.' He had risen through the youth ranks, from rejected ground staff member to club captain, all whilst playing alongside a tight-knit group of players, many of whom he was close to. The decision to hand in a transfer request was not an easy decision, then. He had a good relationship with both the club's fans and his teammates, but by the summer of 1948, he had been so worn down by criticism from Bob McGrory and the local press that he sought employment elsewhere.

His disagreements with both McGrory and the local press essentially revolved around one thing: his style of play. Both wanted Neil to alter the way in which he played the game, and that wasn't something that he was prepared to do. The way Neil saw it, he had become the best centre-half in the country and an automatic selection for England playing that way, so why should he change now? If Stoke City didn't like the way he played, then they could sell him. Both the club and player knew that if Neil Franklin was made available, there would be no shortage of interest in the transfer market.

Neil wrote, 'For a long time I had felt that Stoke City did not like my style of play. There had been a lot of criticism of it, but it was the only style I knew and I had no intention of changing it. I therefore thought that the only solution was for me to move to another club.' This may seem stubborn or big-headed to some, but whilst the local press and his own manager picked holes in his game, he was drawing both national and international acclaim for his performances from newspaper writers outside of the Potteries.

'I raise the Cunningham bowler to Neil Franklin, England's centre-half and the big man in their defence yesterday. His play all through had international stamp. Never flustered, scrupulously fair, he was the complete centre-half.

'Franklin does not believe in giving the ball boot: he uses it intelligently, and with a gliding header or a slick ground pass to his wing-halves initiates as many attacks for his side as any of the old-time classical pivots did in the old days when the position was less onerous.

'He does not look exceptionally tall for a centre-half, but his timing and accuracy in the air or on the ground stamp him as out-standing among the dominating players of recent years.'

Those were the words of Andy Cunningham in the *Scottish Sunday Express* on 11 April 1948, the day after England beat Scotland 2-0 at Hampden Park with Franklin having been indomitable in defence. The words of Cunningham, who had been a fine player and manager himself, and others like him, reinforced Neil's belief that he didn't need to change the way in which he played.

It seemed obvious to Neil that if Stoke were so displeased with his performances, then why not cash in on him and let him play elsewhere? Yet they rejected his transfer request. It was reported that when Neil was to meet the Stoke City directors to discuss his request, he was kept waiting for three hours whilst they discussed the matter between themselves, and they then refused to see him at all. Despite having his request denied, the questions and criticism were unrelenting, and the result was an increasingly unhappy and unsettled club captain.

'I make no secret of the fact that I was unhappy at Stoke. True, I got on well with the crowd and the other players, but my style of play was not popular with Bob McGrory, who was then the manager of the Club. [. . .] I had previously asked for a transfer, which the Club had refused to grant, and yet the continual niggling about my style of play did not cease.'

An indignant Franklin added, 'I make no apology in repeating that to me there is only one way to play football, and I played it that way. Maybe I was wrong. Maybe I still am. But my style was the only one I knew, and it had brought me a fair measure of success.'

All this uneasiness and tension with Stoke City was entirely contrasted by the recognition Franklin received from Stoke-on-Trent City Council in September 1948. Stoke City players and officials were in attendance for the ceremony, which saw Neil presented with an illuminated address. Despite all the troubles he was going through with the club, the ceremony and gift were the source of immense pride for Neil. The address itself read:

We, the Lord Mayor, Aldermen and the Citizens of the City of Stoke-on-Trent, desire to express our great appreciation of the distinction and honour you have brought to the City by playing for England in 26 successive international matches.

By your activities you have rendered magnificent service to your City, not only nationally but internationally, and we hope and trust that you have many more years to play in the sport of football.

We are gratified that you were born in this City and that the whole of your career has been spent so successfully with the Stoke City Football Club.

Signed: Henry Beresford, Lord Mayor
Harry Taylor, Town Clerk.

As stated, the ceremony was in light of Franklin having made his 26th consecutive England appearance, including wartime internationals. He became only the third sportsperson to be honoured by Stoke-on-Trent council, the others being Stanley Matthews and Norman Wainwright, a swimmer who represented Great Britain in three editions of the Olympic Games and won one Gold at the British Empire Games (now known as the Commonwealth Games).

As much as Franklin was doing Stoke proud on the international scene, their club was struggling on domestic fronts. Having finished 15th in the 1947–48 season, the 1948–49 campaign had begun in rocky fashion. Neil wasn't the only Stoke City player to hand in a transfer request, but the club dug in their heels, with Bert Mitchell the only wantaway Potter allowed to leave the Victoria Ground. On 4 December 1948, Stoke fielded an entire XI of players who had come through the club's youth ranks. Ten of the XI had been born in Stoke-on-Trent, and the other—Frank Mountford—had moved there at the age of three. It was some achievement, but the local lads were beaten 2-1 by Stanley Matthews' Blackpool side.

They made amends a month later though, when they drew the Tangerines in the Fourth Round of the FA Cup. The first leg, which took place at the Victoria Ground, was drawn 1-1. The following week, Stoke went to Bloomfield Road and put Stanley Matthews and his teammates out of the cup with a 1-0 win. It was a real coup for Stoke, who were experiencing mixed form in the league, especially since Blackpool had reached the final in the previous season.

Bob McGrory must have thought his luck was beginning to turn when Stoke were drawn at home to Third Division North side Hull City in the Fifth Round. A crowd of 46,738 at the Victoria Ground saw their team well beaten by the Yorkshiremen though. Perhaps Stoke had underestimated their opponents, who had lost just one of their twenty-nine games so far that season prior to the game. The Tigers were led by Neil's former England teammate

Raich Carter, who was player-manager at Boothferry Park, and he had them playing some excellent football. They put in a masterful performance at the Vic, and thoroughly deserved their 2-0 win. Hull went on to romp the Third Division North that season, winning the title and only being put out of the FA Cup by the holders, Manchester United.

The Tigers' classy display may well have left a mark on Franklin. Significantly, despite their lowly status in the Football League, they were one side who were showing a real interest in signing Neil. Bringing in Raich Carter was a huge statement of intent by the East Yorkshire side, but their ambition didn't stop there. They sanctioned a move by Carter to bring Eddie Burbanks to Boothferry Park. Carter and Burbanks had played together at both Sunderland and in wartime internationals with England, and both players scored in Sunderland's 3-1 win in the 1937 FA Cup final. It was reported that Neil was the next England international being lined up by the Tigers board, with a world record fee of £30,000 on offer should Stoke City accept his transfer request.

Of course, no such acceptance came from the Stoke City board, so the move never materialised. Stoke finished the 1948–49 season in 11th place, having lost one more game than they won. Neil's discontent had been intensified when he was stripped of the captaincy by Bob McGrory, who gave the armband back to his predecessor Billy Mould. Neil's refusal to play the ball quicker or be more physical in defence seemed to have been the reason for McGrory's decision.

Over the summer and prior to the start of the 1949–50 campaign, Franklin didn't re-sign his forms with Stoke. He delayed doing so in an attempt to panic the Stoke board into selling him, but they wouldn't be moved. In an age where player power rules supreme, there may be some readers of this book wondering why a failed transfer request scuppered any hopes of a move for Neil

Franklin. However, back in 1949, a player could not leave a club without the explicit permission of his current side.

Fearing a potential breakaway football association, the FA had yielded and accepted the professionalisation of football back in 1885. A player registration system had been introduced, but a player had to either renew forms or register with a new club at the start of each season. Essentially, the player became a free agent every summer. Three years later, the Football League was born, and the most talented players became highly sought after. Wealthier and more successful clubs began poaching the best talent, and there was nothing the smaller and less affluent sides could do to prevent their star players from leaving.

Naturally irritated by this, a number of smaller clubs approached the FA to complain about routinely losing their best players. The FA themselves were worried about the lack of competition that could be caused if there wasn't a spread of talent throughout the Football League, so they agreed that sanctions were required. These sanctions arrived in 1893 in the form of the retain and transfer system. This new system meant that players were no longer free to leave their club at the end of each season. Instead, once a club held your registration, you wouldn't be able to sign for another Football League club without their permission.

Even if a club that held the players registration didn't offer to renew the player's contract, meaning they were under no obligation to pay or play him, the player still wouldn't be free to move to a new club. This draconian ruling led to some players retiring prematurely and finding alternative employment. And this went right to the top: at the height of Stanley Matthews' transfer speculation, it was reported that he might retire if Stoke denied him of a move to Blackpool, reports which Matthews denied one ought to add. So footballers were understandably displeased with the system, and yet it remained in place for some seventy years.

During the retain and transfer systems early years, some players would leave their clubs to play in the semi-professional Southern League, which was exempt from both the retain and transfer system and the maximum wage. Others would head north of the border to ply their trade in the Scottish Football League, but both these get-outs were soon shut down. In 1910, the Southern League adopted retain and transfer, and once the Home Nations rejoined FIFA, football's governing body prevented players from joining foreign clubs without their current club's permission in the same way they were restricted by the FA.

This was very apparent in 1952, when Tom Finney was offered a lucrative contract by the Italian club Palermo. The £10,000 sign-on fee was enough to pique the interest of the Lancashire-born winger, and in his autobiography Finney describes how he told Preston's chairman Nat Buck that the idea appealed to him. 'Listen to me, if tha' doesn't play for Preston then tha' doesn't play for anybody,' came the response from Mr Buck, and that was that.

It was easy to see why the likes of Preston and Stoke were so determined to keep hold of players like Finney, Matthews and Franklin. Not only were they tremendous players who would prove near impossible to replace, they were also crowd-pullers, who added an enormous amount of money to the club and directors' coffers.

This form of footballing serfdom meant Neil's prospects of leaving Stoke City, having had his transfer requests denied, were incredibly slim. Whilst Hull City may have been willing to put up big money, and a string of other First Division sides were very interested, if Stoke weren't listening to any offers, his hands were tied. It has been claimed that Neil even considered an offer from non-league Chingford Town, who were unbound by the maximum wage of the Football League. By offering Franklin a position as manager, there may have been a way out of the retain and transfer system, but it seems the move never got too far off the ground. Indeed, the ambitious Chingford team were founded in 1947 and had folded by 1950.

As mentioned already, in addition to the retain and transfer system in 1893, a maximum wage was introduced by the Football League in 1901. The cap was set at £4 a week, and was a real blow to some top players, who had been earning as much as £10 a week prior to the restriction being introduced. When Neil began his career as a seventeen-year-old, the maximum wage had risen to £8 during the season and £6 in the off-season, although as a young-ster not yet having appeared in the first team, he obviously earned only a fraction of the maximum wage. A slight rise came again in 1945, before a more significant one in 1947. The post-war atten-dance boom meant gate receipts were up significantly. Footballers wanted their fair slice of the money that was now pouring into the game; after all, they were the ones attracting the crowds in the first place.

In 1946, the Players' Union declared a strike, only to discover that such action was illegal. The Labour Government had crimi-nalised strike action as the nation looked to rebuild from the dev-astation of World War II in order to keep production up. This seemed like a blow for the Players' Union, but it turned out to be a blessing in disguise. Since strikes weren't a possibility, the matter had to go to arbitration with direct government involvement. In March 1947, the National Arbitration Tribunal took just two weeks to make a ruling. The maximum wage would rise to £12 a week in the season and £10 over the summer.

It was heralded as a victory for the union, and it did kick-start a domino effect which saw the maximum wage continually rise until being abolished entirely in 1961. However, in 1949, when Neil was having his struggles with Stoke, the cap remained at £12 in the season and £10 in the summer. Like most regular starters at a

First Division club, Neil received the maximum wage. There were also bonuses, like £1 for a draw and £2 for a win, or a pound per point as it worked at the time. There were further ways a footballer like Neil could supplement his weekly wage at the time, such as loyalty bonuses and international caps. A maximum loyalty bonus of £750 could be given to a player by their club every five years. Note the words 'maximum' and 'could' there, as many players never received the bonus at all, and those who did often saw a fraction of the £150 a year their club was allowed to pay them.

Those talented and fortunate enough to represent their country received £50 from the FA for every cap they won with England. That's a hefty sum to a footballer on £12 a week, although England only played an average of seven games a season. So an ever-present in the England team, and therefore we can assume a top player, could add around £7 to his weekly wage and £350 to his annual salary. Lastly, there were competition-related bonuses. A prize fund would be shared between the top four teams in the league. The First Division title winners, for example, would have £550 shared between them. Win bonuses increased in the latter stages of the FA Cup and, as mentioned earlier, £280 would be shared between the winners.

From all this, we can get a pretty accurate gauge of what Neil or any of his teammates were earning at the time. Below is a generous breakdown of what he could be expected to earn during the 1948–49 season:

40 weeks earning £12 per week = £480
12 weeks earning £10 per week = £120
League bonuses (41 points won) = £41
FA Cup bonuses (reached Round 5) = £6
England internationals (played in all 8) = £400
Loyalty bonus (if paid maximum amount) = £150
Total = £1,197

Inflation has changed so radically since then that you could be forgiven for having little to no idea what those figures meant in real terms. The Bank of England estimate that £1,200 in 1949 would be the equivalent of almost £39,000 today. Figures released in 2007 claimed that the average weekly wage in 1950 was £7.08 a week, or £368 a year. By the same Bank of England inflation calculator, that would be just shy of £12,000 a year today.

There was one other way in which Neil looked to increase his earnings, and it was one reserved only for the star players—advertisement. The use of footballers as a means to sell a product was still in its infancy. Dixie Dean may have got the ball rolling, but it was Neil's teammate Stanley Matthews who first started making real money out of advertising. Matthews put his name to products such as cigarettes and football boots. 'The cigarette for me' boasted an advert for Craven A cigarettes back in 1952, alongside an image of Stan, a teetotal non-smoker. Neil looked to follow in Stan's footsteps in the late 1940s, striking a deal with Colman's Mustard.

The Norfolk-based company may seem like an unusual match with a star footballer today, but they were pioneers in terms of featuring sports people in adverts. Their 1895 advert featuring England's finest cricketer, W G Grace, accompanied by the slogan, 'Colman's Mustard Heads the Field' is thought to be the first British advert to feature a sportsman or woman. When the people from Colman's arrived to get some shots of Neil, however, there was one small problem. After a comprehensive shuffle through the kitchen cupboards, it became clear that the Franklin household was not home to any Colman's Mustard. The quick-thinking photographer suggested that Neil use jam instead, and the ad went ahead. It's unclear how much money Neil earned through this one-off endorsement deal, but his son Gary suspects it was not a significant amount.

So, in a good year, Neil was probably earning three times as much as his father would have done at the local gasworks. What did he and other elite footballers have to complain about, then? Well, first, there's the amount of money they were earning for other people. As alluded to earlier, attendances were up just after the end of the war, and gate receipts were growing rapidly. In 1947, a full house at Wembley would rake in around £35,000. By 1950, gate receipts of £50,000 were not uncommon for international matches and cup finals.

The £50 that each player received for an England cap may have seemed like a lot when the maximum weekly wage was £12, but it still only added up to a total of £550 between all eleven players. That leaves a rather substantial amount of £49,450 that is going elsewhere. Unsurprisingly, Neil felt the fee for representing your country ought to be higher, writing, 'Fifty pounds might seem, at first glance, excellent pay for an international match, but consider the fact that many of these internationals draw gates of £40,000 to £50,000, and, of course, an international appearance is the peak of any player's career', adding, 'In the light of those facts, I don't think £50 is a tremendous amount of money, and I should like to see it increased substantially. After all, the Football Association can afford it and I am convinced that a player who plays for his country is worthy of a very high fee.'

When Great Britain took on a Europe XI in 1947, a crowd of 137,000 at Hampden Park took in over £30,000 in gate receipts, yet the players involved were paid just £14 each. It was a similar story at club level. Whilst the maximum wage was capped at £12, rising to £14 with a win bonus, crowds reached record highs across the country in the late 1940s.

Newcastle United averaged more than 56,000 in the 1947–48 campaign, Aston Villa and Sunderland averaged just shy of 50,000, and both Charlton and Wolves averaged over 40,000. The average attendance in the First Division in the 1948–49 season was 38,792, and the average across the entire Football League was 22,318. Hull City averaged almost 37,000 in the Third Division North, whilst Manchester United and Everton both set their record attendances, which still stand, of 83,260 and 78,299 respectively.

Footballers pay packets simply didn't reflect the money coming in at the gates. An acute sense of unfairness surrounding this was the first bone of contention for footballers of the day. Such grievances could be multiplied tenfold among the top players. For stars like Matthews, Finney, Mannion and, of course, Franklin, the maximum wage seemed especially cruel. The £12 maximum, or close to it, was being earned by the vast majority of regular starters in the First Division. So the best players of the day, a man like Stanley Matthews whose mere presence alone was thought to add as many as 10,000 spectators to a gate, was earning the same as a bog-standard First Division starter.

In his 2004 autobiography, Tom Finney described himself as a life-long advocate of 'star pay for star play'. The two-time FWA Footballer of the Year pointed out the fact David Beckham earned considerably more than a number of other players at Manchester United due to his ability and star appeal, which wasn't the case in Finney and Franklin's time. Finney recalled how people used to say that it was good for team spirit and morale for everyone to earn the same, before adding that whilst that might have been true for the rest of the team, it didn't do a great deal to boost the morale of the star players themselves!

Franklin, and many like him, saw themselves as entertainers at the peak of their profession. Great music artists were not paid the same as mediocre music artists, and certainly great actors were not paid the same as mediocre actors; why should footballers be any different? At the same time Franklin and Matthews were picking up £12 a week, the biggest stars of the screen were earning in excess of £80,000 a year, equal to more than £1,500 a week.

Clearly footballers couldn't hope to earn such sums prior to lucrative TV deals, but they had a reasonable claim to be paid their worth. England players in particular were also aware of what their European counterparts were earning, through speaking with them whilst on international duty. Italy star Giuseppe Meazza shocked some English players in 1939 when he told them of his £35 a week salary, which was more than four times the domestic maximum wage in England at the time.

The issues of wages and freedom had been contentious right from the introduction of both the retain and transfer system and the maximum wage. Many players sought alternate means of income, and it was not uncommon for clubs to find them paid positions that didn't involve them doing any actual work in order to supplement their income.

By 1912, a challenge had already been made to the courts regarding the legality of the retain and transfer system. Outside-right Herbert Kingaby had been signed by Aston Villa for £300, but failed to impress at Villa Park. Reluctant to lose out on all their investment, the Birmingham club demanded at least £150 from any potential suitors. With no offers forthcoming, Kingaby took the fairly common route of players in such circumstances at that time, and headed to the Southern League. However, once the Southern League got on board with the Football League's restrictive system, Villa demanded £350 for the player who was still registered with them.

His new side, Leyton Orient, were unable to pay the fee, and Kingaby brought legal proceedings against Aston Villa. Unfortunately, his legal team employed a poor strategy. They argued that Villa were demanding the fee in revenge for his departure, but the judge threw out the case on the grounds that motives cannot render a lawful act unlawful. Had they argued that the system itself was an unfair restraint of trade, the outcome might have been very different. As it happened, it would remain in place for more than half a century after that trial, until a similar case involving George

Eastham and Newcastle United, in which Eastham's representatives did argue restraint of trade successfully.

It's easy to see why Neil Franklin could find himself incredibly frustrated in 1949, then. He was being heavily criticised by his manager and local press; his wages were not in line with his talent or importance; and he was tied down by a system which left his fate entirely in the hands of Stoke City. During the 1949–50 season, he was so dejected with his predicament that he was considering staging a one-man strike, just as Wilf Mannion had done at Middlesbrough in 1948. Neil wrote, 'I also thought of refusing to re-sign at the end of the 1949–50 season and staging a one-man strike. It may well have come to that, although I don't think I would have been able to afford the financial complications.'

It was around this time, in November 1949, that a letter from Luis Robledo of Independiente Santa Fe arrived in Neil Franklin's hands via Stoke City FC. Obviously unable to send the letter directly to Neil, Mr Robledo had sent the letter to Stoke City but addressed it to Neil. Unbeknownst to them, Stoke had handed a letter offering vast riches and a route out of the Potteries to the thoroughly disgruntled star of their side.

The initial letter enquired whether Franklin would consider joining Santa Fe, and outlined the financial benefits that would come with such a move. In regard to that first letter, Neil wrote, 'It all seemed most attractive, so attractive, in fact, that only a fool would have turned it down without going into the matter fully.' Whilst greatly intrigued, Neil wasn't getting carried away. As stated, the retain part of the retain and transfer system extended throughout all FIFA affiliated nations, so he still thought the Bogotá club would have to make an offer to Stoke City, and that offer then be accepted, before any move could happen.

Neil stated this and explained why it made any move impossible in his reply to Mr Robledo, but he received a swift reply from the Colombian. Robledo explained that the Colombian league was not affiliated with FIFA, and as such, there would be no obstacles. All that was required was a contract being agreed between Franklin and Santa Fe. Suddenly, there was a way out. What had seemed impossible for the past year or more was no longer thus, and the seeds of Neil Franklin's trailblazing move to Bogotá had well and truly been sown.

CHAPTER 9

The Ball is Mightier than the Sword

Home to part of the Amazon rainforest, vast grasslands and both Pacific and Caribbean coastlines, Colombia is an extraordinary country. However, its outstanding geographical beauty could not be more firmly at odds with the brutality and violence which has plagued much of the nation's history.

On 9 April 1948, a day after Neil played arguably his finest game for England in a 2-0 win over Scotland at Hampden Park, Jorge Eliécer Gaitán was gunned down in Bogotá. Gaitán was the leader of the nation's Liberal Party, and strong favourite to win Colombia's 1949 presidential election. His assassination sparked immediate outrage and violence, and ultimately a bloody civil war, which officially spanned ten years, although some have claimed the conflict lasted more than five decades. It also led to the creation of a national league and the introduction of professionalism to Colombian football.

Having gained independence from Spain in 1819, Colombia's two leading political parties had been set up in the mid-1800s. These two factions, the Conservative Party and the Liberal Party, were at loggerheads right from their inception. A civil war between the two parties claimed an estimated 120,000 lives between 1899 and 1902. The Thousand Days' War, as it became known, was a particularly violent period, although peace didn't seem to have entered Colombia's lexicon at this time.

Even in some of the years that are generally described as having political stability and relative peace would be described as barbaric by most nation's standards, with news of massacres which claimed the lives of twenty, thirty or forty people not uncommon in the morning's newspapers. One of Colombia's most significant massacres occurred on 6 December 1928. Colombian workers for the United Fruit Company had gone on strike, and the United States responded by threatening to send in the Marine Corps unless decisive action was taken by the Colombian government.

In what became known as the Banana Massacre, Colombian troops set up machine guns on the roofs of buildings and opened fire into a packed crowd of strikers and their families, including children. Jorge Eliécer Gaitán, then a young lawyer who was becoming increasingly interested in politics, called for accountability, and became a noted public figure following his support for workers' rights and the deceased.

Nineteen years later, Gaitán became the leader of Colombia's Liberal Party. A champion of workers' rights and increased social welfare, Gaitán was an exceptional orator, and something of a demigod to many Colombians. Whilst he was an enemy to the nation's elite and seen as disruptive by some, he was heavily tipped to win Colombia's 1949 presidential election.

It was 1 April 1948, not long after 1 p.m., that Gaitán and his friends and colleagues left their office to make the short walk to the Hotel Continental. As they stepped out onto the bustling streets of Bogotá, they could only manage a few steps before three shots were fired at Gaitán from behind. Fifty minutes later, he was declared dead in hospital, and chaos ensued. Riots broke out immediately, and in the ten hours which followed, an estimated 5,000 people were killed. Violence consumed Colombia once more, as the fighting spread from the country's capital of Bogotá and into the countryside, where it would intensify and persist for more than a decade.

The catastrophic riots that night left Bogotá in ruins, with much of the city being destroyed. The events became known as El

Bogotazo, and the violence which continued in the nation's countryside is now referred to as La Violencia. Conservative estimates put the death toll of La Violencia at 200,000. More shocking than the number of people killed was the manner in which thousands lost their lives: cruelty and barbarism on such a scale that it is difficult to believe.

Hangings, beheadings and crucifixions were commonplace. Meanwhile, more gruesome methods included slowly chopping up a living person's body or making small punctures in their flesh until they bled to death. Extraordinary torture and maiming was inflicted on men, women and children. It was sickening savagery masquerading as a form of art.

A country that always seemed to be red hot, full of tension and on the brink of boiling over into violent clashes had done just that. The left was already angered by suspected election fraud and the increased influence of the United States and multinational companies, and Gaitán was to be the perfect tonic to their woes. It's little surprise his assassination sparked such outcry, then. To this day, Gaitán's murder—like so many significant assassinations—is shrouded in mystery.

Juan Roa Sierra is the man widely believed to have fired the shots which killed Gaitán. He was chased down and brutally kicked, beaten and stabbed to death by an angry mob shortly after the shots rang out. The 'official' line was that Roa was a disturbed schizophrenic who had been a supporter of Gaitán's and was possibly angered by the Liberal Party leader's refusal to meet with him or offer him a job. This all seemed a little too convenient to some. The Conservative Party and their leader, Mariano Ospina Pérez, were among those to have fingers pointed in their direction. So too were the CIA, who Gaitán's daughter Gloria felt had to have been involved. Other conspiracies attempted to implicate the Soviet government, Fidel Castro or Catholic priests who were angered by

Gaitán's atheism and his likely ascent to office. A large number of people suspected Roa Sierra wasn't even the killer.

Whoever killed Gaitán, and whatever their motives, the re-elected Conservative Party of Colombia and their leader Mariano Ospina Peréz had a crisis on their hands. Peréz began a devastating campaign of repression which accelerated the violence and anger of the nation. Authorities reportedly encouraged peasants who sided with the Conservatives to seize the land of Liberal peasants, hence the reason the majority of the conflict took place in the countryside. It was clear to Peréz that the nation needed a distraction.

Edward Bulwer-Lytton wrote that 'The pen is mightier than the sword' in 1839, but in Colombia in 1948, Peréz and the Conservative Party had other ideas. Football was identified as a potential tool to distract the masses from politics and conflict, and it didn't take them long to put their plans into action. Colombia had been very late in coming to football, at least in comparison to their South American neighbours such as Argentina, Brazil and Uruguay.

Whilst the first South American Championship took place in 1916, Colombia didn't make their debut until the 1945 edition of the tournament. When they did finally make their bow, they won just one of their six games, suffering a 7-0 humiliation at the hands of Uruguay, and an equally embarrassing 9-1 thrashing against Argentina. At this time, the country still didn't have a centralised league. Regional divisions and local cups made up the country's football scene, and the game remained entirely amateur.

Many campaigned for a national division and the introduction of professionalism, but power struggles between the regional leagues and any newly formed national league hampered progress. Alfonso Senior and Humberto Salcedo had spent years striving to make it happen, but to no avail. Yet, once Peréz became involved, a national league had been formed and professionalism introduced just 126 days after Gaitán's assassination. It is amazing what a bit of intervention by the head of a civil-military dictatorship can do.

So, on 15 August 1948, Colombia's new top flight Campeonato Profesional kicked off its inaugural season in Medellín, 5,000 miles away and one week before Stoke City began their season in the First Division at home to Charlton Athletic. In its first season, the league was just beginning flex its financial muscles. The aptly named Bogotá club of Millonarios led the way, with a couple of prolific Argentine forwards on their books even before the formation of the division, both signed from Argentino de Mendoza. One of them, Alfredo Castillo, was the runaway top scorer in the division's debut season with 31 goals, 11 more than his nearest rival. Seventy years on, he remains Millonarios' all-time leading goal scorer.

This kind of recruitment made Millonarios favourites to win the 1948 Campeonato Profesional, but it was their Bogotá rivals Independiente Santa Fe who won the first championship, winning 12 of their 18 games. The season ran from August to December, but it was during the close season that things really started to heat up. Millonarios, disappointed with their fourth-place finish, were keen to invest further. Thirty-two foreign players had taken part in the league's debut campaign, thirteen of them from Argentina.

It was Argentina that Millonarios turned their attention to once more, but whilst they had signed some talented Argentines to date, now they wanted stars. Carlos Aldabe was one of their first recruits, arriving from the Buenos Aires club of Quilmes, title winners of Argentina's second tier in 1949. Aldabe became player-manager, and Millonarios' president Alfonso Senior was keen to use him as a lure for other Argentine players. Tensions between Adefútbol (Colombia's football association) and DIMAYOR (who oversaw the newly formed national league) were at breaking point in early 1949. On 15 March, the two organisations disaffiliated.

THE BALL IS MIGHTIER THAN THE SWORD

Adefútbol had affiliated with FIFA in 1936, and they remained affiliated, but the split with the league meant the Campeonato Profesional—and its teams—were no longer tied to FIFA. Whilst this might have been seen as damaging to the reputation of most leagues, Colombia's new league, not yet having celebrated its first birthday, saw it as an opportunity. This was the beginning of the 'El Dorado' era in Colombian football, and Millonarios' president Senior wasted no time putting his plans into action.

His target? Adolfo Pedernera. Outside of South America, his name may not resonate a great deal today, like so many players who plied their trade before football became widely televised. But in 1949, Pedernera was the South American equivalent of Stanley Matthews. Between 1941 and 1947, River Plate of Argentina assembled an outstanding side. Nicknamed La Máquina, or 'the Machine', they won ten trophies, including four league titles, in seven seasons. Renowned for their exceptional five-man forward line, they were a formidable unit as their nickname suggests, but Adolfo Pedernera and José Manuel Moreno were often cited as the team's most exceptional talents.

Having started out as a fleet-footed left-winger who would tie full-backs in knots, River moved him and into a more central free role in his early twenties. Quick, elegant and intelligent, Pedernera had starred for Argentina in both their 1941 and 1945 South American Championship triumphs. Yet, in 1946, following a fall-out with the club's hierarchy, he left River for crosstown rivals Atlanta, and Huracán soon after that. He remained one of the finest players on the continent, and the idea of a move to a team founded little more than a decade earlier in a league that was only a year old must have seemed unthinkable.

The whole story of the El Dorado period, though, is a triumph of timing. Juan Perón had been elected President of Argentina in 1946, and the country was undergoing major reform under the lieutenant general. Orchestrated by Argentina's equivalent of the

PFA, Futbolistas Argentinos Agremiados, the country's footballers went on strike in 1948. As defeated Nazis entered Argentina via the infamous ratlines, many prominent footballers departed.

Alfonso Senior was a wily operator, and he sensed the opportunity. Conveniently, his player-manager Carlos Aldabe was a friend of Pedernera. Now freed from the shackles of FIFA, Senior could bypass the clubs and go straight to the players. He sent Aldabe on a plane to Buenos Aires with a suitcase containing $5,000 in cash, an enormous amount of money at the time. The suitcase full of cash would become a common negotiating technique for Colombian clubs throughout the years of El Dorado.

Pedernera was thirty, and his future in Argentina seemed precarious. He was willing to talk to Millonarios, but he wouldn't come cheap. The Argentine international was all too happy to accept the $5,000 sign-on fee, but demanded a $200 a month salary as well. Millonarios obliged, and possibly the biggest transfer coup in the history of the game was completed. Pedernera didn't disappoint: following his first game, a Colombian newspaper column described him as 'phenomenal, an artist, a master of passing, and a show of intelligence', adding, 'After the debut of El Maestro, everything is possible.' Any legitimacy that may have been stripped from Colombia's top flight with their disassociation from Adefútbol had been restored and multiplied ten-fold by the arrival of one of the finest footballers on the planet.

Argentines were outraged, Colombians overjoyed, and the scenes at both the airport when he arrived and his first game against Deportes Caldas suggested Pérez's distraction may have been starting to work. It didn't take long for the masterful Argentine to grow frustrated though, and he approached Senior about further strengthening Millonarios' squad. Whilst Pedernera's arrival was huge for the Colombian game, it quickly exposed the dearth of talent in the rest of the Millonarios squad and the league as a whole.

Senior concurred, and off Pedernera went to bring back some

talent from his home country. A striker had been top of his list of priorities, but he arrived with two men, both from River Plate and both Argentine internationals. Néstor Rossi, nicknamed 'Pipo', arrived to pivot the side, and Alfredo Di Stéfano was brought in to spearhead Millonarios' attack. The 23-year-old Di Stéfano had already been named Argentina Primera División top scorer in 1947, then aged 21, and had a record of 6 goals from 6 caps for the national team.

Both players arrived midway through the 1949 season, but would prove crucial in helping Millonarios win the second Campeonato Profesional. Di Stéfano scored 16 goals in 14 games, as the club finished joint top of the league with Deportivo Cali, but got their hands on the trophy following a two-legged play-off, in which Pedernera scored twice and Di Stéfano once. The number of teams competing rose from ten in 1948, to fourteen in 1949, although there would be no Atlético Junior. Runners-up in the inaugural season, DIMAYOR suspended them for acting as the de facto Colombian national team on behalf of Adefútbol in the 1949 South American Championships. They finished in last place, although their two-year suspension was later reduced to one.

Determined not to be left behind by Millonarios, the country's other teams got out their cheque books and began recruiting. Their Bogotá rivals Santa Fe pulled off one of the biggest signings, bringing in Héctor Rial from San Lorenzo. A classy and complete forward who could lead the line or play a little deeper with equal proficiency, he would later win five European Cups as a teammate of Di Stéfano's at Real Madrid. Deportivo Cali targeted Peru, signing a whopping fourteen Peruvians, a handful of which were full internationals. Peru had finished fourth at the 1949 South American Championships, and could boast some real talent. Valeriano López, one of the nation's all-time greats, was among those to join Deportivo Cali. He had averaged better than a goal a game in Peru, and maintained that form in Colombia. Deportivo's crosstown rivals América de Cali had similar ideas, signing up another Peru international—Félix Castillo—who had scored against Colombia in a 4-0 defeat at the recent championships.

Independiente Medellín were the next team to pick off the remains of Peru's top talent, and in no time at all, every player in Peru's national team was playing their club football in Colombia. Atlético Junior created a hybrid of Brazilians and Hungarians, most notably Heleno de Freitas, a flawed genius and prolific scorer from Botafogo who had a record of 19 goals from 18 caps for the national team, but would die of syphilis aged only 39. Cúcuta Deportivo really didn't mess about, bringing in seventeen Uruguayans, two of whom won the World Cup in 1950, and another, Ramón Alberto Villaverde, who went on to become a legend in Catalonia with Barcelona.

Clubs with slightly more modest budgets had to set their sights a little lower. Deportivo Pereira brought in a few Paraguayan internationals, along with Luigi Di Franco from Italy's third tier, who became their player-manager. Deportes Caldas brought in three players from Argentina, although one of them—Vytautas Krisciunas—was actually a Lithuanian, whose family had moved to South America during World War II. Perhaps most incredible of all were Deportivo Samarios, who took on ten Hungária FC players when the Central Europeans had the misfortune of being disbanded whilst on a tour of South America. Samarios also had the greatest diversity, with ten Colombians, eight Hungarians, two Yugoslavs, and one player each from Argentina, Austria, Italy and Romania. Not that it ever did them much good: they finished 11th in their best campaign despite the presence of player-manager Gyula Zsengellér, a wonderful centre-forward whose goals had helped Hungary reach the final of the 1938 World Cup more than a decade earlier.

Other than Deportivo Samarios, every team seemed to target

one or occasionally two nationalities or regions. The result was many little microcosms dotted around the league and, more often than not, within individual squads as well. Into the 1950s, more than half of all the leagues players were foreigners, and the numbers continued to rise.

One football-crazed region of the world that wasn't yet represented in the Campeonato Profesional was a small group of islands just off the north-western coast of continental Europe. South America's footballing meccas of Argentina and Brazil had been plucked of many of their stars, as had a number of European nations, but the birthplace of the beautiful game had remained as yet untouched by the tremors emanating out of Colombia's El Dorado experiment.

That was all about to change. Luis Robledo, whose father was a millionaire cattle rancher, had been one of the founders of Independiente Santa Fe in 1941. Part of Colombia's wealthy elite, Robledo was educated in England from a young age: first at Downside School in Somerset, and later at Cambridge University, where he had begun to take an interest in football as a supporter of Arsenal. Once he had finished his schooling, he became the first secretary at the Colombian embassy in London. Two years younger than Neil, he controversially married Lady Bridget Poulett in 1948. The daughter of Earl William Poulett, Bridget Poulett was a socialite, model, and one of the most photographed women in Britain in the 1930s.

It is widely believed that Robledo's fondness for Arsenal was the reason Santa Fe made red and white their team colours. They also happened to be the colours of the country's Liberal Party. Whilst this was unintentional, the fact that their Bogotá rivals, Millonarios, were founded by prominent Conservative Party members and played in the colours of the Conservative Party, the rivalry eventually—and naturally—began to carry political tendencies. Well dressed and well spoken, Robledo originally served as the club's vice-president, but he would soon be the one calling the shots at Santa Fe.

If Pedernera, Di Stéfano and De Freitas were not off limits, then why should the English be? Robledo began to plan a raid of English talent, and he was soon eyeing up an unsettled centre-half at Stoke City.

CHAPTER 10

Six Games for Santa Fe

Six games. That is all it was for Neil Franklin at Independiente Santa Fe. A transfer which rocked the British game and led to changes that would alter it forever, resulted in only nine hours of competitive football on Colombian soil.

If you recall, by the end of 1949, Neil Franklin and Luis Robledo had begun correspondence, and the former Cambridge student had assured Neil that due to DIMAYOR not being FIFA affiliated, he would face no obstacles in leaving Stoke City to join Independiente Santa Fe. Robledo promised a great deal in his letters to Neil, from vast riches to spring-like weather all year round.

To the press, players and supporters, Franklin's eventual move in May 1950 had come entirely out of the blue. It appeared sudden and shocking, but Neil and Santa Fe had in fact been in contact for six months by the time he boarded a plane for Bogotá. Once Neil discovered that he required no permission or clearance from Stoke City, FIFA or the FA, he had become pretty set on the idea of a move to South America.

With every one of McGrory's jibes, every disparaging local newspaper column, and with every instance in which he felt he wasn't being properly treated by the Stoke City hierarchy, Franklin edged closer to a move to Bogotá. Neil wrote in his autobiography, 'Whenever I thought of the way my style of play was criticized at Stoke, I became even more interested.' He made no secret of his eagerness during his correspondence with Mr Robledo, and there seemed to be little in the way of negotiations, not regarding the finances of the deal at least.

Just how much money Independiente Santa Fe offered Franklin to travel halfway across the globe and leave the English game behind was a topic of great interest among sports writers and supporters of the time. The most conservative estimates claimed a £1,500 sign-on fee, whilst the most optimistic went as high as £10,000. That's some gulf, but either way, it was a hefty improvement on the maximum £10 sign-on fee in place in the Football League. In his autobiography, Stanley Matthews cited figures of a £3,400 sign-on fee, plus £170 per match and free accommodation when discussing Neil's salary in Colombia. Charlie Mitten, a fellow Colombian exile, claimed he signed on the same terms as Neil, which were a £5,000 sign-on fee, £5,000 per year, plus bonuses, accommodation and various other perks. Other publications have stated a £2,000 sign-on fee with a £60 a week salary, or a £1,500 sign-on fee, plus £150 a month, a £7 win bonus and a £5 draw bonus.

Clearly, there is a great amount of variation in the figures stated, and since Neil Franklin respected the confidentiality of the terms he signed, we cannot know for sure which—if any—are in fact accurate. It is highly unlikely that he was offered a sign-on fee in excess of £5,000. His yearly salary was most likely very similar to his sign-on fee and the oft-quoted £35 win bonus seems to have some validity, but he was certainly not given free accommodation.

What we can say with some certainty is that even the most miserly of estimates would put his annual earnings wildly in excess of what any footballer could hope to earn in the Football League. Even a £3,400 sign-on fee alone would be more than three times what Neil could hope to earn in a good year in Britain, including England cap fees and win bonuses.

It's easy to see why the move appealed financially, then, and also why Franklin didn't barter a great deal with Robledo when it came to money. The one sticking point in negotiations came further down the line. Neil was content with the terms on offer from Santa Fe, and terms had been agreed in principle but not yet in writing when Neil's wife Vera became pregnant with their second child.

That news put the move under serious jeopardy, and Neil quickly contacted Luis Robledo to inform him of the situation and his concerns. Neil and Vera worried about the conditions of the hospitals in Bogotá, and whether the child being born in Colombia would impact his or her nationality. Not only were they keen for their child to be recognised as British, if their status was put down as Colombian, they would most likely be required to partake in compulsory national service.

Robledo had an answer for everything though, telling Neil that Vera would receive first-class medical care, the baby would be British, and assuaging any other lingering concerns the player and his wife might have had. The wealthy Colombian certainly seemed to be very convincing, and Neil saw no reason to distrust him.

Around the same time that Franklin told Robledo of his wife's pregnancy, he also informed the FA. With that information in mind, he told them that he would prefer not to be selected for the 1950 World Cup, England's first time competing in the tournament. It was an enormous blow for the national team to lose a mainstay in the team and their defensive pivot, upon which so much of the side was built. The disappointment was tinged with understanding though, as Vera was due to give birth not long after the time of the finals in Brazil.

However, when Franklin and his family took flight to Bogotá, an almost identical journey in terms of distance travelled, it appeared that he had given a false excuse to the FA as his reasoning for not wishing to be selected. Neil maintained his innocence.

'Some people think I was silly to do that [ask not to be selected], but I don't think I was. I could not have gone to Rio and given my best for England when I knew that my wife was having a baby thousands of miles away at home. It would not have been fair to my wife. It would not have been fair to myself, and probably, most important of all, it would not have been fair to England.'

Despite his protestations, people were, unsurprisingly, doubtful. Once he had received assurances regarding his baby though, Neil agreed terms with Independiente Santa Fe. The deal was done and dusted at the back end of March 1950, three weeks before Franklin played his final game for England against Scotland at Hampden Park. There was no evidence of a distraction playing on his mind that day; he provided a masterful display for the 133,000-strong crowd as he bowed out in style, unbeknownst to any of his teammates or coaches that it would be his last game.

It was on 7 May 1950 that Neil Franklin boarded a flight from London Airport (now named Heathrow Airport) to Shannon Airport in Ireland, the first leg of an onerous journey to Bogotá. Neil's party included his pregnant wife Vera, his son Gary, George Mountford, George's wife Phyllis and the Mountfords' two young daughters. The short flight from London to Shannon was just one of seven flights the heptad had to embark on in order to reach their final destination. London to Shannon was followed by Shannon to Goose Bay Airport in Canada, then on to New York, followed by Miami, from Miami to Cuba, Cuba to Kingston, Jamaica, then from Kingston to Barranquilla, and finally from Barranquilla to Bogotá. Having taken off from Heathrow on the Sunday, they wouldn't touch down in their final destination until Tuesday.

Today, you can fly from Heathrow to Bogotá in a little over eleven hours, but the world's first commercial jetliner wasn't introduced until 1952, kick-starting the 'Jet Age'. As such, the longest of Neil's seven flights was the one from Shannon Airport to Goose Bay Airport, clocking in at around nine hours.

It was the first flight from London to Shannon that began the media frenzy though. The plane was still in the air when the media caught wind of the story. FRANKLIN'S SECRET FLIGHT SENSATION read the headline in the local evening newspaper, the *Evening Sentinel*. Accompanying the story was a quote from the Stoke City manager Bob McGrory, which read, 'The news has come as a complete shock to me. I had no idea that either of the players was going by air.' The other player, of course, being George Mountford, who had somewhat harshly been overlooked in the *Sentinel*'s headline.

McGrory wasn't the only one. The news came as a shock to virtually everyone. Players, staff and supporters were gobsmacked. Only a day earlier, Saturday 6 May 1950, Stoke City had played their final game of the 1949–50 season, losing 5-2 to Arsenal at the Victoria Ground. A Doug Lishman hat-trick for that season's FA Cup winners consigned Stoke to a 19th defeat of the season, ending the campaign only two places above the relegation zone, and a murky shadow of the side they had been only a few seasons earlier. The only people informed of their impending departure were a very small number of close family and friends.

'I can say though, that there were one or two people in Stoke who knew that George and I were going with our families and that we were not coming back. Not for a year, at least. Those few people kept our secret wonderfully well. Not a word leaked out, so I can see no reason why I should betray their confidence and mention their names here.'

The public interest in Mountford and Franklin's flights to Colombia was enormous. They were not the first British players to have made a move overseas. The Football League's first top scorer John Goodall had spent a couple of seasons in France at the end of his career, once into his forties. A handful of Scots, such as David Robertson and Bobby Curtis, swapped Scotland for the United States during the interwar period. There were others too: Tommy Muirhead was lured from Rangers to Boston Wonder Workers in 1924 following a lucrative offer to become player-manager, where he was joined by former Greenock Morton star Alex McNab and future Hearts hero Barney Battles Jr, all Scottish internationals.

It wasn't just the Scots. Sam Chedgzoy, a flying right-sided forward who played 300 games for Everton and won 8 caps for England, swapped Merseyside for Massachusetts in 1926, spending four years in the United States and a further nine in Canada with Montreal Carsteel. Then there were the pioneers, like Herbert Kilpin and Alexander Watson Hutton, less accomplished players but highly significant individuals who were born in Britain but had a gargantuan impact on the development of the game overseas.

What set the Colombian exiles of 1950 apart then, and Franklin in particular, was that it was the first time a top-class player and a full England international had left behind a First Division club. Even in the case of Chedgzoy, he hadn't won a cap in two years. Franklin held the record for consecutive caps (jointly with Billy Wright) and was the most irreplaceable member of the England side. Further to that, the story captured the public's imagination because of the destination. He wasn't leaving England for Italy or Spain; it wasn't the United States or even the established South American footballing nations of Argentina, Uruguay or Brazil. It was Colombia. You could scarcely have picked a more exotic location with a globe in front of you. Many British people had never even heard of the country, let alone its Campeonato Profesional or the Bogotá club of Independiente Santa Fe who were snatching one of the nation's star players.

The first three flights passed without incident, but the Franklins and the Mountfords would meet their first problems during a stopover in New York. The flight to New York itself was not a problem; in fact it was the most enjoyable leg of the journey. The two families were joined on the flight from eastern Canada to New York by the American actor, singer and dancer Gene Kelly. The Hollywood star was returning home from filming the musical *An American in Paris*, a movie which won six Academy Awards, saw

Kelly nominated for a Golden Globe and propelled his co-star Leslie Caron to stardom.

This was a real thrill for Neil's wife Vera, who was an avid movie fan during the era of Classical Hollywood cinema. Her love of all things Hollywood was so great that she named her son after Gary Cooper, a Golden Globe and Academy Award-winning actor who found fame in movies like *Mr. Deeds Goes to Town* and *Sergeant York*. She was rather star struck to meet Gene Kelly, and was keen to talk to him. The actor was very friendly, and Gary—the only one in the Franklin family with no idea who Gene Kelly was—soon found himself sat on the actor's knee.

It was a welcome pick-me-up for the pregnant Vera, and somewhat befitting of her expectations of the direction in which the family were heading. It is a sign of how little was known of Colombia among the common man or woman on the street in Britain in 1950, that Vera would talk of 'going to America' prior to their departure. Of course, the family were going to South America, which was a world away from the 'America' that she had seen in the movies, but at this time her hopes were still high of their new home. However, the first bump in the road arrived in the Big Apple.

Having landed at New York International Airport, then known as Idlewild Airport and now known as John F. Kennedy International Airport, the Franklins and Mountfords were due to meet a contact from Santa Fe in the United States' most populous city.

'This was at a flat in Manhattan. We were told we should find a contact there and he would give us all the help we needed during our ten hours' stay in New York, but when we got to the flat, complete with our mountain of luggage, we found no one at home.

'Fortunately, the gentleman in the next-door flat came out and took pity on us when he heard our story. He was a student and he invited us to use his flat and rest. He was extremely kind to the children and took them out and bought them ice cream.

'But for this extremely thoughtful student we should have been in a real fix, because I had very little American currency. Fortunately, I did have a cheque, which the Santa Fe officials had given me, so I was able to cash it and avoid being absolutely broke.

'At the time, both George and I were annoyed at the breakdown in the arrangements, but we thought that it was just one of those things. Little did we know that it was only the first of the many examples we were to get of the complete lack of organization in Bogota.'

Following their half-day stopover in New York, the two families were airborne once more, travelling from New York to Miami this time. Blisteringly hot and humid, Miami was where they would be spending the night, before an early flight to Cuba the following morning. George Mountford tried to brighten the trip by enquiring where the boiler-room was once they arrived at their hotel, but not everyone was in such high spirits. The combination of the heat and travelling was taking its toll on Neil's heavily pregnant wife.

The next day would do little to alleviate her struggles. At 7 a.m., they made the short flight from Miami to Cuba, and then from Cuba on to Kingston, Jamaica. It was even hotter on the Caribbean island than it had been in Miami.

'Here [in Kingston] the heat was even worse, and Vera was beginning to feel the effects of it all. She was terribly exhausted and most unhappy, but we had only two more stages of the journey before we arrived in spring-like Bogota.'

The next flight would see them touchdown on Colombian soil for the first time, in the northernmost major city in the country, Barranquilla. Here, they found the hospitality offered by Santa Fe much more satisfactory than it had been in New York. The club sent a doctor to accompany Vera, who Neil described as taking 'his duties most seriously', and he insisted on sitting next to Vera for the final leg of their two-day journey. Below are Neil's reflections on the doctor's presence and finally landing in their new home city.

'We were glad to have him, too, because the last stage of our journey was the roughest flight I have ever experienced. I don't think the aircraft flew on a level keel for more than a minute at a time, and we were all tossed about like so many corks in a rough sea.

'This sort of thing, of course, upset my wife more than ever, although I am thankful to say that she never needed the attentions of the doctor. However, we were all glad when the aircraft finally touched down at Bogota, where we found waiting for us a reception worthy of visiting monarchy.'

Just as the famous Argentine stars had been upon their arrival in Bogotá, the Stoke City duo were greeted by large numbers of joyous Colombian football fans. 'Everyone who was anyone appeared to be at the airport, including newspaper and radio correspondents,' Neil noted. Franklin may have been surprised that the duo were greeted like royalty, but the English were in fact considered to be footballing royalty across much of the globe at the time, although that reputation was to take a fairly sizeable dent when the Franklin-less England team were dumped out in the first group stage of the 1950 World Cup.

The Colombians weren't the only ones taking a great interest in Neil and George's arrival in South America. Back home, the story dominated the national newspapers back pages, even as the England team trotted off to Portugal and Belgium in preparation for their World Cup debut. Shortly after the news had broken, the *Daily Express* had managed to get a quote from Daniel Ferro, a fellow founder of Santa Fe and then club secretary. Ferro was quoted as saying, 'They have been engaged to coach our team, but they may play some games. We should like to show them off in front of the crowd. We shall put them into a hotel for a couple of days. Then we hope to get them into a house. They will be well looked after.'

The same newspaper even sent a reporter to meet the two

players during their ten-hour stopover in New York. Both players decided not to reveal all, and as such, the early indications remained that they were only temporarily engaged in Bogotá, possibly only to train, and that they could be back in Blighty before long. Other newspapers were hot on their trail, eager for a scoop on the sensational story. *Empire News*, a Sunday newspaper that merged with the *News of the World* in 1960, sent their sports writer Capel Kirby out to Bogotá. Kirby met up with the duo in Colombia to get a better idea of the reasons behind their intriguing flight to South America.

It's testament to the fascination and shock in the story in Britain at the time that the newspapers thirst for Franklin and Mountford was this great. Transatlantic flights alone for their reporters would have come at a significant cost, and this at a time when football was afforded a fraction of the column inches dedicated to it today. The *Sentinel* even had maps showing their departed stars' flight routes; the story was truly a sensation.

It quickly became clear that this was not a coaching expedition, and that the two Stoke City footballers had signed for Independiente Santa Fe as players. The English press reacted quickly and angrily. There was panic in the upper echelons of the FA, the Football League and its ninety-two members. Why had they left? Why Colombia? How could they leave without the permission of the clubs that held their forms? Was this the beginning of a mass exodus?

These were all questions coursing through English football when the news broke. Once it came out that the players would be financially rewarded far better for their work in Colombia than they would in England, the press had a field day. Suddenly, they were mercenaries, greedy working-class footballers with the nerve to seek out greater financial security. It had been a similar story when Argentina had lost so many of their finest players around the time of their player strikes. Below is an extract from an Argentine newspaper at the height of their players' defections to Colombia.

> This latest case announces itself as a real hawk with a cannibal appetite. The question for us is, what we are going to do to safeguard our coveted pigeons . . . just how long will the suicidal zeal of the Colombians last? And we declare it a suicidal zeal because one day this will all collapse. Which castle of cards doesn't? The spectacle of football as business and not as sport can only give so much and so there will be many that will return with tears in their eyes and confessing to their dangerous adventure.

There may have been an element of foresight to the article, but just as the English press would come to the immediate aftermath of their own departures, it entirely overlooked the legitimate concerns of those players in their domestic leagues and their reasons for seeking such a move. There was little talk of whether these star players who drew supporters in their thousands, only to line the pockets of club chairmen (and the tax man, in Britain at least), perhaps deserved to see more of that money themselves. Few thought to posit whether a system less draconian than that of retain and transfer might have seen the Football League retain their best defender. The language the press used was enough to sum up their narrow views, labelling those players who had moved to the Campeonato Profesional as the 'Bogotá Bandits'.

Franklin and Mountford were not the only two players from these shores to wave the British game goodbye and try their hand in the FIFA-exiled league. There was Charlie Mitten from Manchester United, a super outside-left who had come through the youth ranks with the Manchester club. Mitten was an outspoken star who had confidence in his ability and was highly frustrated with the Football League's wage structure. He was uncapped, but he was one of the key men in a talented Manchester United side that was playing a vibrant brand of attacking football under their young manager Matt Busby.

During his four seasons in the Manchester United first team following the war, Mitten and his teammates had finished as First Division runners-up three times and won the 1948 FA Cup with victory over Stanley Matthews' Blackpool side in the final. According to Mitten, Robledo had approached him on the recommendation of Franklin himself. Unlike Franklin, it was a call Mitten had been waiting on and one he had hoped would arrive. Like everyone else with even a fleeting interest in football, Mitten had heard about Franklin and Mountford's moves to Santa Fe. The figures quoted in the press had turned more than a few heads, and Mitten was one of them.

'The press had been full of it when Neil Franklin and George Mountford signed for Bogota Santa Fe. I thought: a £5,000 contract, plus £35 win bonuses—what the hell are we doing here! We'd toured the United States, beaten their best teams, yet we'd nowt in the bank to show for it. We all felt this way.'

The above is a quote from Mitten, and it makes it easy to see how he was even easier prey for Robledo than Franklin had been. When he did receive the call, he was only 2,000 miles from Colombia, whilst Neil had been 5,000 miles away in Stoke-on-Trent when he received his first correspondence from the club. This was because Manchester United were on a highly profitable tour of the United States. On 10 May 1950, they had flown stateside to play twelve games in a little over five weeks in the United States and Canada.

The tour proved to be an enormous success. United beat a Canadian All-Star XI 5-0 in their first game, followed by a 9-2 win against a New York All-Star XI. The side from the Big Apple were spearheaded by Joe Gaetjens, who would soon immortalise himself by scoring the winner versus England at the 1950 World

Cup. Wins against Besiktas and LA All-Stars followed, before Matt Busby's men suffered two defeats in their last two games, going down to an All-England XI, who were preparing for the upcoming World Cup, and Swedish amateurs Jönköping. They ended the tour with eight wins, two draws and two defeats to their name, along with a significant amount of cash in the club coffers. Mitten had scored eight goals, and seeing the crowds turn up in their thousands in the United States, just as they did in England, only aggravated the sharp-shooting wide man further.

According to Mitten, the offer from Santa Fe had been the result of Robledo asking Franklin who the club should sign at outside-left. Mitten's response to the club's offer was, 'How do I get there?' It's fair to say there didn't seem to be too much doubt in his mind. The club arranged flights from New York to Bogotá for the following morning, and Mitten went off to tell Busby of his decision. Though initially angered and apprehensive, the Manchester United boss supposedly enquired, 'Do they want a manager?' when Mitten revealed his potential Colombian salary, and ended the conversation with the words, 'Okay. You'd better go, or you'll die wondering.'

Before Mitten, there had been a couple of other exiles. From north of the border, Bobby Flavell had agreed terms with Santa Fe's Bogotá rivals Millonarios, much to the annoyance of his club, Hearts, who had paid £10,000 to acquire his services from Airdrie only three years earlier. A diminutive but determined centre-forward with a knack for scoring goals, the lad from North Lanarkshire would spend much of the 1950 season as Alfredo Di Stéfano's strike partner in Bogotá, before returning to Scotland and scoring in successive Scottish League Cup finals for Dundee.

The other Colombian exile from Britain was the Irishman Billy Higgins, who was probably the least well known of the players from the British Isles to try their luck in South America. Higgins had played just forty-nine games and scored only nine goals in the four seasons which had followed the war, all spent with Everton. The Tranmere-born forward's less established reputation in comparison to the likes of Franklin and Mitten was reflected in the terms offered to him. His deal was reportedly worth less than a third of what the former Stoke City and Manchester United stars would be earning.

Millonarios were actually snooping around a handful of Everton players, including future long-time Toffees boss Harry Catterick, who won two First Division titles and one FA Cup as a manager on Merseyside. Catterick rejected a deal, but one Everton player who was very interested in Millonarios' advances was Jack Hedley, a solid club full-back who had made sixty-one appearances in three seasons at Goodison Park.

Hedley was keen, but he wanted to know what he was signing up for, so he flew out to Bogotá before making any formal agreements. He didn't travel alone: with him was Roy Paul, a Welsh international who had recently won promotion to the Second Division with Swansea Town. Higgins, Hedley and Paul had all been approached by Jock Dodds, who was acting as an agent for Millonarios. Dodds had been a superb player. He wasn't the most gracious of footballers, but he was quick, strong and never gave a defender a moment's peace, scoring prolifically for Sheffield United, Blackpool and Everton.

By 1950 though, he was thirty-five, and looking to gain some financial security as his playing days neared an end with Lincoln City. It has been said that Dodds played a part in Neil's move to Sante Fe, but this was not the case. Dodds represented the interests of Millonarios, and if anything, Neil was counteractive in his efforts to recruit players to join the Bogotá side.

In the cases of Jack Hedley and Roy Paul, they both spoke to the British expats to get an idea of what life in Bogotá was like. Franklin and Mountford gave honest accounts of their brief experiences of Colombia thus far, but it was the scathing testimony of Hedley's former Everton teammate, Higgins, that really put them off. The Millonarios forward was having a terrible time of things in Colombia, and his struggles were enough to put both players off a move. The duo returned to England after just a week, but they couldn't have expected the reaction they got on their returns. Both players were transfer listed, with Hedley leaving Everton for Sunderland and Paul making the move from Swansea to Manchester City. It proved to be a blessing in disguise for Paul, who became one of the most accomplished half-backs in the First Division at Man City, lifting an FA Cup as their inspirational captain in 1956 and amassing 30 caps for Wales.

So that was it: Neil Franklin, George Mountford, Bobby Flavell, Billy Higgins and Charlie Mitten. They were the five British players who made moves to Colombia during the El Dorado era, all in 1950. It could nearly have been very different though. Jock Dodds once boasted of having letters from 250 top-class British players all enquiring about moves to Colombia, and Neil didn't believe it was all hot air from the Scot.

'Then there were the stories of Jock Dodds, who was reputed to have been asked by many well-known players to fix them with contracts. I can well believe it, because I received countless letter from many famous players at home. They all wanted to come and join us. If only 10 per cent of those players had made the trip, I doubt whether English and Scottish football would have recovered from the shock for years.'

What would life be like for those players who had taken the plunge, though? Well, things had got off to a rocky start for Neil and George. Although they had been impressed by the turnout for their arrival at the airport, there were already indications that Luis Robledo had perhaps oversold Bogotá.

Despite having been in contact with one and another for six

months, Robledo and Franklin met for the first time when Neil landed at Bogotá Airport on 9 May. Robledo's first words? 'Watch your pockets.'

'I wondered what he meant, but I soon found out. Bogota was full of the world's most expert pickpockets. I remember on one occasion walking down the street when a newspaper seller came up to George Mountford and tried to sell him a newspaper. While he was delivering his sales patter he was actually taking George's pen out of his pocket!'

Those first three words from Robledo set off a few alarm bells. The wealthy cattle rancher had failed to mention pickpockets in the six months that they had been talking; what else might he have 'forgotten' to bring up? On the journey from the airport to the hotel, too, which included a quick tour of the city, there were surprises in store.

'Already we were beginning to realize that Bogota was not all it had been cracked up to be,' Neil noted. 'As we saw the hovels and shacks in which people lived in abject poverty, we could not help but remember the glowing descriptions we had been given.

'We had been led to expect a bright, modern city on the lines of, say, Rio de Janeiro. We found that Bogota was nothing like that at all.'

The journey concluded at the Hotel Granada. In a city obsessed with image, the Granada was the ultimate status symbol. The height of luxury, it was the gathering place of not just the city but the nation's elite. A 1941 article in the *Los Angeles Times* likened it to the Waldorf-Astoria in New York, adding, 'There hasn't been a thing of that sort here since the depression got in its early hard licks.' The Hotel Granada boasted 310 guest rooms, apartments for permanent residents, two nightclubs, four bars, four elevators, twenty shops and under-street parking.

Even the Hotel Granada though, the jewel in the crown of Colombia's capital, bore the scars of the country's ongoing violence.

On the night of Gaitán's assassination, when the riots known as El Bogotazo broke out, the hotel was heavily damaged. There was, and still is, a rigid class system in Colombia, with incredibly limited social and economic mobility. Although the country gained independence from Spain in 1810, the white descendants of the colonial era maintained control of its politics and economics. Since much of the political discourse surrounded this issue, the Hotel Granada, as the epicentre of Colombia's 'elite', or 'entitled' as the opposition may put it, was a natural target during the riots.

When I told Neil's son, Gary, that the hotel had been the scene of significant civil unrest, violence and fatalities less than two years before the Franklins and Mountfords moved in, he responded by saying, 'Oh, is that what it was? Ah, you see, well part of it was closed off.'

Gary was only five years old at the time, soon to turn six, and he had a hard time adjusting to life in South America. Days after their arrival, he came down with dysentery, whilst doctors sent by the club had told Vera to rest in bed for a few days following her travels. Gary's problem was not an unusual one in Bogotá, so much so that it had nicknames, such as 'Bogotá Tummy' or 'Bogotá Belly'. To this day, stomach parasites and other such ailments can be quite common in the city, with visitors advised to avoid drinking tap water and to be very cautious with where and what they eat.

The Hotel Granada was luxurious, but Franklin and Mountford's suites were nothing to write home about. They were comfortable enough, but not particularly large, consisting of only a bedroom, a bathroom and a sitting-room. With Vera restricted to bed and Gary very unwell, there was another challenge facing the two families from the Potteries—altitude sickness. Bogotá is 2,600 metres above sea level, and visitors from less geographically extreme parts of the world were known to suffer from altitude sickness. The symptoms, which are similar to that of a bad hangover, can kick in at 1,500 metres, and can become severe at over 2,400 metres.

It was reported in some news outlets that the poor air quality in Stoke-on-Trent had been one of the reasons behind Franklin seeking a move elsewhere. If that were true, Bogotá would have been a poor choice of alternatives, but his son Gary assured me that such suggestions were nonsense anyhow.

Both the doctor and the British embassy warned the players of the potential hazards presented by Bogotá's high-altitude level, particularly in relation to Vera's pregnancy and both Neil and George playing competitive sport at that height. Despite the advice having come from a doctor sent by them themselves, Santa Fe were dismissive of such concerns, and eager to thrust their new stars straight into the action.

'Both George Mountford and I were willing to take the advice of the British embassy about the height, but the Santa Fe Club were terribly anxious that we should play on the Sunday, although we had only arrived the previous Tuesday. The officials wanted to show us off to the public, and one could hardly blame them for that because they had gone to a lot of trouble to sign us, and our arrival had received tremendous publicity.

'The whole town was alight with the news. Crowds gathered outside our hotel, and we were rocketed into the same sort of position television stars find themselves in after a few successful appearances, but we had not yet appeared.

'So it would have been a terrible let-down if it had been announced we were not in the side for the game on Sunday. Knowing that, both George and I decided to turn out, and in our very first game we beat Medellín by three goals to two.

'I couldn't help thinking during the game how strange it was that we should play at Victoria Grounds, Stoke, one Saturday and lose 5-3 [the actual scoreline was 5-2] to Arsenal, and eight days later we should be playing in Bogotá, a city no one had ever heard of in a country few people knew existed!'

Medellín were a decent side, but they weren't littered with stars, having only signed a couple of Peruvian internationals. Santa Fe, on the other hand, were expected to be battling it out at the top end of the Campeonato Profesional. Whilst Millonarios were considered the nation's big spenders who could just about name a full team of internationals, their Bogotá neighbours had been just as zealous when it came to player recruitment.

As well as their three Englishmen (Franklin, Mountford and Mitten), they had invested heavily to poach players from Argentina. Where Millonarios had Di Stéfano, Santa Fe had Héctor Rial. The two would go on to become teammates at Real Madrid, where they won five consecutive European Cups, but in Colombia they were local rivals.

Rial, who liked to play as a second striker or in attacking midfield, was an elegant footballer who played with verve and swagger. A wonderful playmaker renowned for his perfectly weighted passes, pinpoint deliveries into the box and fine close control, he left Santa Fe for Nacional in 1952, before his move to La Liga in 1954. He scored 26 goals in 53 games during his time in Bogotá, and was similarly prolific at the Santiago Bernabéu. Born in Argentina to Spanish parents, Rial won five caps for Spain following his move to Madrid, and scored once against England in a 1-1 draw.

The biggest name signing at Santa Fe, other than Franklin at least, was René Pontoni. A magical footballer who had quick feet and a quick mind, he had scored goals for fun in Argentina for both Newell's Old Boys and San Lorenzo. Regarded as one of the best footballers in South America, Pontoni scored 19 goals from 19 caps for the Argentine national team between 1942 and 1947. He won three Copa América titles with La Albiceleste, but in 1948, a brilliant career came crashing down. A devastating tackle by Boca Juniors defender Rodolfo De Zorzi fractured Pontoni's kneecap, his meniscus and the ligaments in his right leg. It was a horrific injury, and it forced one of Argentina's brightest stars into an early retirement, aged twenty-eight.

Santa Fe managed to convince him to make a comeback in 1949 though, and the man they nicknamed 'La Chancha' spent the next three years in Bogotá. Niggling injuries kept returning, but he did manage 36 goals in 54 outings, and was always a joy to watch when fit. Pontoni has the rare distinction of being the childhood hero of Pope Francis. The leader of the Catholic Church is a life-long San Lorenzo fan, and he was twelve years old when Pontoni suffered his career-threatening injury. As recently as 2013, Pope Francis was given a photo of his favourite player, and recalled a famous goal the centre-forward scored against Racing back in 1946. So, if you are among those who believe in papal infallibility at least, Pontoni was some player.

The third and final Argentine international in the Santa Fe side was Ángel Perucca. He was Santa Fe's answer to Néstor Rossi at Millonarios, and probably more talented than his compatriot. A steely but elegant defensive midfielder, Perucca won 26 caps for Argentina, and River Plate spent years trying to add him to their formidable 'La Máquina' squad. Instead, he joined San Lorenzo. He was into his thirties when he signed for Santa Fe following the players' strike in Argentina, but he still strolled around the pitch with the aura of a player who was a class above most around him.

There were other internationals too, like Enrique Álvarez Castillo. A skinny but technical midfield ball player, Álvarez had previously played for Lanus in Argentina, and was one of Santa Fe's first big signings, joining the club in 1947. He left the club in 1948, but returned for another season in 1950. Capped seventeen times by Ecuador, he represented his country in three South American Championships. Between the sticks, Santa Fe had Julio Gaviria, a charismatic shot stopper who had won Gold whilst representing

SIX GAMES FOR SANTA FE

Colombia's football team at the 1946 Central American and Caribbean Games.

Clearly the Independiente Santa Fe side was not lacking in international experience or pedigree, but even in this mishmash of global stars, one man stood out. Hermenegildo Antón was his name, and he had enjoyed a far less illustrious career in Argentina, never receiving a call-up never mind a cap for the national team. In Bogotá though, he endeared himself to the Santa Fe supporters even more than the combined talents of Mitten, Rial and Pontoni.

He thrived in El Dorado, with a goal-scoring record similar to Di Stéfano's at Millonarios. Having joined the club as a 23-year-old, he scored 91 goals in 118 games for Santa Fe. A virtuoso forward who could score all kinds of goals, Antón was a particularly talented header of a ball. All in all, Santa Fe had six current or former internationals on their books in 1950, two uncapped Englishmen from the First Division, and one incredibly prolific uncapped Argentine. Whilst the Millonarios side of Di Stéfano, Pedernera, Rossi, Cozzi, Villaverde and more were known as the 'Ballet Azul' (Blue Ballet), due to their fine play and dark blue shirts, Santa Fe were known as the 'El Expreso Rojo' (The Red Express).

The two sides met in one of Neil's six games for Santa Fe, in what is now known as the 'Bogotá Clásico'. The attacking duo of Pedernera and Di Stéfano were shut out by Franklin. The game ended in a 0-0 draw, making it Neil's only draw in Colombia. The former Stoke City man's verdict on these South American superstars? He didn't seem overly impressed.

'Without being too hard on them, I should class Santa Fe and Millonarios as no better than the average Third Division side at home, so you can imagine the success any average First Division player would have achieved in a Colombian season. A team composed of players from the Football League or the Scottish League would romp away with the Colombian Championship, and in the meantime send the crowds into ecstasy with its football.'

Neil doesn't even mention playing alongside Héctor Rial or marking Alfredo Di Stéfano in his autobiography, which came out at the same time as both players lifted their first European Cup together. Gary said it was a similar story at home. Neil never spoke of being impressed or underwhelmed by Colombia's South American imports, just generally unmoved. Even whilst Real Madrid conquered Europe with consummate ease, Franklin's son never heard him mutter a word about Di Stéfano or Rial.

Charlie Mitten was rather more complimentary of football in Colombia, calling it 'an entirely different type of game out there', but not necessarily inferior to the English game. The former Manchester United man described his Santa Fe teammates as 'first-class performers'. Below is his account of the South Americans he played alongside in Colombia.

'The number one thing I saw in South America was that they learned first to become the absolute master of the ball. Every footballer there was a ball-player—there wasn't a kick-and-rush player in the country. Of course, some footballers are better ball-players than others, but *all* could trap a ball, kick it dead with a flick of the foot. All could pull the ball down on their thigh or on their chest—and after that, they all knew what to do with it.'

Clearly there was a big difference between how Mitten and Franklin rated the Colombian game, but both agreed that there was a greater onus on a player's ability with a ball at his feet than there was on his physical fitness. Mitten wrote, 'The emphasis all the time was on control of the ball, that is, having possession as well as a mastery of it.'

It seemed to fit perfectly with Neil's ideals of how the game should be played. Whilst the England centre-half remained unconvinced by the talents of his teammates and the rest of the players he saw in the Campeonato Profesional, he did reserve praise for some of their training methods.

'The training was vastly different to the training we had been used to at home. It was much more varied and included much more ball practice, both of which are good points. Training in Britain is usually much too stereotyped, and there is nothing like enough ball practice.

'Not only were the South Americans fanatics about practising with a football, they also included a lot of other ball games, such as basketball. But whatever ball games they chose, they made sure they were games played at speed, so that you had to keep agile, your eye had to be good and your stamina had to be good.

'I think we in Britain can learn a lot from this system. We place too much reliance on golf, which is a good enough game and a pleasant enough relaxation, but it is useless for sharpening up the senses of a footballer. Footballers need to play games of quick movement so that they develop their ball sense and develop it at speed.

'We also did a lot of mountain climbing, which was invaluable for developing stamina. When I was doing it I could not help thinking of the stories I had read about Scandinavian athletes, who train by running through the snow-bound forests. Tramping up a mountainside has pretty much the same effect. It toughens the muscles, improves the stamina and helps considerably in building up the general physical fitness of any athlete.

'So one good thing about Bogotá was the training programme. The only pity was that everyone was too lackadaisical about timing and too many of the players did not buckle down to the programme seriously enough. But for those two faults it was the sort of system which, with the right coaching, would have lifted Colombia high in the list of international soccer rankings.'

Having been fairly dismissive or uninterested in the talents of Bogotá's South American stars, Franklin is pretty scathing of their training attitudes. But why is there such a great discrepancy between Mitten and Franklin's accounts of Colombia's standard of football? And which was the more accurate?

Well, one reason might have been the fact that Charlie Mitten hung about for a full season, rather than six matches like Neil. There had been such an enormous influx of players into the league that summer, and it's inevitable that football teams need time to gel. So the fact that Mitten arrived later and stayed much longer means it's not unlikely the overall standard of football in the Campeonato Profesional improved following Franklin's departure.

That wouldn't explain Neil's lack of compliments for players' individual talents though, particularly those he played alongside. As we know, Neil certainly wasn't arrogant or blinkered when it came to football outside of Britain. He was quick to compliment the stars of the continent and quick to criticise the English game for failing to act as other nations surpassed us, particularly in terms of technical ability. So it's safe to assume that he wouldn't disregard a player's talents due to British hubris. One reason Neil may have been slow to praise the Argentine players in Colombia was because he never got on with them, well not those at Santa Fe at least.

'Most of our players came from Argentina, and they rather resented the intrusion of George Mountford and myself. Before we arrived, the Argentinians had held the monopoly, but when they realised that English, Scottish, Irish and Welsh stars were likely to invade Bogota they became insanely jealous, because they realized the British players would train and train hard. Training was not quite the strong point of the Argentinians. They were very good ball players, very good exhibitionists, but they were incredibly lazy in the training sessions. George and I naturally trained hard, just as any British player does, and when the Argentinians saw us throwing ourselves whole-heartedly into the training sessions they took a poor view of it.'

Neil's claims are corroborated by the likes of Billy Higgins and Adolfo Pedernera himself. When Roy Paul and Jack Hedley were in Bogotá weighing up a move to Millonarios, Pedernera reportedly went to Alfonso Senior and said to him, 'A quick word Don

Alfonso, I want to know something—are we a team of Englishmen or Argentinians? Because, if these English guys play for Millonarios, I'm off.'

Higgins, meanwhile, claimed that, 'The Argentinian players boycotted me and made me play as a reserve.' The Irishman added, 'The Argentinians at Millonarios have been acting like this for some time because they understood that the English were going to take their places in the team.' Higgins left Millonarios shortly after Pedernera was appointed as player-manager.

The hostile relationship between Franklin and the Argentine stars may have somewhat blinded him to their talents, or at least made him more reluctant to wax lyrical about them. Then of course, there is the distinct possibility that he really wasn't that impressed by them. Franklin typically reserved high praise for only a select few footballers, and in his six games in Bogotá, it's quite possible that no one stood out. After all, Di Stéfano and Pedernera had failed to get the better of him for Millonarios, and whilst Charlie Mitten called Héctor Rial a 'brilliant' player, he still regarded his former Manchester United teammate Stan Pearson as being superior to him.

In truth, there were clearly some exceptional footballers in Colombia during the El Dorado era, but the standard was almost certainly poorer than that of the First Division, and most likely the Second Division in England, too. Whilst the star players were real talents, as some went on to prove in Europe, the overall quality of the division was not great.

The Campeonato Profesional's best players did prove their class shortly after Franklin returned to Britain, taking on Uruguay's national team in 1950. Uruguay had shocked the world by beating the hosts Brazil at the Maracanã, so they were big favourites when they flew into Bogotá. The country had little footballing pedigree on the international stage, but few Colombians would be involved in this game. The star-studded team representing the Colombian

league featured Argentines and Englishmen, and ran out 3-1 winners against the world champions, courtesy of a brace by Alfredo
Di Stéfano and another by Héctor Rial.

That showed the class that was in the league, but hardly painted
a full picture. In contrast, George Mountford went from being a
winger who averaged a goal every five games at Stoke City, to one
with an average of better than a goal every other game in his season in Colombia, a stat which was in no small part thanks to his
willingness to head a ball. The South Americans weren't all that
fond of heading the ball at the time, and as Charlie Mitten put it,
'George Mountford used to score a lot of goals with his head
because he'd be the only one of our players going up to head the
ball in the goalmouth.'

Even Franklin himself managed to score his first peacetime—
if you can call Colombia in 1950 'peacetime'—goal in his six outings for Santa Fe. The notoriously goal-shy Franklin had gone 142
league games without finding the back of the net for Stoke City,
but it took him only half a dozen games to head home his first official league goal for Independiente Santa Fe.

Then there were the antics that went on away from the pitch,
but all too often influenced matters on it. Football may have been
seen as a means of distraction by the nation's government, but
instead of curbing Colombia's tensions and violence, it often simply moved it into the stadiums themselves. Neil had experienced
some vociferous crowds in his time, from the roar of the Scots at
Hampden Park, to the passionate and full-voiced Dubliners at
Dalymount Park, but nothing like the crowds he encountered in
Colombia.

'A Colombian crowd in action has to be seen to be believed.
Everyone is so excitable and so biased. We all know that in Britain
you stick up for your favourite team and get into tremendously
heated arguments about the merits or otherwise of a team or player,
but in Britain it is all done in a friendly spirit. In Colombia there

is nothing friendly about it! You hit a man over the head with a bottle with the same sort of nonchalance as you would say, "Don't talk rubbish!" here at home.

'The players are just as bad. Their tempers are always at exploding point, and it only needs a tiny spark to turn a football game into a brawl. I remember one occasion when 20 players got to grips in a terrific scrap. The only players who stood aloof were George Mountford and myself.

'On another occasion, one of our opponents was penalized for a foul, and our goalkeeper raced past me on his way to join in the scuffle, about which he could have known nothing. But a fight to a South American is a fight, and he must be in it.

'The atmosphere is so electric that every ground has netting to keep the spectators off the playing pitch, but in my six games with Santa Fe I never knew that netting to succeed in its purpose. The spectators even got into the dressing-room before the start of a game!

'In Britain, dressing-rooms are private. No one is allowed to enter them before a match except the players, the manager, trainer and directors (and few directors ever come in), but in Bogota, the dressing-rooms before a match were the scene of a gathering of the clans. Scores of people would jostle about, jabbering away excitedly in all sorts of languages, and it was a miracle that we players ever got on to the field at all.'

Had Franklin lasted a full season, he would have witnessed more than mere scuffles in the ground and fans invading the pitch. Before any footballers set sail for Colombia's El Dorado era, six English referees had already arrived. The professional game was still in its infancy, but the Colombians wanted a more professional feel across the board. English referees were regarded as the best in the world, hence the reason they were targeted, although certain supporters and players in Colombia didn't always seem to share that view.

Referees in England are used to having mud slung in their direction, particularly today with the advent of social media and pundits analysing their every decision on large electronic screens. However, the mudslinging is always of a metaphorical nature, whilst it was rather more literal in Colombia. Bill Brewer, one of the officials drafted in by DIMAYOR, had a large clump of earth thrown at him after giving a decision against one of the feisty South Americans. The Englishman's response? He returned the favour of course, and the match went on as if nothing had happened.

Another, Tom Pounder, had an even tougher time of it in Colombia. On one occasion at the start of a match when he called the two captains over to him, the home team's skipper pulled out a small knife and declared, 'We win, or else!' The players weren't the only ones at it though. Colombian referee José Antonio Sundheim was reportedly detained by police following a match between Cali and Millonarios, having also been found in possession of a knife.

Pounder seemed to have a particularly rough time of it. During one Santa Fe match against Cúcuta, which lies on the Venezuelan border, he awarded a goal to the away side, which seemed to have been a clear offside. The Englishman consulted his linesman though, and the decision stood. The home team and their supporters were incensed, but the game went on. Based in Bogotá, Pounder had been scheduled to fly back to the capital with the Santa Fe party after the game. With no sign of the English ref, George Mountford and Charlie Mitten went on look about. They eventually found him lying on the floor of his changing room. When he came round, Pounder told them, 'One of those bastard gendarmes hit me with his rifle butt!' It turned out the referees so-called 'security' supported the home side, much to Pounder's misfortune. It may seem like a fantastical and humorous story now, but it must have been a terrifying experience for those referees, and it's a wonder that they managed to last longer out there than Neil!

SIX GAMES FOR SANTA FE

One thing that Neil noted during his short time in Colombia is that you *had* to win your home games. Here in Britain, we are used to managers' rhetoric about making their home ground a 'fortress', and throughout Europe's major leagues, teams tend to have better records at home than away from home. Across the board though, the difference tends to be marginal. As I write this, there are a few teams in the Premier League who have picked up more points on the road this season than at home. In Colombia, this was not the case.

For Santa Fe, every away game in the Campeonato Profesional required a flight, with the exception of Millonarios with whom they shared a ground. League games took place at 3 p.m. every Sunday, so teams would typically fly to the nearest airport of their opponents on the Saturday. The road and rail system in Colombia was very poor, and the arduous journeys to away games could partly explain why visiting sides often came unstuck. A more obvious explanation would be the hostile home crowds and belligerent players taking their toll.

English referees admitted turning down substantial bribes to fix games during their time in El Dorado, but we've little way of knowing if the Colombian officials acted as honourably. In the six games Franklin played for Santa Fe, the club won all three of their home games, lost both of their away games, and drew their only neutral game against Millonarios at their shared 35,000-seater stadium, Estadio El Campín. Of course, that's a pretty limited sample size, but it was a similar story over entire seasons.

Even today, a quick glance at a home and away Colombian league table suggests teams enjoy vastly improved points' hauls at home than they do on their travels. One weekend after Gary and I had joked about the contrasting fortunes of home and away teams in Colombia, I put a small accumulator on every home side to win in what is now named the Categoría Primera A, and bizarrely it came up trumps.

With games on a Sunday, training took place every Tuesday and Friday, and that was it. The combination of twelve games fewer in the Campeonato Profesional, only two days training a week, and the relaxed nature of the South American training sessions meant the Bogotá Bandits had a lot of spare time on their hands. How to fill that time would present its own problems. Charlie Mitten used his new-found wealth to purchase a racehorse, fulfilling a lifelong dream which helped the days pass by.

One problem for the Englishmen was the language barrier, both on and off the pitch but particularly off it for Neil and his wife, and another was the city's curfew. Colombia's bustling capital of Bogotá would practically fall dead by 9 p.m. every night. Although La Violencia was still claiming lives in barbaric fashion on a regular basis, most of the fighting was now restricted to the countryside. As such, Neil never witnessed death or seriously violent encounters, but there were still signs in Bogotá that this was a country in the midst of a civil war.

A drive around town would involve regular stops at checkpoints manned by soldiers who were dotted around the city, and ID cards had to be carried at all times. Martial law had been proclaimed throughout the nation shortly after the aforementioned riots broke out in Bogotá in April 1948, and they remained in place during Neil's time there. Franklin and Mountford found this out the hard way, as they were arrested shortly after arriving in Bogotá for failing to carry their relevant documents.

The standard of football was not the only area where Neil disagreed with Charlie Mitten's accounts of Colombia. Their descriptions of the place itself are entirely at odds with one another. Mitten paints a picture of a tropical paradise that his children saw as a year-long holiday, whilst Neil talks of a dark, seedy city which was a million miles away from the place Luis Robledo had described in their six months of exchanges. Even the weather was a bone of contention. You will recall that Luis Robledo boasted of 'spring-like weather all year round' in Bogotá.

'Perhaps the biggest disappointment we had in Bogota was the weather. Even now I laugh when I think of the promises of spring-like weather. All I can say is that the Colombians have queer ideas about what constitutes spring-like weather. We found nothing but rain, rain, rain. I can hardly remember a day without rain, and if you are thinking of beautiful moonlit nights, you can forget Bogota. It suddenly goes dark around six o'clock in the evening, and the darkness plus the incessant rain spells abject misery.'

It didn't help that the Franklin's arrived in May, one of the wettest months of the year in Bogotá, but clearly they had been misled. Bogotá averages twenty-three days of rain in May alone, compared to just six days of rain in May in Stoke-on-Trent, and there are more than double the number of rainy days over a calendar year. It was clearly a real grievance for Neil, but one can't help noting how typically British it is to go to a country experiencing civil war, political unrest and regular outbreaks of violence, and still take particular exception to the weather.

Everything from the altitude to the food, and the great political unrest, made Neil's short time in Bogotá thoroughly unenjoyable. One of the most troubling issues for the centre-half was the cost of living. Whilst his pay packet in Colombia was far greater than his salary at Stoke City, his outgoings were enormous by comparison. One element of his time in Bogotá that Neil was always keen to clarify was that he did not get free accommodation, as was commonly reported both at the time and following his return to Britain.

'Here let me explain that we had to pay our own rent and pay for our own food. I mention that because so many people thought we got everything free of charge.

'Even when we eventually found a house on the outskirts of

the city—the Mountfords shared it with us—we had to buy all the furniture.

'Obviously, we did not have the capital, so we bought it on a hire-purchase agreement with the Club. It was all terribly expensive, as was everything in Bogota.

'The shops were full of good things to buy, but they were at prohibitive prices. Tea, for instance, was ten shillings a pound [equivalent to £16 in 2019], a plastic mackintosh, which can be bought here for now under a pound, cost four guineas in Bogota. That, I should say, was the usual standard. The cost of everything in Bogota was some four times the cost at home, and the quality was no better. Sometimes even it was worse.'

Mitten, too, described the cost of living as very expensive, but didn't find it as much of a problem as Franklin. He stated, 'although the cost of living was perhaps double what it was in Britain then, we still lived very well since I was earning five times more than I did with Manchester United.'

Fellow 'bandit' Billy Higgins, who was on less money than Charlie, George and Neil, found getting by in the city to be even more of a struggle. Upon his return, he declared, 'The cost of living was much too high and we spent every penny.' It was a similar story to the one he relayed back home whilst out there, telling a friend, 'We have to watch every penny of our money, particularly when we don't get a bonus.' Adding, 'You will probably have guessed by now that I am not particularly happy. Having taken the plunge, however, I was quite prepared to stick it out until I was told I would have to pay the passages from England of my two children.'

The Irishman had been told by the Millonarios club that all flight and travel expenses would be seen to by them, and for Higgins, like Franklin, broken promises became a theme of their time in Bogotá.

It is worth noting that unlike Neil and George, Charlie Mitten—having joined Santa Fe after the Stoke City duo—had no problems regarding his accommodation, and was very happy with the hacienda-style property that the club found for him. Neil had been irked by the club's inability to arrange proper housing for him, bemoaning, 'our hotel suite was comfortable in its way, but we had been promised a house, not an hotel, and certainly we were not promised a fifth-floor room, which meant that Vera was almost a prisoner because she could not climb the stairs at that time.'

The lack of any semblance of organisation, planning or well-kept arrangements was something which none of the British players could ignore during their time in Bogotá. Even the team coach, which would pick the players up to take them to training every morning, was often two hours late! Billy Higgins lamented how often he would hear the words 'manana' and 'momentico', which mean 'tomorrow' and 'just a minute', adding, 'Each time you ask to see the directors, you are met with this.' Neil echoed that, writing in his book, 'Time means nothing to them. It is nothing for them to be a couple of hours late for an appointment, and if you ask for anything to be done, the stock answer is always, "Tomorrow".'

One matter in which Mitten, Mountford, Franklin and any soul who has visited the city of Bogotá could never disagree on, is that the city was incredibly divided, and the conditions some people lived in were heart-breaking. 'We found that the country had a huge social divide: there was the great mass of poor people, and above them a tremendously wealthy millionaire elite,' was how Mitten put it, whilst below is how Neil summed it up.

'How, then, did ordinary people live? Well, they didn't, unless they had plenty of money. But then Colombia is one of those places, so typical of South America, where you are either very rich or very poor. The very rich have a comfortable time, but the poor live in conditions that we would not offer to animals at home.

'On our way from the airport to the city we saw them living in hovels and shacks, and we later found that their staple diet was rice and fried bananas. Sometimes they had coffee.'

ENGLAND'S GREATEST DEFENDER

When recalling England's trip to Bogotá in 1970, Gordon Banks wrote in his book, 'From the moment I set eyes on it I didn't like Bogota'; he went on to describe the harrowing sight of 'cardboard shanty towns where exhausted mothers clutched babies with distended stomachs and stick-like limbs'. England's greatest-ever goalkeeper concluded his thoughts on Bogota with the sentence, 'To us the place seemed like a living hell.'

Everton legend Brian Labone wasn't much more complimentary, stating, 'It looked like the end of the world.' In 1970, the writer and novelist Brian Glanville described Bogotá as 'a sombre city of criminals and cripples' in the *Sunday Times*.

Charlie Mitten may have been the staunchest defender of Bogota at times, calling it 'a big modern city with department stores, cinemas and office blocks', as well as boasting that he 'lived like a millionaire' during his year there, but his comments wear a little thin under examination. We can take his word that his house was luxurious and his staff helpful, but he was far from immune to the perils of Bogotá.

Within weeks of his arrival, his pride and joy—the family's brand-new Ford sedan—was stolen. The car was found two days later, but every removable part, from the wheels to the windscreen wipers, were gone. The 1948 FA Cup winner even conceded that theft was a common occupation in the city, stating, 'Some people were so poor, it was their way of life'.

Another comment by Mitten that would have led to a raised eyebrow and a wry smile from Neil Franklin was his compliment of Luis Robledo. 'If Luis Robledo promised you something, you got it,' he declared. Well, this certainly wasn't true for Neil, and one finds it unlikely that he didn't promise twelve months of spring-like weather to Charlie too, and we know for a fact that he 'forgot' to mention the fact that Colombia was in the midst of a civil war.

During their lengthy discussions, spanning half a year in Neil's case, a full and frank description of what the players were signing up for would surely include a mention of the brutal violence that was occurring in Colombia, even if it had mostly been restricted to the countryside. Of course, Neil and his fellow Bogotá Bandits ought to have been more diligent in researching the state of what would be their new home for what they believed would be at least a year, but Robledo's failing to inform them of the reality of the situation was a rather major omission from a man as open and honest as the one Mitten describes.

Ultimately, it would be the incompetence, broken promises and inability to make proper arrangements by the Santa Fe officials that would cost them their famous English centre-half.

CHAPTER 11

Facing the Music

The greatest mistruth that Luis Robledo ever told Neil Franklin was that there would be no question marks regarding the nationality of his child should he or she be born in Colombia. That had been paramount to the move taking place, and the discovery that this was untrue was the first step towards Neil Franklin's return to England.

Vera was deeply unhappy in Bogotá, and considering flying back to have the child. However, it was the news that the child could be claimed as Colombian that finally convinced both Neil and Vera that the baby should be born in Britain. As Neil put it, 'We had been assured that there would be no nationality trouble whatsoever, otherwise we would not have gone in the first place, and it was this news of possible Colombian nationality that made Vera decide to have her baby back at home in Stoke.'

This deception alone, one might think, could have been enough to convince Neil Franklin to cut his misbegotten South American adventure short. He knew the anger surrounding his departure in England though, particularly within the FA, and he was keen to at least see out his contract with Santa Fe. As such, Neil went to the club and told them that Vera would like to return home, along with Gary. Much to his relief, Santa Fe seemed understanding, agreeing to arrange Vera and Gary's flights home as well as allowing Neil to accompany them as far New York, before returning to Bogotá.

It was a generous gesture by the club, and went some way

towards rebuilding the relationship between the player and the club, following the damning nationality revelations. It was in early July, shortly after England's humiliating group stage departure from the 1950 World Cup, that Neil, Vera and Gary boarded a flight from Bogotá for New York.

That journey went smoothly, but there was bad news waiting for them in the sweltering heat of New York City. At Idlewild Airport, airline officials told them no reservation had been made for Vera and Gary on the flight to London. Just as they had been a couple of months earlier, the Franklin's were stranded in New York thanks to the failed arrangements of Santa Fe.

'I pleaded with the airline officials, but although they tried to be co-operative, even the most co-operative of airline officials cannot crowd two extra people on to a full airliner.

'Fortunately, I knew that Mr. Robledo made frequent business trips to New York and he had told me that he always used the St. Regis Hotel. So we went there and I telephoned Mr. Robledo to tell him that not a single arrangement had been made for Vera and Garry [sic]. I was very annoyed and told him straight that I wasn't going back on the midnight and that I was staying in New York until I saw my wife and son fixed up with a passage home.

'He pleaded with me to go back, telling me that his reputation depended on my playing the following weekend. I told him flatly that I didn't care too hoots about his reputation. All I cared about was seeing Vera and Garry safely on their way home and that I was staying in New York with them until that had been arranged. I did, however, promise him that as soon as they were safely on their way I would catch the next aircraft for Bogota.'

Whilst the Franklins did not seem to encounter much luck in New York, they did encounter some kind-hearted individuals. Once more, they were welcomed into a stranger's apartment, Evelyn Webster this time. Webster was a reporter for the *Daily Express*, and she had taken pity on Neil, Vera and Gary. By this stage, Vera was quite distressed. She was unwell, unhappy about the lack of flight arrangements and struggling with the heat wave that had taken over New York. She was also anxious of the fact that her family would be waiting for her at the airport in London. Vera knew they would be worried when they discovered she wasn't on the scheduled flight, but had no way of contacting them.

'Now I ask you, what would be the reaction of any normal man to all that? I was so annoyed at the way I had been let down over Vera's trip home, and I was so worried about her health that I made up my mind on the spur of the moment—I would fly with her to London.'

That same day, Neil, Vera and Gary, managed to catch a flight to London. Neil would never return to Colombia. He insisted that he had every intention of returning, but Santa Fe were not convinced. To those who doubted his credibility, Neil pointed to the fact that he left behind all his clothes and belongings in Bogotá. 'No man who was running away would run away without his clothes and his possessions,' as Neil put it in his book.

Neil could be a little naive at times, and he couldn't quite see what all the furore was about. As far as he was concerned, all he had done was fly the full length of the journey rather than only accompanying his wife and child halfway. Sure, he would miss that Sunday's game, but he had told Luis Robledo that would be the case anyway, as he planned on remaining in New York following the lack of flight arrangements made. Neil contacted Mr Robledo and assured him that once Vera's situation was in order, he would be on his way back to Bogotá. He both cabled and wrote to Luis Robledo and George Mountford, explaining why he had made the journey to England and attempting to put their nerves at rest.

It was no use. Luis Robledo was a proud and image-conscious man, and the rapidly emerging news came as a blow to his reputation. Santa Fe announced that Franklin would not be returning, and stated that the player had broken his contract. Neil could still have returned to Bogotá, but even if he did manage to convince the Santa Fe officials that he was telling the truth, his name had been denigrated. The club and local press had taken great offence to his flight to London, and his name was dragged through the mud. In fact, the English in general were painted as being disloyal or untrustworthy, and the club's anger at Neil was briefly taken out on Charlie Mitten and George Mountford. Below is Charlie Mitten's recollection of the time after Franklin's departure.

'Santa Fe officials were furious when news reached Bogota that Franklin had returned to England. There were some hard things said to George Mountford and myself about Englishmen breaking their word. For weeks afterwards, private detectives followed us around everywhere, obviously checking up that we weren't going to leave town. Even the British consul was concerned, and asked whether we were happy in Bogota, and whether we intended to honour our contracts. He said British prestige was at stake.'

One does not doubt that Charlie Mitten enjoyed his year in Bogotá, but it tends not to be the warmest of organisations that hires detectives to keep tabs on someone in case they plan on defecting. Mitten would last a season in Bogotá, but ultimately terminate his contract, too, as his wife was less content with life in South America, feeling increasingly homesick and concerned for their child who had been unable to find an English school.

So in the space of two months, Neil Franklin had made two cataclysmic moves, both of which had caused uproar in the nation he was departing, and both leading to some less than complimentary words being written about him. The impact of his departure from Bogotá was seismic, and actually led to Luis Robledo resigning.

Robledo felt he had lost face when Neil left Bogotá for London, so the man who had been at the forefront of Colombia's El Dorado era, trying to build a team that would be respected across the globe, took a step back from football. A keen footballer—and polo player—he left the game for good following his resignation in 1950, retreating to his business interests up until his death in Bogotá in 1987, aged sixty-three.

Without their charismatic and cosmopolitan chief, Luis Robledo, and their marquee English centre-half, Neil Franklin, Santa Fe stumbled to a disappointing eighth placed finish, thirteen points behind the title winners Deportes Caldas. Defending champions Millonarios finished second, but Caldas, from the coffee capital of Manizales, were the surprise package winning their first championship. Whilst the 1950 campaign ended in shock, Millonarios continued to spend, and things clicked the following season. They won the next three league titles relatively comfortably, and even beat Real Madrid in 1952, but Colombia's 'castle of cards', as the Argentines had put it, was indeed to come crashing down.

The countries that had lost their star turns to the Campeonato Profesional had not done so quietly. The likes of Argentina and Brazil had urged FIFA to become more involved, but when those calls fell on deaf ears, they turned to their governments, demanding sanctions be placed on Colombia until they got their footballing matters in order. FIFA eventually turned up the heat, setting up a special commission tasked with resolving the 'Colombia problem'.

Negotiations were long and messy, but in August 1951, five months after talks had begun, DIMAYOR made concessions. They agreed to stop poaching players and to allow their foreign imports to return to their former clubs, becoming FIFA members once more in the process. The fine print stated that they could keep their South American and European recruits until October 1954. It wasn't until July 1953, when Alfredo Di Stéfano jumped ship to join Real Madrid, that the mass exodus began, and the El Dorado era of Colombian football was over.

As much as Santa Fe's declaration that Franklin had broken his contract with the club dissuaded Neil from returning to Bogotá, he was hardly itching to get back. His return had reminded him

◀ A young Neil in the Cannon Street School team photograph

▲ England's number five proudly dons his national team shirt and cap

▲ Neil Franklin in action for England against Ireland

Neil, Vera and Gary Franklin pose for a photograph on the streets of Bogota, Colombia in 1950. ▶

Stockport County players pose for ► a team photograph prior to their shock FA Cup win against Luton Town, but wearing borrowed Wolverhampton Wanderers shirts. [Neil one in from the left, top row]

England's former pivot pulling pints for ▼ some cheery patrons.

▲ Neil playing for Stockport County against West Ham in the FA Cup Fourth Round at Upton Park, 1958.

Franklin and his deputy keep an eye on a training session at ▼ Colchester United.

Not your average pub landlord: Neil's caps on display at the ▼ Dog & Doublet

◀ Neil playing Sunday
league football.

Neil [bottom left] shares ▶
a drink with some
famous faces.

◀ Neil walks along the
street with the likes of
Raich Carter and John
Charles, both of whom
made the 'Franklin XI'.

Neil [centre] alongside his old friend ▶
and celebrated Manchester United
manager Sir Matt Busby [left].

◀ Franklin [right] and Billy Wright [left]
at Sir Stanley Matthews' [centre]
70th birthday party.

The Dog & Doublet Inn, Sandon. ▶

◀ The author alongside Neil's son
Gary Franklin.

of all the home comforts he had missed in South America. He met up with his Stoke City pals and played alongside them in a Stoke City representative cricket match against Port Vale. Neil insisted that he would have returned to Santa Fe if they had believed his account of what happened, but it's fair to say he did not miss Bogotá.

'If I was so sure that I was going back to Bogota, what made me decide to stay in England? The simple fact that the Santa Fe officials announced I was not returning, said I had broken my contract and let them down. They just would not understand my point of view, so I decided it would be foolish to go back.

'They would have made misery for me. I would have been let down on the field by my Argentinian colleagues, and they would have seen to it that the crowd turned against me. And when a Colombian crowd turns against you it is time to duck.

'I decided that I would rather be an unpopular character here in Britain than an unpopular character in Bogota. It is safer.'

Was Neil Franklin an unpopular man in Britain? Well, as is so often the case when it comes to the world of football, opinion was largely divided. The press had tended to be very pejorative in their coverage of the move, but not everyone was convinced. To some, the Bogota Bandits were mercenaries, to others they were just professionals looking to ensure the best deals and maximum security for themselves and their families.

Neil, like pretty much all of the players who went off to Bogotá, returned worse off than when he had left. As was the case with his salary, the amount of money Franklin actually made during his eight weeks abroad is unclear. Certainly he didn't bring back his lucrative sign-on fee, and Stanley Matthews wrote in his autobiography that Neil only ever received one week's wages, which would have been no more than £60.

Although the public opinion was relatively split when it came to the question of the Colombian exiles, as is always the case, it was the most disapproving and outraged voices which could be heard the loudest of all. Just like the officials in Bogotá, most people in England didn't believe that Neil had any intention of returning to Colombia. It seemed as though he had jumped ship expecting to discover untold riches but returned home with his tail between his legs . . . and in many respects that was true. Some revelled in his failure though, and he even received hate mail back in Staffordshire.

'Even some of my own countryfolk thought that [I never intended to return to Bogotá]. Many of them wrote long and abusive—and, of course, anonymous—letters to Vera and me, and I can only hope that they did not represent the majority opinion in Britain.'

Neil Franklin's brief stint in Bogotá was a significant chapter in his life, as well as being a significant chapter in this book and in the history of English football in general, but it was just that—a brief stint. Less than eight weeks passed between Neil and his family touching down in Bogotá and their return to Stoke-on-Trent.

He returned home with mixed emotions. On the one hand, he was rid of all the ills of Bogotá, Vera was much happier and more comfortable, and Gary could get back to school. On the other, what had seemed like the opportunity of a lifetime had proved to be a false dawn, and he returned with a damaged reputation and a precarious-looking cloud hanging over his career.

It's important to remember that Neil returned after two months, but other Colombian exiles were still in Bogotá. The shock, the anger and the fear of the FA was still very raw, and they still had people like Jock Dodds boasting of English footballers who were keen to get out of the Football League. Therefore, Neil Franklin would not be welcomed back into the English game with open arms, and nor did he expect to be. His deception and defection hadn't been taken lightly, and the FA knew an example had to be made of their finest centre-half.

Once Neil made the decision to remain in England, he was of

course eager to return to football, but he wasn't quite sure how to go about it. This was unknown territory for him, or any English footballer for that matter, so there was no real protocol for him to follow. He was too scared to go straight to Stoke City. Bob McGrory was still in charge at the Victoria Ground, and quite what he'd say to the steely Scot, he did not know. When the Potters kicked off the 1950–51 campaign with a defeat at home to Newcastle United, Neil spent the day fishing.

Perhaps the FA suspected that Neil felt as though he was left in a bit of a lurch, as less than a week later, on 25 August, Stanley Rous, who had served as the Football Association's secretary since 1934, sent him a letter. The message to Neil was pretty terse, and told him flatly that he had been suspended, and if he wished to change that, he would have to be the one going to them. The entire letter read:

> I am writing to inform you that for leaving their clubs while under contract and for playing in unaffiliated football in Bogotá in contravention of the Football Association, Football League and Club rules and regulations, the following players are suspended forthwith:
>
> N. Franklin (Stoke City).
> W. C. Higgins (Everton).
> C. Mitten (Manchester United).
> C.F. Mountford (Stoke City).
>
> The suspensions must remain effective until the players apply to this Association for, and are granted, reinstatement.

That removed any doubt then! Neil was naturally disappointed but not at all surprised to learn of his suspension. However, his disappointment with any footballing matters were rather overshadowed at this time, as two days before he received that letter Vera had given birth to the family's second child. Elizabeth Franklin was born at Haven Nursing Home in Porthill on 23 August 1950.

It wasn't until the start of September that Neil Franklin applied to be reinstated by the Football Association then, and it wasn't a difficult decision. Franklin was only twenty-eight, and the best centre-half in the country; he was hardly going to call it a day. For the time being, all he could do was try his best to stay fit. The lax and infrequent training sessions in Bogotá already meant he was not as fit as he would typically have been, and he was keen to get back out on the training ground.

For the first couple of weeks, Neil trained on his own at Stoke City, but soon that would be taken from him, too. Following his appeal to the FA, the club informed him he could no longer use their facilities. Undeterred, Franklin found a police recreation ground where he continued to carry out all his drills and exercises in solitude.

The finest English defender of his generation had been banished into the footballing wilderness. He had won his 27th consecutive cap for England only four months ago and anchored Stoke City's defence a little over two months ago, yet now he was a footballing outcast training at a police recreation ground. It was some fall from grace, and others would have been humiliated in similar circumstances, but Neil Franklin got his head down and worked hard on his fitness and his game, like he always had.

'It was a change from what I had been used to, but I had no grumbles. I had gone to Bogota of my own free will. I had come back of my own free will, and I had asked for reinstatement of my own free will. So I had to be prepared to be an outcast until the powers-that-be decided what to do with me.'

It was an attitude typical of Franklin. Make no mistake, he was gutted that Bogotá hadn't proved the utopian adventure of a lifetime, and he had deep regret, describing the move as a 'ghastly mistake'. And yet, despite having been at the centre of a footballing sensation that had ended in disaster, 'It's no use crying over spilt milk' is perhaps the proverb which best describes Neil's reflection on the whole ordeal, both in the immediate aftermath and for the rest of his life. Even once he was handed a hefty fine and ban by the FA, he never seemed angry or bitter. Sad, perhaps, and certainly rueful, but never the genuine resentment that would be expressed by Charlie Mitten upon his return.

The date set for the joint Football Association-Football League enquiry into the case of Neil Franklin was 2 October 1950. Neil hadn't expected to get off scot-free, but he did find the whole thing a bit of a charade. It felt a bit like he was back at school, as eight representatives—four each from the Football Association and the Football League—gave him a jolly good telling-off, before dishing out an almost certainly pre-arranged punishment.

The 28-year-old 'naughty schoolboy' was not entirely hung out to dry. Stoke City's vice-chairman Arthur Preece attended the enquiry along with Bob McGrory on behalf of the club, and he told the various administrators that Neil was, 'the nicest player Stoke ever signed.' Sir Stanley Rous was also sympathetic to the player's plight, although he wasn't about to go out on a limb to defend him.

That was the view Neil took of Stanley Rous anyway, and Charlie Mitten seemed to agree. In his account of Mr Rous, Mitten stated, 'He was a decent, down-to-earth chap and seemed to be on the players' side, but for the sake of his job he kept quiet.'

The enquiry took place at the Adelphi Hotel in Liverpool, and coincided with the annual Footballers' Golf Tournament on Merseyside, meaning Neil had the chance to catch up with some familiar football faces from outside the Potteries too. The entire proceedings lasted less than half an hour, and Neil spoke for about fifteen minutes. He gave a frank and candid account of why he had wanted to leave Stoke, how he ended up in Bogotá, the broken promises and ultimately his return home.

The next day, he received a letter from Sir Stanley Rous informing him of the FA's decision, it read as follows:

A report of a Joint Commission appointed to hear an Appeal by N. Franklin, a professional player of Stoke City F.C., against a suspension imposed on him for leaving his Club whilst under contract and for playing in unaffiliated football in Bogota in contravention of the Football Association, the Football League and Club Rules and Regulations.

The Commission met at the Adelphi Hotel, Liverpool, on Monday, 2nd October 1950. The members of the Commission were:

Messrs. A. Book Hirst (in the Chair), A. E. Ansell and Sir Leslie Bowker (the Football Association) and Messrs. A. Drewry, W. J. Harrop and J. Richards (the Football League).

Sir Stanley Rous (Secretary, the Football Association) and Mr. F. Howarth (Secretary, the Football League) were also present.

The following also attended before the Commission: Mr. T. A. Preece (Vice-Chairman), Mr. R. McGrory (Manager) and Mr. N. Franklin (Player) of Stoke City F.C.

The Commission, having questioned Franklin on all the aspects of his case, decided that his suspension will be removed as and from the 31st January, 1951.

In the meantime, Franklin remains a retained player of the Stoke City F.C., but may not receive wages or payment of any kind from his Club in respect of the period of his suspension.

The Commission also decided that no payment should be made by the Stoke City Football Club to Franklin in respect of the unexpired period of his contract from the date of his leaving this country.

FACING THE MUSIC

In communicating the foregoing decision to Franklin, the Chairman informed him that the Commission deprecated his actions for:

1. Giving untrue reasons to the Football Association for not wishing to be considered for International matches.
2. Deceiving his Club and breaking his contract.
3. For making statements to the Press and allowing articles to appear under his name likely to bring the game into disrepute.

Since he had initially appealed at the start of September, the commission's verdict essentially meant that Neil would be banned for four months, having already served one of them. The unprecedented nature of the case meant Neil wasn't quite sure what to expect, but the four-month suspension didn't come as any great shock.

'It could, of course, have been worse. I could have been kept out of the game for ever, whereas I knew now that I would soon be back where I wanted to be—playing in the Football League and, who knows, for England.'

Neil soon learned that he had no future at Stoke City, with the club announcing that it 'would be better if we parted company'. Of course, that may have been why they were so complimentary during the disciplinary proceedings. They had a dog in this fight. Neil Franklin had been the subject of a world record bid prior to Stoke City losing him to Santa Fe for nothing. He may now have been 'damaged goods' in the eyes of many, but he was at least back under contract at the Victoria Ground, and he would still command an enormous fee from any potential suitors.

Yet again, Neil found himself in an unusual and divided position. Finally, Stoke City were happy to sell him, which is what he had wanted for so long, but only after his name had been dragged through the mud in the newspapers. It was the outcome he had long craved, but it was a million miles away from the route he would like to have taken to get there. The financial rewards offered by Santa Fe had been highly attractive to Neil, but if Stoke had simply sanctioned a move for their wantaway centre-half, he felt he would never have taken the plunge and headed to Bogotá.

Naturally these were the type of thoughts swirling around Neil's head, and as he put it, he was 'left with a lot of time to ponder on the tragedy of the situation'. When news of his suspension reached Bogotá, and it didn't take long, an outraged Charlie Mitten told the press, 'Franklin is not under contract with Stoke; he isn't drawing any wages; he is not allowed to train with the club. Yet the club are negotiating to sell him. Is there any other business in the world whereby a person is sold, yet is not under contract?'

Mitten had a valid point, and the courts would later rule in favour of players' freedom of contract in the landmark cases of both 1964 and 1995. However, Neil still felt a sense of acute sadness rather than anger or spite at the powers that be. He was generally a positive and forward-thinking person, but there is no doubt that the whole episode had hurt him. Tom Finney wrote in his 2003 autobiography that Neil 'was never quite the same after his heartbreak in Colombia', and Finney knew him better than most.

Neil probably summed up his post-Bogotá feelings best of all, writing, 'I went there a happy and expectant man. I came back a sadder but wiser one.' He made no bones about regretting the move, describing it plainly as, 'the greatest mistake of my career', but he maintained that he had sound reasons for seeking pastures new.

'I didn't go out of spite for Stoke City, England or anyone else. True, I had my differences with Bob McGrory. True, I was not altogether happy with Stoke City because of the differences of opinion over my style of play, but all those reasons were secondary to the vastly superior conditions of work and pay I was offered by the officials of the Santa Fe Club.

'Unfortunately, those conditions did not come up to the standard of the prospectus! Colombia, which had seemed a Shangri La when viewed from Stoke-on-Trent, turned out to be not even as good as my birthplace, the Potteries.'

The tragedy of the whole situation was that it could so easily have been avoided. Whilst his trust in the words of one man shows a great faith in humanity, Neil had been incredibly naive. He should have journeyed to Bogotá, just as Jack Hedley and Roy Paul had, to get an impression of the place, the people and the club before agreeing terms. That simple procedure would have opened his eyes to the fact that Colombia was a nation at war, that Santa Fe were incredibly disorganised, and—of course—that Bogotá did not enjoy spring-like weather all year round! It would have been an obvious precaution, and it is one Gary and I have spoken about a number of times.

Stanley Matthews expressed similar woe on Neil's behalf. If Charlie Mitten is to be believed, Matthews himself had been attracted to the idea of a move to Bogotá. Stan was out-earning any of his fellow pros through his lucrative endorsement deals, but a move to Colombia supposedly still peaked his interest at one time. However, Matthews was a little older, a little wiser and a little shrewder when it came to such matters. Whilst discussing Neil and the other Bogotá Bandits in his 2001 autobiography, Matthews bemoaned, 'No one could blame them for being captivated by such an offer, but I feel they should have at least made an initial trip to check the place out before signing on the dotted line.'

It's difficult not to note the tragic irony of aggrieved footballers from Britain seeking a better life in a country that was in the midst of a bloody civil war which, by the time of its conclusion, had claimed 200,000 lives.

One slight relief for Neil was the fact that, whilst Bogotá had not been the money-making expedition of a lifetime that he had hoped, he was financially secure. Prior to his move to the Colombian city, Neil had been on a winning streak at the bookies. Like a number of footballers, he enjoyed gambling a few quid on the horse racing. In the first half of 1950, every horse he picked seemed to come up trumps, and he won literally thousands of pounds. Gary still has some of his betting slips, the dearest of which included bets of up to £500, equivalent to over £16,000 in 2019. His combined Stoke City and England salary totalled less than £1,200, remember. At one stage, his bookie was so indebted to Neil that he offered him a share within the bookmaker's itself, an offer Neil refused, and later expressed regret at doing so. His success at the bookies had given him further confidence to take the risk of a move to Bogotá, and that cash would come in handy during his twenty-plus weeks without pay.

Others weren't so fortunate. The former Everton forward Billy Higgins, who had signed for Millonarios, returned to Britain virtually penniless and property-less. His contract was terminated by the Ballet Azul after five months in Bogota, and he and his family returned to Merseyside with only £19. Upon hearing of their plight, one Everton supporter offered him the temporary use of his cottage in south Wales. Soon after, Higgins left Everton to join Bangor City, and little is known of his life and career after that.

Charlie Mitten lasted a full year in Bogotá, but when he returned, he was hit with an even harsher suspension than the one dished out to Neil. Should Mitten return to the Football League, he would have to pay a £250 fine and be ruled out of action for six months. He accepted, but with great anguish. Presumably, the more severe terms meted out to Mitten were the result of his behaviour both in the press and during his commission hearing with the FA and the Football League.

Mitten wasn't one to bite his tongue. He felt passionately that footballers were getting a raw deal in Britain. He thought they should be paid more, they should have far greater freedom of contract and that he had done nothing wrong in going to Bogotá.

During his time at Santa Fe, the press had often come to him for comments and sound bites, and rarely did he disappoint. This behaviour was seen as deliberately antagonistic by the FA. Equally unhelpful to Mitten's cause was his attitude and approach to his joint enquiry. The already irritable Manchester United winger was not as forthcoming with information as Neil had been. He despaired as the various administrators quizzed him solely on the finances of the deal, eager to talk about footballing matters, such as what he had learned in South America and how the English game could benefit from it instead.

The other positive which could be taken from both the joint FA/Football League ruling and Stoke City's stance on Neil was the fact that he at least now knew where he stood. He would be leaving Stoke City, although where he would be heading he did not yet know, and he would be back on a football pitch just past the halfway mark in the season.

He may have been a 'sadder' man than the one who had departed for Bogotá a few months earlier, but his love of the game had not diminished. Neil was determined to train hard and get back onto a football pitch, whatever colour shirt he'd be wearing.

CHAPTER 12

Reunited with Raich

'From Boothferry to Wembley' is a chant often sung by Hull City fans. Well, for Neil Franklin, it would be the same journey but in the opposite direction. Despite firm interest from First Division side Derby County, the England international made a somewhat surprising transfer to Hull City, setting a world record fee for a defender in the process.

Talk to any footballer about facing a lengthy spell on the sidelines and they'll tell you how frustrating and depressing it can be. Neil Franklin was no different, and it was doubly frustrating for him as his body was in perfect shape, yet he could not step onto a football pitch or even train with fellow professionals.

Neil spent his four months out getting as close to the game as he was physically capable of doing. One of the traits which made him the player he was, was his constant eagerness to learn and improve. Even though he had reached the pinnacle of the game, his relentless appetite to keep getting better never diminished. It's a quality that you will find in just about every top-level footballer and athlete. So whilst he was out of the game, Neil watched football religiously. He had never sustained a seriously long-term injury, so it presented a chance for him to step back and view the game as a spectator for the first time.

'I watched all the football I possibly could, trying to spot faults and pick up tips. One great thing I did learn was that you can see more from the stands and terraces than you can from the field of play itself. Your field of vision is much wider. You can see the pattern of the game. You can see how moves are built up, how they can be counteracted, and how there can be an antidote to every antidote.

'That is not to say, of course, that the spectator knows more about a particular match than the players. He should do, but the average spectator has not the knowledge of the game to benefit by his excellent field of vision.'

Watching football may have provided a tonic of sorts for Neil, but it also served to further whet his appetite for a return to action. He may have seen football as his profession, and one for which he ought to be rewarded fairly, but don't be fooled into thinking he had lost his boyish love of the game. Neil Franklin was a football obsessive. He loved the game, along with all its intricacies and machinations. This is how he described his love affair with the beautiful game:

'Football, you see, is my life. I chose the profession myself, and I have loved every minute I have spent in the game. Some people think that just because you do a thing professionally you cannot love it, but that certainly does not apply to football players in Britain. I have yet to meet one who doesn't love the game.

'There is nothing strange in that. Maybe the ordinary working man gets fed up with his daily stint at the desk or at the factory bench, but anyone who is in any branch of the entertainment industry, of which professional football is very much a part, must love his job. I read once that Danny Kaye had said to a reporter: "Good gracious! Don't think I do this just for the money. I love every second of it".

'Whether Danny actually said that or not doesn't matter. I am sure he would not disagree with it. Neither would any other entertainer–singer, dancer, actor, sportsman. We love our jobs, we love playing, and when we are "resting" we are always itching to get back on the job.

'That is certainly how I felt during my suspension. That was why the suspension was the hardest part. For to be happy I must be playing.

'During my suspension, I felt irksome. I was itching to get my boots on again, to feel the thrill and tingle of a really exciting league match in my bones, to hear the cheers and the counter-cheers of the crowd in my ears. I even missed such seemingly unimportant things as the smell of liniment in my nostrils.

'Perhaps football is a drug. Once you have tasted it you cannot leave it alone. Sitting in the stand or standing on the terraces watching your pals go through the motions is not enough. You find yourself playing the game with them and for them. Your neighbouring spectators look at you with queer looks on their faces as you mutter to yourself: "Take it this way, boy. Body swerve past him. That's right. Now a feint to your left . . . slip it with the outside of your foot . . . No, not that way." And so you go on. You even move your legs and your body as your imagination transports you from your seat or position on the terraces right out there on to the field.

'Frankly, this playing the game from the stand is even more tiring than being in the actual match. Many former players who have become managers have told me that, but I never believed them until it came to me.

'And many managers who are ex-players do play the game from the stand. Stan Cullis, they tell me, never sits still during a game. George Kay, who played for West Ham United in Wembley's first Cup Final and then managed Liverpool, was like a cat on hot bricks throughout a game.

'Yes, football is a drug. Once it has you in its clutches it never lets you go, but there cannot be a pleasanter drug, or, indeed, a more beneficial one.

'So throughout my suspension I counted the days until I would be back in the fighting-line.'

Neil's likening of football to a drug might have been seen as hyperbolic back in the 1950s, but it's pretty commonplace now. Today, a third of all British footballer's divorce within a year of retiring from the game, and a staggering 35 per cent go on to suffer from anxiety and/or depression, which is twice the national average. The thrill and buzz of the crowd, the sense of identity from belonging to a team and the regimented routines dictated to you by staff and coaches can all be difficult to replicate.

As Neil Franklin eagerly anticipated his return to the Football League, still not knowing which club he would return with, he knew his game would come under increased scrutiny. Neil said himself that he knew many people 'were already throwing me on the scrap-heap as a has-been', and he was determined to prove them wrong. Prior to his suspension, one prominent sportswriter had even written in his column that he had it on good authority that Franklin would never play in the Football League again. This 'scoop', of course, was completely untrue, and for the first time in his life, Neil Franklin had to get in touch with a solicitor. In the end, the newspaper and journalist in question printed a full apology, but it certainly strengthened Neil's belief that he wouldn't be getting an easy ride from the press upon his return.

'I knew that my past reputation would not help me one little bit, for the average sporting follower, or rather sport follower, has an incredibly short memory. When you are on top you are his idol, he worships the ground you walk on, he writes to you, he cheers you, he greets you in the street.

'But once you are out of the game you are out of the limelight, and overnight you can be forgotten. That is not just a peculiar phenomenon of football. It applies to all sport and, indeed, to all branches of the world of entertainment. There is nothing more "ex" than an ex-entertainer.

'I knew, then, that I would come back as "Neil Franklin, the man who went off to Bogotá". I knew that people would watch me critically, be only too glad to find faults with my speed or with my play, and be quite unconcerned about writing me off as finished.

'So I trained, and trained hard.'

As every footballer knows though, no amount of work done on the training ground can fully help you rediscover that sharpness required to play first-class football. To make matters worse, Neil Franklin couldn't even compete in training games and team drills. All his training was done on his own, or 'in the wilderness', as he put it.

That kind of training can ensure physical fitness though; and Neil Franklin knew that was what he'd have to do. He was typically one of the first out and last in on the training ground, and now that he was the only one training on a police recreation ground, he was training harder than ever.

In the immediate aftermath of his suspension, and Stoke City announcing that they would sell him, Franklin was linked with a whole host of clubs. Having previously made a world-record bid for him, Hull City were still said to be in the hunt. The 1946 FA Cup winners Derby County were also strongly linked. Half of the First Division were linked at some stage or another, as a number of England internationals went to managers and chairmen of their clubs and pleaded with them to sign Franklin. Below is Tom Finney's recollection of having just that conversation with the Preston North End manager, Cliff Britton:

'"I understand Neil Franklin is heading back and looking for a club. What an excellent signing he would be for us," I said. The manager shrugged his shoulders in a gesture of "thanks but no thanks" and I couldn't believe it.

'I suffered the same fate when I tried to persuade Preston to recruit the great Jackie Milburn. I had heard that Wor Jackie was to leave his beloved Newcastle and checked the story with the man himself.

"'I've had an offer to go over to Ireland and I'm seriously considering it," Jackie told me.

'I was incredulous. Here was a truly outstanding forward who had averaged a goal every other game over a decade at the top with Newcastle in danger of slipping out of our game—and he was only thirty two into the bargain. The opportunity to play in the same forward line with Milburn at club level was very appealing, but Cliff Britton, who always knew best, was again unimpressed. Daft or what?

'Managers should have been killed in the rush for the signatures of Franklin and Milburn. To see them as unwanted men was criminal.'

Within a month of Franklin's suspension though, he was no longer making headlines. The Home Championships got into full swing in October and November, whilst Tottenham Hotspur won all the plaudits by going on a run of eight straight victories at that same time. Spurs had only won promotion from the Second Division the previous season, but under the 'push-and-run' tactic pioneered by their manager Arthur Rowe, the North Londoners won a historic first title that season.

Behind the scenes, Hull City had made their first post-Bogotá bid for Neil Franklin in October. The fee on offer was £20,000, significantly lower than the £30,000 bid the Tigers had tabled months earlier. Stoke were holding out for £25,000, but with no other clubs willing to outbid Hull City, one of the club's directors, Kenneth Percival, telephoned Stoke on 9 November and asked them to reconsider their original offer.

In the end, the two clubs met in the middle, and a gentleman's agreement was made for the transfer of Neil Franklin from Stoke City FC to Hull City AFC for a fee of £22,500. It had to be a gentleman's agreement, rather than a sanctioned deal, because under the terms of Neil's suspension, he could not agree terms with a new club. If Neil could not agree terms, then obviously the transfer could not go through in full.

On 1 February 1951, straight after his suspension finally expired, Neil travelled up to Hull to sign on the dotted line. Although he was joining a Second Division club, the transfer made him the most expensive defender in the history of world football. Sunderland's great Welsh international centre-forward Trevor Ford held both the British and world record fee at that time, following his £30,000 move to Roker Park in October 1950, but never before had a defender commanded a fee in excess of £20,000. When discussing the amount of money Hull City had paid to acquire his services, and the validity of the reported £22,500 fee, Franklin said, 'I just wouldn't know, and I just wouldn't care.'

Although Hull City had been linked with Franklin for some time by then, the move still came as a shock. After all, the nation's best centre-half surely ought not be playing outside the nation's top flight. As far as Neil Franklin was concerned though, that's where Hull City was heading, and there were a few factors which made a transfer to Boothferry Park attractive to the now 29-year-old.

For one, Hull had shown an interest in him right from the off. They had made a world record bid for him before his move to Bogotá, and renewed their interest upon his return, whilst others considered him to be damaged goods. Everyone wants to be valued by their employers, and footballers are no exception. Hull City had shown emphatically that they held him in very high regard, and their faith in his commitment and ability had not been tainted by the whole Bogotá affair.

Then there was the man at the helm, a certain Raich Carter. Reuniting with Raich was very appealing to Neil. He was one of the finest footballers Neil had ever played alongside or against, and the two shared a similar footballing philosophy. Carter was the only man to win an FA Cup either side of the war, the first with Sunderland and the second with Derby, but the war cut like an axe through the prime years of his career, meaning he only won thirteen peacetime caps for England, his first and last caps coming more than thirteen years apart.

Carter was a cultured inside-forward, who was intelligent both on and off the ball, and capable of hitting a blistering shot with either foot. He had an enormous presence on a football pitch, revelling in his role as star and entertainer, an approach which led to some labelling him as arrogant. 'He was a nice man but he loved himself,' was how John Charles summed him up. Raich had captained Sunderland to league and cup glory by the time he was twenty-four, before taking his magic to Derby County.

When he decided to leave the Rams in 1948, there was no shortage of interest. Carter wanted a role as both a player and coach, with a view to taking the reigns as first-team manager once his playing days were numbered. There were offers from Second Division duo Leeds United and Nottingham Forest, but Carter dropped down into the Third Division North, becoming Major Frank Buckley's assistant at Boothferry Park. Buckley was one of the most celebrated managers in the game following his time at Wolverhampton Wanderers, and he was one of the factors behind Raich choosing Hull City over his other suitors.

However, within two weeks of Carter's arrival, Buckley was gone, taking the managerial position at Leeds United. So Carter was fast-tracked into the top job, and in 1948, aged thirty-four, he became Hull City's player-manager. The 'Silver Fox' proved to be as confident and calm a manager as player, and he brought a delightful style of play to the Yorkshire outfit. In his first full season, the Tigers won the Third Division North title, as well as being the top scorers in England that year.

That brings us to the third, and most important, reason that Neil Franklin was—as he put it—'only too happy' to sign for Hull City. They were a club on the up. Title winners in Carter's first season, you may also remember that they recorded a shock FA Cup

Fifth Round victory over Stoke City, a game in which Neil was involved and couldn't help but be impressed by the third-tier side.

When they were knocked out of the FA Cup by Manchester United in the following round, a record crowd of 55,019 supporters packed into Boothferry Park. Their average attendance that season in the third tier was 36,763, which was higher than almost half of the clubs in the First Division, including Stoke City, and that average rose in the Second Division the following season.

The reason for Hull City's post-war ambition was their chairman, Harold Needler. The Needler family had generously taken over the club and put up the £10,000 it needed to survive, but they wanted to see it thrive. They completed the building of Boothferry Park, brought in Buckley—and later Carter, and began investing in the playing squad. They allowed Carter to bring in wartime England international Eddie Burbanks from Sunderland, along with the Danish international Viggo Jensen. Soon after that, they saw off competition from the likes of Arsenal and Manchester City to secure the services of Leicester City's brilliant deep-lying forward Don Revie for a whopping £19,000. Their ambitious recruitment policy had 'shook the footballing world', as Neil himself put it.

Big names were arriving and Hull City were a club making noises in English football, and it looked like an exciting project for Neil Franklin to step into. It was a move which made sense for the club too; it would be another statement of intent. Whilst other managers shied away from the prospect of signing the 'troublesome' Franklin, Carter had played alongside him. He did not need nudging or persuading by any of his players that signing Neil Franklin was a smart idea.

The city of Kingston upon Hull itself needed something to shout about after the war. It was the second most bombed city after London during the Blitz, and the most severely damaged in relation to its size and population. The city's multi-purpose dockyards had made it a prime target for the Luftwaffe. In addition to the targeted bombing attacks, Hull's geography meant they often became secondary targets: when the Luftwaffe abandoned raids on Manchester, Liverpool, Leeds and other major northern cities, they would often dump their bombs on Hull as they flew back to Germany.

The result was 95 per cent of all homes in Hull suffering damage during the Blitz. The city was under air raid alert for more than 1,000 hours over the course of the war. In 1939, Hull had a population of approximately 320,000, and the Nazi bombing campaigns rendered 152,000 of them homeless by the war's end. A further 1,200 people were killed, as communities and the local economy lay in ruins. The damages sustained during the Hull Blitz were believed to total around £20 million, equivalent to £820 million in 2019.

If the abusive mail Neil had received at his home in Staffordshire had him worrying about how the footballing public would respond to his return, the people of Hull soon put his mind at rest. From his first day in the city, he was welcomed with open arms and celebrated as a star. It was widely considered to be the biggest coup in the club's history. Although they had already signed stars like Carter and Burbanks, both were well into their thirties, whilst Franklin was still considered the finest centre-half in the country. Neil may have been dying to cross that white line, but the Hull City fans were just as eager to see their new signing take to the field.

'Vera and I received kindness after kindness, and one young girl, sixteen-year-old Marie Clipson, voluntarily gave up her chance to see me in my first match. She looked after the children while Vera went to join the cheering throng.

'When you remember that Marie was a great fan of Hull City you will realize the sacrifice she made. Even the consolation of a second-half broadcast could not have made up for the disappointment, but I hope Marie realized how much Vera and I appreciated her kindness, which was so typical of the people of Hull.'

That first game came just two days after Neil Franklin had joined Hull City, as the Tigers faced Blackburn Rovers on 3 February 1951. Neil described himself as feeling 'like a schoolboy on the first day of the holidays' as he stepped onto the training ground with his new teammates, a refreshing change from the solitary work he'd been doing in the previous months. He wanted to prove his fitness, and when Raich Carter asked him if he felt up to playing in the first team against Blackburn on the Saturday, Neil replied, 'Just try and keep me out!'

Upon Franklin's arrival, Hull City's president Ken Percival was quoted as saying, 'The fee . . . is the highest we have ever paid, but this is yet another indication of our Board's determination to ensure first-class football for Hull.' The 'Club Matters' section of the programme notes for Neil's debut against Blackburn Rovers contained the following message:

> New players always receive a warm welcome at Boothferry Park, as, indeed, does anyone who helps to spread abroad the fame and renown of Hull City and whose object it is to entertain the people who throng week after week to this ground.
>
> It is with considerable pleasure, therefore, that we welcome Neil Franklin, whose signature from Stoke City was obtained earlier this week. If he were merely Franklin N. an unknown junior, he would be welcomed; we know, however, that we have signed one of the outstanding players of the day, a brilliant centre half back who should provide many hours of enjoyment both here and on opponents' grounds.

Almost every national publication sent their best reporters to Boothferry Park that day, and it was a veritable who's who of sports reporters in the press box. It didn't matter that Arsenal were hosting Newcastle United in a top-of-the-table clash in the First Division, 3 February was all about the return of England's centre-half. Neil may have felt some trepidation about the media, but Henry Rose of the *Daily Express* did a lot to alleviate some of those concerns. He wrote the following on the morning of the match:

> Neil Franklin can banish any fears he may have about the Hull soccer public's reaction to his return to the English football scene.
>
> Football fans elsewhere have definite views of the International centre-half's ill-starred Bogota adventure, but the 50,000-powered roar when Franklin steps on the field against Blackburn Rovers behind Raich Carter, his old England team buddy, now his boss at Boothferry Park, will leave him in no doubt that his presence in the City is well timed, desirable and welcome.
>
> One topic commands the talk here. In pub, club and bus it is 'Franklin, Franklin, Franklin'.
>
> . . . I have been asked a dozen times whether Franklin will be chosen by England against Scotland on April 14 if he shows no decline in form after a seven months' lay-off.
>
> My reply was a definite 'Yes'. I am on the side of the selectors and Franklin. The player committed no crime when he went to Bogota to earn more money.
>
> He committed one when he broke his contract and came back. For that, like anyone else culpable, he has paid the penalty— a four months' suspension and loss of wages.
>
> Having paid the penalty, he should not be victimized. I do know the F.A. were deeply impressed by the manner in which Franklin made a clean breast of all the details of his runaway trip and return . . .

Rose was one of the most celebrated football writers in the country. His prose was adored by readers of the sports pages, and his words meant a lot to Neil. Rose would be one of eight sports journalists killed in the Munich air disaster in 1958, along with Neil's former England teammate Frank Swift. At Rose's funeral in Manchester, hundreds of taxis ferried mourners along the route, in what was described as 'the biggest funeral procession ever seen in Manchester'.

Rose was certainly right about the enthusiasm for Franklin in Kingston upon Hull. His arrival was the talk of the town, and that was reflected at the turnstiles on the Saturday. Although a lot of the newspapers claimed there was a crowd of 50,000 at Boothferry Park that day, the official records show an attendance of 38,786. Attendances were down by an average of 10 per cent across all four divisions of the Football League that season, and they were down 15 per cent at Boothferry Park.

The Tigers averaged only 31,872 over the course of the entire campaign, and a mere 20,623 had turned up for their last home league game that wasn't against a Yorkshire rival. Given that Hull were 13th in the Second Division and Blackburn 4th, it's probably fair to assume that the sizeable spike in numbers that day was in anticipation of Neil Franklin making his Hull City debut.

As their league position suggested, Blackburn were a decent side, whilst the Tigers were underperforming. The Lancashire club could call upon players like Eddie Quigley, who had previously moved for a world-record fee, Paul Todd, who would be snapped up by Hull City within a year, and Joe Harris, a young centre-forward that Rovers had brought in from Belfast Distillery. It was Harris who ensured that Neil Franklin's return to English football would not be a peaceful one. The 22-year-old Northern Irishman was robust and busy. He bustled around the pitch, drifting out wide and back in field to cause the Tigers all kinds of problems. Neil certainly considered him a worthy adversary, later commenting that he could 'never understand why Joe never really progressed in the game'.

It was deep into the second half when a relatively smooth transition back into the English game hit a snag for Franklin. Harris drifted out wide and fizzed a low ball into the box. The ball was bobbling at pace when Neil tried to take it under control in his own penalty area, but it slipped under his boot and straight into the path of Paul Todd, who comfortably slotted home to put the visitors in front. Thankfully, the Tigers spared Neil's blushes with a late equaliser, but he was his own harshest critic, and expected the worst with the nation's press watching on.

He was pleasantly surprised the next morning then, as reporters largely overlooked his lone error, complimenting the overall rhythm of his game and the absence of any signs of deterioration to his speed or style. Henry Rose offered some of the most glowing praise once more, writing:

> Franklin played as well as ever, in my judgement. He has always taken risks in the goal-mouth, and the fact that he failed to trap a ball almost on his own goal-line and presented Todd with a scoring chance is to me sufficient evidence that he has not been affected by his long rest.
>
> Only a player confident of his own ability would have dared to attempt to stop Harris's cross. The ordinary man would have belted it away first time.

Alan Hoby, who had recently been appointed chief sportswriter at the *Sunday Express*, a role he would go on to hold until 1986, was almost as complimentary: 'Franklin certainly lacked match practice, but all the old touches and moves were there. The skilful placing, the lovely heading and that perfect positional sense.

. . . In my opinion, Franklin will regain his place as England's centre-half.'

Never one for pomp or bravado, Neil stretched as far as saying he was 'satisfied' with his Hull City debut. After all, trapping a ball was a basic skill in his eyes, and the failure to do so was not easily forgivable. However, he was back doing what he loved! Training with teammates, playing in front of thousands of adoring fans and trying to play his way back into England contention. It seemed that he was out of the woods, but little could he have known that there was another pitfall waiting for him around the corner.

CHAPTER 13

Injured and Overlooked

As the title of this chapter suggests, everything did not go swimmingly for Neil Franklin at Hull City. He would enjoy mixed fortunes, at times playing some of his best football for the club, but he also suffered his first long-term injury, as well as a handful of other setbacks, and his attempts at making a dream return as England's number five would prove unfruitful.

Following the 2-2 draw with Blackburn Rovers, Hull City were turned over 3-0 away at Bristol Rovers in the FA Cup. The defeat was seen as a shock and an embarrassment for the ambitious Hull side, despite the fact that Bristol Rovers went on to lose only one home league game all season, and it would take First Division high-flyers Newcastle United to end their dream cup run. Franklin would have to wait until the next league game—a 3-2 win away at Southampton—to record his second Hull City appearance, as he was ineligible for the cup defeat at Bristol.

The most notable matches of that season, from Neil's perspective at least, were the two games against Leeds United, both coming in March. A fine young centre-half by the name of John Charles had broken through into the first team at Elland Road under Frank Buckley in 1949. By early 1951, Buckley had begun experimenting with the Welsh teenage international as a centre-forward. He played in that role twice against Hull City in March of that year, and both games were remembered for the fierce duels between Franklin and Charles. In the first game at Boothferry Park, Charles was lively, but Neil managed to keep him in check as Hull ran out

2-0 victors. At Elland Road six days later, Charles was unstoppable, bagging two goals in a 3-0 win, with the England selectors present to watch Franklin for the first time since his return from Bogotá.

The rest of the league campaign passed largely without incident for both Neil and the Tigers. They won seven, lost six and drew one, climbing a few places up the league table to finish 10th. The campaign was viewed as a disappointment for Hull, given their recruitment, despite it being only their second season in the Second Division for more than a decade.

Their team was a strong one, boasting the likes of Carter, Franklin, Burbanks, Jensen, Revie and the less nationally renowned but ever-reliable Billy Bly between the sticks. Carter was the star, even at thirty-eight, and still good enough to play for England at that time—in the view of this author's grandfather at least. Raich's intelligence allowed him to continue to be the driving force in the Hull City side well into his late thirties, and his presence still saw Second Division crowds boosted when the Tigers were in town.

South African centre-forward Alf Ackerman had been brought in from Clyde in Scotland, and he and Carter jointly led Hull's scoring charts with 21 goals each that season. Further reinforcements were made for the 1951–52 campaign, as Paul Todd arrived from Blackburn Rovers, along with a talented young Irish outside-right by the name of Paddy Fagan. It looked as though Harold Needler had bolstered an already strong squad, but his new recruits could do little to prevent a disastrous start to the 1951–52 season.

The summer of 1951 would be an intriguing one for the club, coming up against top-class foreign opposition. They lost 3-2 to Serbian side Partizan Belgrade and drew 3-3 with Luxembourgian outfit Progrès Niederkorn, before embarking on a pre-season tour of Spain, where they would face Atlético Madrid, Athletic Bilbao and FC Barcelona. Their first game came against the Spanish champions Atlético Madrid, who had just won their fourth La Liga title, and they proved their class with an emphatic 4-0 win over the Tigers. Atlético Madrid were, at that time, managed by the great Helenio Herrera. Then only a young manager, he enjoyed his first great successes at Atlético, before winning five trophies in two years at Barcelona, and later forming the team known as 'Grande Inter' at Inter Milan to cement his reputation as one of the greatest managers in the history of the game. Hull City, meanwhile, were without a head coach, as Raich Carter hadn't travelled on the tour of Spain due to his wife's recent operation.

Things weren't about to get any easier for the Tigers, who faced Athletic Bilbao in their next match at the San Mamés stadium. The game would see Neil Franklin face Telmo Zarra at the peak of his powers. One of the greatest footballers Spain has ever produced, Zarra had scored 46 goals in 36 games the previous season, and scored 20 goals from 20 caps for the Spanish national team. Bilbao won the game 2-0.

Thankfully for the Tigers, their final tour match was only against the Catalan minnows of Barcelona . . . Fresh off the back of their tenth Copa del Rey title, Barça also proved to be too much for the Yorkshire side, although they did at least manage to find the target, with Alf Ackerman scoring one and Don Revie bagging twice in a 5-3 defeat. Bizarrely, at the final game against Barcelona, Neil spotted a familiar face from his time in Colombia. One of the Independiente Santa Fe directors was at the Camp de Les Corts stadium watching Barcelona's star centre-forward, the great László Kubala, who they were hopeful of signing. The Hungarian didn't leave though, staying at Barcelona for the next decade, where he would become an idol.

The new season began about as successfully as the Spanish tour had gone, and five games into the campaign, there was a fallout between Raich Carter and the Hull City directors. The former England international resigned, which came as a huge blow to everyone associated with the club. In his three and a half years at the helm at Boothferry Park, Carter had come to define the club: playing a distinct style of play, bringing in his own players and leading by example with his wondrous individual performances. Without him, they looked rudderless. Between 20 September and 1 December, they went on a run of twelve games without a win, losing ten of them. They dropped down to second bottom in the table, and relegation to the Third Division North was looking like a genuine possibility.

The Tigers board had essentially removed Carter from the playing squad following his resignation, and in the meantime, he had been playing non-league football in Leconfield, as well as running a sweet and tobacconist shop on George Street, Hull. Desperate times called for desperate measures though and, on 27 November, the directors called for a meeting and invited Raich. It was decided that Carter would return to training and to the playing squad, much to the delight of the city, and some 14,881 fans turned up to watch him make his return for the club's reserves.

He made his league return on 8 December, and Hull City won their first game in three months against Doncaster Rovers. There is always chaos around the corner at Hull City though, and the winter of 1951 was no exception. Just after Raich's return, Don Revie was sold to Manchester City for £25,000, Neil Franklin sustained the worst injury of his career to date, and the Tigers went into the new year in last place in the Second Division. Revie would go on to become a central figure in what was known as the 'Revie Plan' at Maine Road, winning an FA Cup with the club in 1956.

For Franklin though, it was heartbreak. He had never suffered a genuinely serious injury before. Of course, he had taken the odd whack and his fair share of bumps and bruises, but the worst injury he'd previously had was a minor ankle break, and he'd made a remarkable return to action in just three weeks after that. His injury fortune had run out though, and the injury he sustained was a perennial career ender for footballers: knee cartilage damage.

Cartilage injuries can vary in severity, but as soon as the diagnosis came back in December 1951, it was clear his knee was not in good shape. After his four-month suspension, Neil had finally felt like he was getting back to playing some of his best football, and that he was on the cusp of England selection. This was a bitter blow. A stoic Franklin recalled, 'So just when I was getting back into my stride, I went down with the injury we all dread, and packed my bags ready for the visit to the operating-table and the date with the surgeon's knife.'

So severe was the damage to Neil's cartilage that the first operation proved inadequate, and he had to go through the whole thing once again. Franklin would play no further part in the 1951–52 season, but he was determined the setback would not end his career prematurely. Both operations were carried out in Newcastle, and Neil paid tribute to the 'skill of the surgeon', who specialised in football-related injuries and took on the challenge of what Neil called his 'wretched knee'.

Thankfully, the second operation seemed to have done the trick, but it would be a long route back to competitive football, or even the training ground for that matter. Neil spent hours upon hours sat in a chair lifting his leg up and down, as he attempted to get some strength back into the 'injured part'. It was a mind-numbingly tedious process, but Neil knew he had to commit fully to recovering if he was to return to the Tigers first team.

His teammates went the entire season without a manager, but with Raich Carter back in their ranks, they narrowly escaped relegation to the Third Division, finishing three points above relegated duo Coventry City and Queens Park Rangers. The highlight of a chaotic campaign was undoubtedly a 2-0 win away at Manchester United in the FA Cup Fourth Round. The Red Devils won the First Division at a canter that season, but goals by Syd Gerrie and Ken Harrison ensured a famous win for the Yorkshiremen. When the season drew to a close though, Carter did finally bring an end to his more than four-year association with the club, ironically leaving to replace Major Frank Buckley as the new head coach at Leeds United.

The Tigers had been ambitious in their appointments of Buckley and Carter, and they continued that trend with the next man through the door at Boothferry Park. Bob Jackson was brought in from Portsmouth as the Needler family sought desperately to make Hull City a First Division club. Jackson arrived with a big reputation, having guided Portsmouth to consecutive First Division titles in 1949 and 1950, which remain the club's only two top-light triumphs to this day.

Franklin made his return to training during the summer break, and he was delighted to inform his new boss that he felt great. He could jump, tackle and sprint at full intensity, and his knee was holding out fine. Relief and joy were the overriding emotions for Neil, who described the opening day of the 1952–53 season as being 'like a birthday, wedding, anniversary and Christmas Day all rolled into one for me.'

The much-anticipated opening day of the season saw Hull City travel to Merseyside, where Everton awaited them at Goodison Park. The focus had moved away from marquee signings that summer, as a number of youth players were promoted to the first team. Andy 'Jock' Davidson, Brian Bulless and Brian Cripsey, among others, were all handed first-team duties under Jackson, and all three would go on to become club legends.

Going into the game against Everton, Bob Jackson handed Neil Franklin the Hull City captaincy, telling him, 'I know you can do it, Neil, and to show you the confidence I have in you, I'm making you skipper.' The faith of the two-time title-winning manager meant a lot to Neil, and he repaid it with an excellent performance. He wasn't the only one: the whole team put on a virtuoso display for their new boss, beating Everton 2-0.

The Second Division was no place for semi- or half-fit

centre-halves, and Franklin faced the stern test of Dave Hickson in the Toffees forward line. Everton's sixth-highest scorer of all time, Hickson was a big strong centre-forward, renowned for his aggressive approach to the game. He wasn't one to shirk a challenge and was particularly dominant in the air. If Neil could come through ninety minutes against him unscathed, it would surely bode well.

And come through unscathed he did! Not only had his knee held up, but Franklin had run the game from the back for Hull City. Ray Raymond wrote in the *Sunday People* that Franklin was 'the focal point of this triumph', whilst Henry Jones of the *Sunday Express* called him 'the kingpin in a great Hull City victory'. They weren't the only two; Henry Rose was full of compliments for Neil once more, describing his performance as 'a display of the best 1947–48–49 England vintage'.

Everton were one of the pre-season favourites for promotion, and although they went on to have a poor campaign, no one was to know it then. Bob Jackson didn't mess about when he took the reins at Boothferry Park. Carter had been a colourful character, a real entertainer who was known for his on-field antics as well as the indelible mark that he had left on the club as a manager. Jackson couldn't replicate Raich's on-field magic, but he wasn't one to twiddle his thumbs when it came to tactics and team selection.

He orchestrated a positional shake-up that was something akin to a footballing version of a cabinet reshuffle. The team remained largely unchanged, but markedly rearranged. Someone had to replace Raich Carter as an inside-left for a start, an unenviable task if ever there was one. Jackson handed that role to Viggo Jensen, the Danish international who had been playing as a full-back for the Tigers. Jensen was a talented footballer and a willing runner who would put in a seven out of ten performance whichever position he was put in.

Neil too found himself in a new position. The newly appointed skipper was moved from centre-half to half-back by Jackson, who was keen to get the most out of his technical and creative capabilities. The role of the 'half-back' or 'wing-half' was similar to that of a modern-day defensive midfielder. Bill Harris, who had played as a half-back under Carter and would later be capped by Wales, took Neil's role at the heart of the defence.

The positional shifts seemed to work, and Hull City made a promising start to the season. The victory at Goodison Park was backed up by a late home winner against West Ham, before draws against Brentford and West Ham once more. Neil moved back into the centre-half position for the visit of Brentford, where he would be tasked with keeping his old England teammate Tommy Lawton quiet. Lawton was player-manager at Brentford, and Neil managed to keep him in check on this occasion. The former Chelsea centre-forward had caused controversy at Boothferry Park the previous season. When Notts County put him up for sale, Hull City had a bid accepted. The two parties failed to reach an agreement since Lawton was reluctant to move, yet the people of Hull could see Lawton sat happily in the director's box for their next match against Nottingham Forest. As Lawton later put it in his autobiography, *My Twenty Years of Soccer*, 'This, it was thought, would show the supporters that the management was at least trying to do something to remedy the faults.'

Although he had received plaudits for his performance against Lawton, the Brentford game had been the first time Neil had felt some pain in his knee following his lengthy lay-off. He made it into September unscathed, until he turned out in a benefit match at Sincil Bank stadium in Lincoln. One sharp turn and the excruciating pain returned. Only ten games into the campaign, and it was another season-ending injury for Neil. He was shattered.

'I always thought the period of my suspension was bad. I then thought that nothing could be worse than my first period on the injured list, but this second dose was worse than anything I have ever experienced.

'Another operation, to remove some foreign body from my knee, was called for, and then began the long, uphill road to fitness. I had massage, I paid three visits a week to a therapist, but nothing seemed to work.

'The annoying part about it all was that I would train as hard as anyone and suffer no ill-effects, but whenever I tried to cope with the usual Tuesday morning private practice match, I had to hobble back to the dressing-room with the wretched knee swollen to an alarming size. It was heartbreaking.'

Without Neil, Hull City's form fell off a cliff. Three defeats and one win in October were followed by a run of five straight defeats in November. Heading into the New Year, the club were plagued by injuries and boardroom disputes. There was a growing frustration surrounding Neil's constant inability to play, but it was a frustration he shared.

'I knew I had cost Hull City a lot of money, and I knew I had given them precious little service in return, but what could I do? I had suffered my injury during my career with Hull City and I just had to keep on trying to get back to perfect fitness, but it was galling to have to shake my head every time Mr. Bob Jackson asked me whether I was fit.'

Neil was determined to return to action, especially as Hull City were in the midst of a second consecutive relegation scrap, but he feared that a premature return could end his career for good. Around January 1953, Neil was approached about the possibility of taking over a pub in Staffordshire. Although he was determined to make a return to the game, with such a precarious injury situation, the offer appealed to him.

He approached the Hull City directors, and asked whether he could take over the pub and move back to Stoke but still play for the Tigers. With the club languishing at the foot of the Second Division, and having got little football out of their £22,500 investment, they weren't in a particularly giving mood, and Neil's request was denied. He played no further part in the 1952–53 season, as Bob Jackson's team managed to dig out a trio of wins in March, which helped them on their way to avoiding the drop.

Over the summer, Neil did become a licensee, taking over the Blue Bell Inn in Hanley. He and the family moved from Park Road in Hull to Hanley, meaning Neil would no longer be able to train with his Hull City teammates. He asked both Stoke City and Port Vale if he would be able to train with them, but both teams said no, so Neil was left in the wilderness as he had been a few years earlier. Luckily, this time he was joined by Jock Kirton, who you may remember from Neil's time at Stoke.

Kirton had left Stoke to join Bradford City in 1952, but was still living in Staffordshire. The two players, both former Stoke City captains, found themselves in similar boats, so they decided to train together at the Michelin Sports Ground in Stoke. By July of 1953, Neil Franklin hadn't kicked a ball in a competitive game of football for ten months, but he felt that rest was required if he was to make a smooth return to the sport he loved with a well-healed knee.

By the summer, he felt happy and sharp. He played in two pre-season games for Hull City and emerged unscathed from both. Despite their struggles, Bob Jackson's team had a decent defensive record at the end of the previous season, and full-back turned centre-half Tom Berry was doing a great job. As such, he retained his place for the first two league games of the season, in which Hull lost to Birmingham and drew with Oldham. Two injuries paved the way for a Franklin return to the first team, as Everton journeyed to Boothferry Park, but this time the Toffees came out on top in a 3-1 win.

That, as they say, was just about that for Neil Franklin in the 1953–54 season. Tom Berry, by and large, retained his place at the heart of the Hull City defence, whilst Neil turned out in the Midland League for the Tigers reserves. He did make a rare outing for the Tigers in February 1954 for an FA Cup Fifth Round replay against Tottenham at White Hart Lane, in which the home side won 2-0. Three days later, *Soccer Star* magazine gave their tuppence on Neil's performance, describing him as 'much slower, but as polished as of old and bearing the touch of a master'. The season was an unusual one for Neil, who had never found himself not starting games other than during his injuries and suspension. It has to be said that Tom Berry was putting in admirable displays for the club at this time, but there may have been more to Neil's omission.

It is fair to say that the relationship between Hull City and Neil Franklin had become a little fractured by this time. During his lengthy injury lay-off, they had even asked him to consider retirement, as they looked to cash in on his insurance and recoup some of the £22,500 they had spent on him. Neil refused. As he said, football was his life, and he wasn't ready to end his love affair with the game. Then there was the fact he had moved back to Stoke and was no longer training with the first team. It's not unreasonable to think Hull City may have been irked by that and consequently reluctant to hand him first-team football.

He was transfer-listed at Boothferry Park, but whilst the likes of Preston and Arsenal were said to have been interested, no solid bids are known to have been tabled. So at Hull City he remained, playing second-string football. It is yet another situation where you might expect a former England international to have been outraged and humiliated, but Neil's injuries had been so great and so tortuous that he would have been happy playing Sunday league football by this point.

'I had never believed that I was finished. Despite the setbacks and heartbreaks, I was always confident that I would pull through.

'And playing in the Midland League side did me the world of

good. Football in that league is tough, and I took many a hard knock and a lot of what we call "clogging", but never once did I break down. Never once did I so much as flinch. This proved to me, and, no doubt, to others, that Neil Franklin was back to 100 per cent fitness.

'Proving I was fit did me the world of good. I felt happy. I felt relieved, and I knew in my own mind that my form was improving. "This," I kept saying to myself, "is the old Neil Franklin."

'I enjoyed every second of my football. I knew I had found the old touch, and when you know that it doesn't matter what sort of opponent you meet, you can come out on top.

'But I never won a regular place in the first team, although my form was the talk of the fans and of the newspaper writers. I didn't complain, though. I knew I would play my way back into favour.'

His prophecy was correct! The summer of 1954 began with Port Vale allowing Neil to train at their ground, and there was just a hint that his fortunes might be starting to turn. Hull City had a pre-season European tour to Denmark and Germany, and prior to the opening day of the 1954–55 campaign, Neil was told that he would not only be restored to Hull City's starting XI, but that he would also be reinstated as captain.

It was great news for Neil but also for the Hull City fans. Back in the 1950s, reserve team games did not receive the lowly gates that we see today. Several thousand would turn up every week, with bigger games occasionally attracting over 10,000 paying spectators. Those who went to watch the Midland League games had been impressed by Franklin's recovery, but his return to the first team would be a baptism of fire. The Tigers travelled to Elland Road to take on a Leeds United team managed by Raich Carter, who now had John Charles as their regular centre-forward.

Hull City lost that game 2-0, but then went on a really promising run of four consecutive wins followed by a couple of draws away at West Ham United and Birmingham City. The 25th September 1954 brought a significant day for Neil Franklin. He led Hull City onto the field at the Victoria Ground, the first time he had returned to the famous Stoke City ground since his escapade to Bogotá. Stoke had been relegated from the First Division in 1953, but Neil had missed both of Hull's games against them during the previous campaign.

His acrimonious departure, twinned with the angry letters he had received upon his return from Bogotá, meant Neil made the short journey to his old home ground with some trepidation regarding the reception he would receive. The 27,201 crowd gave him a warm welcome though, which Neil described as putting his 'mind at rest'. In typical Franklin fashion, Neil wanted to put on a show at the Victoria Ground—not to prove anyone wrong or make a point—but to thank the supporters for the reception they had given him. This was a man who believed the game was all about entertainment, lest we forget, and this could be the last chance he got to entertain his homefolk.

The newspaper reports suggested he did a pretty good job. The game ended all square, with Neil keeping the Stoke City forwards at bay in a 0-0 draw. Bill Frycr gave his thoughts on the former Stoke City man in his match report for the *Daily Dispatch*: 'Neil Franklin may or may not be England's best centre-half . . . but at least I have not seen a better one this season.

'How pleasant it was to see a centre-half with his thoughts constantly on attack, even from his own penalty, how pleasant to see such calmness under stress.'

Hull City's good form and Neil's accomplished individual performances led to renewed calls, not just in the regional but national press, for him to be restored to the England setup. Through all the injuries and setbacks, that had been one of Neil's most burning desires, to pull on that famous white shirt one more time. He was back playing at centre-half; he felt quick, fit and strong, and close to the level he had been at the end of the 1940s. No such call was to come, though.

In my conversations with his son Gary we spoke about Neil's sadness at never being recalled by England, and Gary told me he suspected no amount of good form or on-field brilliance would have changed the FA's minds. There were, of course, a number of factors which counted against Neil. He was playing in the Second Division for starters. Of the final seventeen-man squad that Walter Winterbottom took to the 1954 World Cup in West Germany, only Syd Owen (Luton Town), Gil Merrick and Ken Green (Birmingham City) played outside of the First Division.

Then there was the question of fitness. England liked to have a settled side, and Neil's injuries perhaps raised one or two doubts as to whether he could provide that stability, especially at thirty-two. He had also played a handful of games whilst not fully fit, such as Hull City's 5-0 defeat to Everton in 1952, in which he played nowhere near the level an up-to-scratch Neil Franklin would expect of himself. After that particular game, Leslie Edwards of the *Liverpool Daily Post* wrote that, 'In the game Horatio Carter and Neil Franklin retain their glamour but that is not to say that either is measurably as he was. Indeed, the thought crossed my mind more than once that there should be a law against former England players prolonging their careers to the point at which they gently fade away, showing no hint of the greatness they once possessed.'

Of course, Raich Carter and Neil Franklin rank among the greatest players to ever play for Hull City, and the tens of thousands who headed to Boothferry Park every other Saturday most certainly would not have agreed with Mr Edwards. One such Hull City fan was Geoff Andrew, who was just fifteen when Neil joined Hull City. A regular at Boothferry Park and still a regular at the KCOM Stadium now, he witnessed many of Neil's appearances in black and amber, and still ranks him as the club's best ever centre-half. 'That half-back line was the best we've ever had at Hull City, with Harris, Franklin and Revie,' Geoff declared, adding, 'Franklin was probably the best centre-half we've ever had at the club . . . Tom Berry was very good and Michael Dawson who also played for England is a good defender, but Neil Franklin was the best, he was a great passer of the ball and reader of the game.'

In spite of the views of Geoff and thousands of other regulars at Boothferry Park, if the England selectors had been present at one of those unfit Franklin 'off days', it may well have put them off recalling their former number five. A final point—by 1954, Billy Wright had moved over from the half-back position and had established himself as England's centre-half, providing a degree of solidity which meant the selectors weren't desperately searching for a new centre-half.

In truth, Gary is probably right. Whilst all those factors are indeed true, Neil Franklin probably could have been injury-free and starring for Arsenal or Manchester United, scoring 20 goals from centre-half in the First Division whilst keeping countless clean sheets, and the selectors still wouldn't have yielded to the calls for him to be recalled. Neil could accept being overlooked for purely performance-based reasons, but the suspicion that there was more to it was incredibly frustrating.

'That [being recalled by England] was my great ambition, and I tried everything I knew to produce the form worthy of a restoration to the England side. The Press rooted for me. Many fans rooted for me, and quite frankly I often thought my chances of selection were good, especially when the England selectors were struggling to solve the centre-half problem.

'But no selection ever came, and I was bitterly disappointed. If the selectors had not been certain how I would react to International opposition, I would have loved to have put their minds at rest . . . if only they had given me the chance. A trial match, a representative match . . . any sort of match would have done. Because I am convinced that given the chance I could have fought my way back to the England team and kept there.

'That chance, though, was never to come.'

Although Neil's disappointment is understandable, and his ambition ought to be commended, it is worth pointing out that although he never regained international status, it was some turnaround. From two season-ending, and potentially career-ending, injuries, and being asked by his club to consider retirement, to getting the captain's armband once more and earning calls for an England recall, is some achievement. More disappointment was to come though, as Hull City's form dipped over the festive period. They didn't win a single game in November, December or January, seeing off any hopes of a promotion push.

The rest of the season was a pretty drab affair for the Tigers. Having won eight of their opening fifteen games, they won just four of the twenty-seven games that followed, as a once-promising campaign ended with the club finishing only six points above the relegation places. Bob Jackson had been sacked in March 1955, and he was replaced by Bob Brocklebank.

A Londoner who had played pre-war football for Aston Villa and Burnley, Brocklebank moved into management with Chesterfield in 1945. He did a very good job at Saltergate, establishing the side in the Second Division and even guiding them to a fourth-placed finish, which remains the club's best ever season. He left for Birmingham City in 1949, with whom he was relegated from the First Division, before rebuilding the side but resigning before they were crowned Second Division champions. Brocklebank brought a less hands-on approach to life at Boothferry Park. He came across as a very relaxed, polite and personable character.

It is fair to say that this approach did not prove an immediate success in East Yorkshire. His first full season began with utterly dreadful form, some of the worst in the club's history in fact. The

Tigers had brought in a couple of former England internationals, Wilf Mannion and Stan Mortensen, to join the one they already had on their books. Both had played alongside Neil for England, and both were among the finest players of their generation.

Wilf was an inside-forward whose beloved body-swerves were a thing of legend up in Middlesbrough. Nicknamed 'the Golden Boy', Mannion is probably the greatest player to pull on the red of Middlesbrough, and a statue of him was erected outside Middlesbrough's Riverside Stadium following his death in 2000. Stan, as you may recall, had played with Neil for Blackpool Services during the war, as well as many a representative match and England international. A wonderfully well-rounded centre-forward, Mortensen joined Hull from Blackpool, where he had spent his entire career up to that point. Just two years before the move, he immortalised himself at Wembley with a hat-trick as Blackpool came from behind to beat Bolton 4-3 in the 1953 FA Cup final. He scored 197 goals in 317 Football League games for Blackpool, and 23 goals from 25 official caps for England.

However, Mannion was thirty-seven at the start of the 1955–56 season, and Mortensen was thirty-four. Both players still had plenty of panache, but clearly they had lost a yard or two of pace. What's more, whilst Mortensen arrived that summer, Mannion had been brought in the previous Christmas, after a dispute with Middlesbrough which ended in him claiming he had retired. Below is Mannion's brutally honest account of the conversation he had with Harold Needler and his thoughts regarding his move to Hull City:

> I hadn't played football for months . . . I knew I was gone really. But [Harold] Needler, the chairman of Hull approached me, I think on transfer deadline day. They were in danger of going down and he wanted me to help them. I said to him, 'I can barely walk, never mind run.' He said, 'All I want you to do is hold the

rest of them together and be a steadying influence.' He wanted me to use my footballing brain. I hadn't done any training or anything, but he said that was okay. I was practically walking around in my first few games.

As Mannion openly admits, he didn't play his best football at Boothferry Park, but he still made sixteen appearances, which aided the Tigers survival. Over the summer though, comments made by Mannion and his subsequent refusal to attend a Football League hearing saw him handed an indefinite Football League ban. The FA, on the other hand, issued no such blanket ban, meaning Wilf was officially no longer under contract at Hull City but could still play football outside the Football League, so he moved on a free transfer to non-league Poole Town in September 1955.

Hull City's treacherous start to the 1955–56 season stretched from August to November, during which time they went on a run of just one win, two draws and twelve defeats from their opening fifteen games, leaving them marooned at the foot of the Second Division. Franklin missed much of these catastrophic opening stages of the season through injury, and although the Tigers won a couple of games in both December and January following his return in October, they had left themselves with too much to do. This would be Neil's last season at Boothferry Park and he didn't even stick around for it in its entirety, as the club which had seemed so ambitious and bound for success when he joined in 1951 were relegated to the Third Division North.

The last game of Hull's season saw the visit of Stoke City to Boothferry Park. The game itself was a classic, as Hull City scored three to Stoke City's two, but the home side had already had their fate sealed and the visitors had nothing to play for. The halcyon days of 35–40,000 crowds at Boothferry Park seemed like a distant memory, as little over 5,000 turned up to witness their final-day defeat of the Potters. By that point though, Neil Franklin was long gone. He left Hull City in late February 1956, his last match for the club being a 2-1 home win over Port Vale.

In a classic case of what Hull City fans might call 'typical City', the torrid 1955–56 campaign actually brought the most impressive performance and result of Neil Franklin's five-year stay at the club, and it could be argued the most impressive in the history of Hull City—certainly the most shocking.

In the early to mid-1950s, there was one nation leading the way in footballing excellence . . . Hungary. The 'Magical Magyars', as they were known, were absolutely electric. The technical brilliance of their side, the transitions between defence and attack and the effectiveness of Nándor Hidegkuti as a deep-lying forward had turned them into an unstoppable force within the beautiful game. Between May 1950 and November 1955, Hungary's Golden Team played 51 games, of which they lost just one. In that time, they beat England 6-3 at Wembley and 7-1 in Budapest, they beat Italy 3-0 twice and thrashed Sweden 6-0.

At the 1954 World Cup, they were overwhelming favourites. In their two group games, they beat South Korea 9-0 and West Germany 8-3. The quarter-finals brought a 4-2 win against Brazil, which was followed by victory over the holders Uruguay by the same scoreline in the semis. In the final they met West Germany, where a combination of torrential rain, dubious refereeing decisions and seemingly divine intervention conspired as the Germans inflicted Hungary's only defeat of that five-plus-year period in what became known as the 'Miracle of Bern'.

It is perhaps unusual that Hungary were so dominant and celebrated throughout this period, yet little is known of their domestic game at that time in Britain. Four teams from Budapest tended to battle it out for the major honours at that time, namely: Budapest Honvéd, MTK Budapest, Újpest and Vasas. The last of those four, Vasas, had a tradition of travelling abroad and pitting themselves against three of the top clubs from said nation. This was an annual excursion that the club had upheld for twenty-five years, during which time they had—remarkably—remained unbeaten.

In 1955, Vasas were to travel to England, where the locals were unsurprisingly keen to banish the woes that the national team's 13-4 aggregate loss of 1953 and 1954 had inflicted. The three sides elected to challenge Vasas were Tottenham Hotspur, Sheffield Wednesday and Wolverhampton Wanderers. Those three were chosen on the grounds that they were the best sides in England with the adequate facilities to host Vasas. Since it was a mid-season tour in October, all three matches would be midweek night games, and only a handful of grounds boasted quality floodlights in 1955.

Vasas' first challenge on their tour of England was provided by Tottenham Hotspur. Boasting a star-studded squad featuring the likes of Alf Ramsey, Ted Ditchburn, Len Duquemin and Bill Nicholson, Spurs had won the league and finished as runners-up in the first half of the fifties. Such greats could do little to suppress the irresistible Vasas though, who found no trouble in matching the exploits of their national side, putting seven past their hosts at White Hart Lane.

Next up for Vasas was a trip to the Steel City for a tie at Hillsborough against Sheffield Wednesday, the lowest ranked of the three sides Vasas were set to face. The Owls inclusion in Vasas' tour was down, in no small part, to the then excellent Hillsborough Stadium and its credentials for hosting a midweek evening game. Wednesday had been relegated from the First Division in the previous season, and following Tottenham's humiliation, many observers in the media were already looking to Wolves to restore some faith in the English game in Vasas' final tie. The fears of the press were soon confirmed as the Budapest side, drilled by their legendary coach Lajos Baróti, maintained their form and put six past Wednesday.

Wolverhampton Wanderers, three-time English champions in the 1950s and two-time runners-up, were unbeaten against European opposition in 1955, having seen off the likes of Real

Madrid two years earlier. However, ravaged by an injury crisis and fearing humiliation, England's great hope pulled out of the game at the last moment.

With Vasas looking to complete their tour, who could step in for the mighty Wolves? Well ... a certain plucky and ever-ambitious Yorkshire club were happy to offer their services. That's right, the Hull City directors saw themselves as the ideal candidates to take the fixture. I mean, why not? Boothferry Park had state-of-the-art floodlights and a playing surface that was widely regarded as the best in the country, better even than Wembley. Officials from the Vasas club made the short journey up to Kingston upon Hull to check the place out, and they were sufficiently impressed. Hull City would play Vasas.

When news of the arranged fixture was announced, the national press were unimpressed. If Vasas put seven past Spurs and six past Wednesday, what would they do to lowly Hull City? The Tigers were at the foot of the Second Division with only one win all season. Their most recent results were a 5-0 defeat away at Fulham and a 3-2 loss at home to Bury. Fleet Street were up in arms, and they tried to put as much pressure as possible on the Hull City directors to pull out of the match, but Needler and co. would not relent.

So on the evening of Monday, 17 October 1955, Hull City played host to one of Europe's elite. Today, one might expect to see a rotated squad in a game seen as such a mismatch of quality, but in 1955—ten years before substitutes were introduced into the English game—squads offered little room for manoeuvre. Vasas had only brought two goalkeepers and thirteen outfield players on the tour, so there would be no gimmes for Hull City. In fact, seven of the Vasas starting XI that day were either current or future Hungarian internationals, at a time when they were undoubtedly the finest national team on the planet. One of those seven, Rudolf Illovszky, has been immortalised by his former club. Vasas are soon to move into their new ground—the Illovszky Rudolf Stadion, the club's second arena bearing his name.

Neil Franklin was not expected to start the game against the Hungarians, as he had been out injured in the early parts of the season. Andy 'Jock' Davidson looked set to start in the centre-half position, but Neil told Bill Brocklebank that he was fit, and was promptly reinstated to the side.

The belittling of Hull City's chances in the game by the media seemed to have put off some locals, as only 13,889 turned up at Boothferry Park for the clash, which was fewer than the number that had come through the turnstiles for the previous Saturday's defeat to Bury. The dozen or so thousand Hull City fans who attended the game would witness a historic and remarkable game. In the month that he joined the club, Hull's new inside-right, Bill Bradbury, scored a hat-trick, as the Tigers ran out 3-1 winners. Bradbury was a fine technician, but not always the most disciplined of trainers. Jock Davidson stated that Bradbury, 'should have played at a far higher level with his ability, but he really was such a clown. He had terrific ability, but I sometimes think he'd have been happier being a comedian.' Despite his jovial attitude, Bradbury still went on to score 89 goals in 190 games for the Tigers, which puts him eighth in the club's all-time scoring charts at the time of publication.

Fleet Street were unerringly quiet after the 3-1 home win. A representative from the Vasas club sent a letter to Hull City once back in Hungary, which was published in the programme notes of Hull's league game against West Ham almost a month later. The letter read:

> I am very much grieved to see that you lost nearly £200 on this match, which should have been a real money-spinner for your Club. There is no doubt that the unreasonable attitude of certain sports journalists had a lot to do with it. Your only conciliation

is that you beat a Club of world reputation and on the day's showing you thoroughly deserved that famous victory. I wish your Club the best of luck and I am sure that by the end of the season your position in the League Table will be very much better.

With kind regards to all of you at Boothferry Park and a special thanks for the sporting welcome given to my party.

Yours sincerely, B. P. MIKLOS.

Given that Vasas had just lost their first game on foreign soil in a quarter of a century, they showed a great deal of graciousness in defeat. Sadly though, their optimism for Hull City's campaign would not come to fruition. In a season which saw Vasas lift the Mitropa Cup, which was the precursor to the European Cup, Hull City were relegated to the Third Division North.

CHAPTER 14

Learning to Lose

Looking back on Neil Franklin's time at Hull City, one would have to categorise it as disappointing. He may have gone down as one of the club's finest ever players, but he had joined Hull with the intention of winning promotion to the First Division and earning a recall to the England squad; and he had done neither. What's more, injuries had seen him play in only 95 of a possible 214 league games during his time with the club. On leaving Hull City in February 1956, it would not be unfair to say that he had joined the worst club in the Football League.

Bringing an end to his five-year spell at Boothferry Park, Franklin swapped the team at the bottom of the Second Division for the team at the bottom of the Third Division North—Crewe Alexandra. The Tigers struggles were nothing compared to that of the Alex. He signed for Crewe on 24 February 1956, exactly one month after celebrating his 34th birthday, for a fee of £1,250. Despite Hull City's struggles, Neil had been one of their better players since returning to fitness in October, so those unfamiliar with the railway town of Crewe and its geography may wonder why he headed there.

It was less than fifteen miles from Neil's home in Hanley to Crewe Alex's stadium, Gresty Road. There had been other interest, particularly from Northampton Town who were in the middle of the Third Division South table, but Crewe's location was attractive. From Johnny King to Neville Coleman, there's a long tradition of footballers turning out for both Stoke City and Crewe, due to their close proximity. By 1956, any hopes of an England recall lay on the scrapheap, and with a public house to run in Stoke, it made sense to join a club a little closer to home.

There was also a great enthusiasm for his signing in the town, and just a general feeling that things had run their course at Hull City. So keen were the Crewe Alexandra fans to see Neil Franklin at Gresty Road, the club's Supporters Association raised £750 in donations to go towards his £1,250 transfer fee. The Railwaymen were far from awash with cash at the time, and without the supporters' donations they most likely wouldn't have been able to fund the move.

Having arrived on 24 February, he made his debut on 25 February, a sign of both the excitement surrounding his arrival and the desperation at the club. Crewe had drawn one and lost eight of their last nine games, so the fact that Neil was yet to even partake in a training session with the club was not considered a stumbling block. He came in at centre-half, and Crewe managed a 1-1 draw against Darlington. The enthusiasm that he had felt upon his arrival in Hull was more than matched in Crewe. Whilst Gresty Road didn't see crowds of over 30,000 like Boothferry Park, there was a 160 per cent increase in gate numbers for Neil's debut. From a crowd of 2,432 for the club's last home game against Scunthorpe United, some 6,344 spectators came through the gates for Neil's debut against Darlington. The numbers remained high for the following home game too, as 6,384 came to witness a rare Crewe win. Within a few games, Franklin had repaid his transfer fee through the extra money brought in at the gates.

Although attendances in general were greatly improved, Crewe's form only picked up a little. The Alex had an excellent March by their standards, with two wins, two defeats and two draws. For the most part though, it was defeat after defeat. Gary put it mildly to me when he said, 'they were not a good team'. They ended that 1955–56 season in last place in the Third Division North, taking advantage of the final years of the regional Football League system, where teams were not relegated from the Third Division North and South, but either re-elected or not re-elected. In Crewe's case, as was almost always the case, they were re-elected.

Neil started the first ten games of the 1956–57 season, in which Crewe won two, drew two and lost six. Following Hull City's relegation, his new club were in the same division as his old one, and Franklin made a return to Boothferry Park on 8 September, where the hosts won 2-0. Neil picked up an injury in a 2-1 win over Scunthorpe United in mid-September though, and the Railwaymen hurtled into a patch of appalling form.

They lost the next nine games on the spin, in which they scored eight goals and conceded twenty-seven. Their dreadful league form was interrupted by the FA Cup, which brought Gresty Road's biggest attendance of the season, as 11,513 fans witnessed a 2-2 draw against Wrexham in the First Round. There were more travelling fans than home fans at Gresty Road for the game, as thousands of Welsh fans made the relatively quick journey east to Cheshire.

Even with the return of Neil Franklin at centre-half, Crewe Alexandra extended their winless league run to 30 games, which remains a record for the club to this day. They then set an even more extraordinary record spanning from October 1954, long before Neil joined the club, all the way to April 1957, during which time the Alex failed to win a single away league game from a whopping fifty-six attempts. That record came to an end on 24 April 1957, with a 1-0 win away at Southport.

Oddly, having won only three games all season, Crewe won all of their last three games, which included both that away win at Southport and a 6-4 home thriller on the final day against Mansfield Town. Those three wins saw the Alex end the season with a record of: 6 wins, 9 draws and 23 defeats, with a staggering -67 goal difference, having conceded 110 goals.

One of Crewe's six goals in their final day victory over Mansfield was scored by Neil. It was the third goal of his Crewe Alexandra career, with one more still to come, and all scored with his head. Despite possessing a great leap and a very accurate header, Neil's four strikes for Crewe were the only goals he scored in the Football League. Whilst today it is not unusual for a central defender to bag a goal every 15 or so games, back in the 1940s and most of the 1950s, far less players would occupy the box for set pieces, and as such, centre-halves rarely got themselves on the scoresheet. Neil scored nine goals at club level in total: four for Crewe, one for Independiente Santa Fe, three for Stoke City in wartime fixtures, one of which came against Crewe, and one for Macclesfield Town. It ought to have been five rather than four for the Alex. On 27 October 1956, with the club trailing 1-0 away at Stockport, they won a penalty. Club captain Neil Franklin was elected to take the spot-kick, only to fire it well over the bar; Crewe lost the game 1-0.

In a dreadful couple of seasons in terms of results for Crewe Alexandra, Neil Franklin still went down as one of the greatest players to have pulled on the club's shirt. I was fortunate enough to speak to Crewe local Bernard Morgan during the writing of this book, an immensely positive and colourful 94-year-old man. Bernard attended his first Crewe Alexandra match in 1936, and after working as a codebreaker for the RAF during the war, he manned the turnstiles at Gresty Road for the first time on 29 March 1947 for a game against Rochdale.

Between that first game against Rochdale and his final match working for the club on 9 May 2004, Bernard missed only one game, and even that was only a reserve game against Buxton. Having clocked up 57 years as a turnstile operator at Crewe, attending somewhere in the region of 2,000 games, it is Neil Franklin who Bernard considers to have been the best player he saw turn out for Crewe. Morgan wasn't the only one from the club to hold Neil in high regard: club historian Harold Finch included Franklin in his book *Crewe Alexandra Football Club: 100 Greats*, stating,

'A classic central defender, had he been in a successful Crewe side who knows where his career may have taken him, or indeed Crewe Alexandra.'

Neil started the 1957–58 season with Crewe, but played in only the Alex's first three games before agitating for and finally making a move away. His final game came on 31 August 1957, against his most favoured goal-scoring opponent—Mansfield Town. Amusingly, the Mansfield player-manager throughout Neil's days at Crewe was . . . Charlie Mitten. Manchester United had refused to let the penalty specialist return to their first team fold upon his return from Bogotá, and after four years at Fulham, he joined Mansfield as a player-manager in 1955. A 6,047 strong Crewe Alexandra crowd witnessed a rare win for their side at Gresty Road, as Franklin scored the only goal of the game in a 1-0 victory, bowing out in style.

CHAPTER 15

Hanging Up His Boots

Waving goodbye to the professional game is not an easy decision to make, and we often see players play well beyond their prime through a reluctance to hang up their boots. The yard of pace deserts you, the niggles become more frequent, and whilst your reading and understanding of the game has often never been better, your ability to make use of that is greatly diminished. It is squaring this circle which has proved the bane of many an ageing footballer's life, and Neil Franklin was no exception.

Having been by far the best player in the Crewe Alexandra side for twenty months, Franklin was in no mood to hang up his boots just yet. Aged thirty-five, he had missed only a handful of games over the best part of two years at Gresty Road, and he still had plenty to offer a Third Division side. That was reflected in the interest in him, and in October 1957, he joined Stockport County for the same £1,250 fee that Crewe had signed him for in February 1956.

It was a welcome relief for Neil. The newspapers began reporting that he was unhappy at Crewe at the start of October, but that the club were refusing to let him go. On 17 October, the *Stockport Advertiser* reported that Stockport had made a bid for a 'well-known ex-international'. Their initial bid of £1,000 was turned down, with Crewe insisting that an incoming forward had to be part of the deal, but the two clubs eventually agreed on a fee of £1,250 a couple of days later. In the end, Stockport only had to pay Crewe £550, as they were still owed £700 for the transfer of Jack Connor a year earlier, which was written off as part of the deal.

Neil left the worst side in the Football League at that time, for a club in the same division, but a far more competitive one. Stockport had finished fifth in the previous season's Third Division North, above his old club Hull City even. The Hatters were hardly world-beaters, but they had a sprinkling of decent players and averaged more than double the crowds of Crewe, with an average gate just shy of 10,000.

Alongside Neil in defence was full-back Barrie Betts. Ten years Neil's junior, Betts was a solid right full-back who went on to rack up more than 100 First Division appearances for Manchester City. At left-half they had Frank Clempson, who joined Stockport from Manchester United, where he had been a bit-part player during United's title winning 1951–52 campaign. Leading the line for County was Bill Holden, an experienced centre-forward who had been a prolific scorer in the top flight with Burnley, and he joined the Hatters from First Division side Sunderland.

The most famous of the lot, though, was the club's manager, and just as he had done under Raich Carter, Neil Franklin would be playing under a fine inside-forward and player-manager at Stockport County. Willie Moir was the man in charge at Edgeley Park, and some of you may recall that he was the man capped by Scotland in their all-important Home Championship game against England, despite the selectors never having seen him play, as the Scots lost 1-0 in Neil's last ever game for the Three Lions. Moir was a former First Division top scorer who had spent his entire career with Bolton prior to joining Stockport, aged thirty-four. A scorer for Bolton in the 1953 'Matthews Final', Moir could play as either a winger or as an inside-forward, and he had a couple of very good years at Stockport, but managed only four games in the 1957–58 season. All in all, though, they'd assembled a decent side for the Third Division North.

The team had enjoyed mixed form at the start of the season, and when Neil made his debut on 26 October away at Chester, they were without a win in their last four games. Despite the introduction of their experienced new centre-half, there was no turnaround in form at Sealand Road, where the Hatters were convincingly beaten 3-0.

Neil's home debut would bring a much-improved performance and result, however, as Stockport ran out 4-1 winners against a very respectable Chesterfield side who had enjoyed a bright start to the season. Stockport followed that up by hosting European opposition in a friendly game under the lights just two days later. Unlike the illustrious European opposition of Vasas and Barcelona that Neil had faced at Hull City, Stockport entertained OKS Odra Opole.

The Polish city of Opole, which is sometimes referred to as 'Poland's Venice', has not been blessed with footballing success. The city's greatest gift to the world of football is probably the fact that it was the birthplace of German international Miroslav Klose, who has scored more goals at the World Cup finals than any other player. Odra Opole were in the top flight of Polish football at that time, although they had flirted with relegation during the previous season, and would ultimately be relegated later that year. In an entertaining match at Edgeley Park, there was nothing to split the Third Division North and Polish Ekstraklasa sides, the game ending in a tie at 3-3.

The 1957–58 season, which would prove to be Neil's last in the Football League, was a significant one. It was the last season in which the Football League had regional divisions. The Third Division North and Third Division South had been introduced at the start of the 1920s, but the Football League announced that from the 1958–59 season onwards, the divisions would be de-regionalised, switching instead to a four-tier system. That meant that there was a lot riding on the 1957–58 season for Third Division North and South teams. Finish in the top half, and you would be in the Third Division next season (except for the champions, who would still go into the Second Division), but finish in the bottom half, and you would find yourself in the new Fourth Division.

For the entirety of the campaign, the Third Division North was an incredibly tightly fought contest. It was also a season in which Third Division clubs recorded a number of extraordinary FA Cup giant-killings, and Stockport County were firmly in on the act. Northampton Town arguably pulled off the upset of the year when they beat Arsenal 3-1 in the FA Cup, at a time when they were only four points above bottom-placed Torquay in the Third Division South.

York City were another, the lowly Third Division North side beating First Division outfit Birmingham City 3-0. Scunthorpe claimed a major scalp a few weeks later with a 3-1 win away at Newcastle United in the Fourth Round, and determined not to be outdone, Darlington pulled off an incredible 4-1 victory over Chelsea in the same round after forcing a replay.

For Stockport County, their FA Cup journey began against Third Division North rivals Barrow. As far as First Round ties go, this was no gimme, since Barrow were fifth in the table at the time, ahead of the Hatters. Just thirty-five minutes into the match, Neil felt some pain in his thigh, and he played out the rest of the tie at centre-forward, his first experience in that position since his school-boy days. Stockport emerged victorious with a 2-1 win though, and Franklin and his teammates drew Hartlepools United in the next round. It was a carbon copy of the Barrow game in many respects. They faced a divisional rival who were above them in the table at home and came out as narrow winners by two goals to one.

In the Third Round, Stockport were tied against Luton Town. Luton may not seem like the most daunting opponents today—their name hardly carries the weight of an 'Arsenal' or 'Liverpool', for example—but back on 4 January 1958, when they faced Stockport County, they were above both of the aforementioned duo. In fact, going into the game, Luton were sixth in the First Division, whilst

Stockport were twelfth in the Third Division North. Few gave the club from Greater Manchester a chance.

In the 'battle of the Hatters', however, Franklin and co upstaged their top-flight opponents in remarkable fashion. A crowd of more than 18,000 raucously cheered their team out at Edgeley Park, and the team soon gave them something to really shout about. Age had not wearied the adventurous side of Neil's game, and three minutes into the match, Stockport's 36-year-old centre-half picked up the ball out on the right flank before whipping a sensational cross that was just begging to be put in the back of the net into the box. Arnold Jackson did the honours, nodding home as Stockport took an early—and unlikely—lead.

Centre-forward Bill Holden had been experiencing mixed form, but he picked the right day to turn on the style. A quarter of an hour into the second half, he received the ball not far into the Luton half, before going on a long, mazy run. He committed and beat two Luton defenders, before firing past a helpless Ron Baynham in the Luton goal; an England international goalkeeper, one might add.

An upset now looked to be on the cards, and a panicked Luton side resorted to the long ball tactic. Neil had long bemoaned such an approach, partly because he felt it was incredibly easy to defend against, and that is exactly what he and the rest of his Stockport comrades continued to do. In the dying embers of the game, as Luton became increasingly gung-ho, Frank Clempson sensed an opportunity. He set Arnold Jackson away, who in turn played in Ken Finney, and finally the ball was squared to Bill Holden, who grabbed his second and Stockport's third.

It was one of the finest displays and results in the long history of Stockport County, and still is to this day. The *Stockport Advertiser* were full of it the next day, their headline reading: COUNTY, IN WOLVES CLOTHING, LEAD LUTON SHEEP TO SLAUGHTER. The reason behind that headline being that as well as sharing a nickname, Stockport and Luton also shared home colours. They also shared away colours, and in the end the FA bemusingly decided Luton could wear their second strip, but Stockport would have to find a new kit from elsewhere. Wolverhampton Wanderers offered the home side their strip, and so it came to be that it was in eleven Wolves shirts that the Hatters pulled off a historic win.

There was only one gripe from the Luton Town manager about his team's shock exit from the cup in his post-match interview. Dally Duncan, capped fourteen times by Scotland and a very accomplished left-winger in his playing days for Hull City and Derby County, had orchestrated Luton Town's rise up the footballing pyramid. After the defeat, he referred to the crucial moment three minutes into the game, when Neil had delivered that sumptuous cross for Arnold Jackson to head home. 'What's a centre-half doing down the right wing?' Duncan queried. Well, he was assisting a goal, would have been Neil Franklin's most likely response. And why shouldn't he?

The result was a big national story, even in a season packed with notable upsets, yet it is rarely spoken about as one of the great 'giant killings' today. The reason for that is the fate that has befallen the respective clubs since 1958. During the 1990s, Luton dropped into the Third Division, whilst Stockport reached the second tier and even pushed for promotion to the Premier League. Although Luton have still tended to be a better team than Stockport, they have been a lower league and even non-league club for much of their recent past. This often taints people's perceptions of great upsets, shocks and giant-killings.

The Hatters were handed another tough tie in the Fourth Round, being drawn away at West Ham United. The Hammers were leading the Second Division at the time, with Charlton Athletic and Liverpool in hot pursuit. They were also among the top scorers in the country, with their new partnership of John Dick and Vic Keeble really starting to flourish. Dick was a talented

Scottish inside-left, but it was the arrival of Keeble, a prolific target man who was superb in the air, that transformed the Hammers into Second Division title winners.

Willie Moir recalled himself once more to the starting XI for cup action at inside-right, meaning it would be the same eleven that had beaten Luton three weeks earlier. The Hatters put in an impressive showing at Upton Park, with the possible exception of their goalkeeper, Ken Grieves, who had a day to forget.

A multi-sport athlete, Grieves was a brilliant cricketer, and an especially accomplished fielder. Born in the suburb of Burwood, 10km west of Sydney, the Australian first-class cricketer moved to England in 1947, where he began playing football as a goalkeeper. He recorded an incredible 608 catches over the course of his career, 555 of which came for Lancashire, an all-time record for the county. As well as representing England against his native Australia in the Ashes, Grieves also played football for Bury, Bolton, Wigan and Stockport. He spent the 1957–58 season at Edgeley Park as the club's regular number one, making forty-three appearances in all competitions. He conceded three goals as Stockport were narrowly beaten 3-2 at the Boleyn Ground, bringing their cup run to an end.

Upon his return home, Neil joked that Grieves could catch cricket balls for fun, but struggled with footballs at Upton Park. Some saw it a little differently, since Vic Keeble seemingly bulldozed the Aussie shot stopper across the goal line for West Ham's opening goal. Keeble was a hellishly strong centre-forward, and the goal was typical of his robust approach, but it left 1,000 travelling County fans feeling a little hard done by. Keeble was a very effective front man, but he was forced into retirement the following season due to a back injury at the age of thirty. He scored 51 goals in 84 games for West Ham before his career ended prematurely, yet he never won a cap for England.

It was a 36,000-strong full house for the match, and the 1,000 there from Greater Manchester had sold out their allocation, with at least one special train having to be put on down to London. Ken Finney and Bill Holden bagged a goal each for the Hatters, but a brace by Eddie Lewis, who had previously played for Manchester United and would go on to manage Kaizer Chiefs in South Africa, put West Ham into the next round.

Stockport lost heavily away at Rochdale the following week, before an emphatic win over Neil's former club, Crewe Alexandra. Five different players got on the scoresheet for County in a 5-1 thrashing of the Railwaymen. Just over a month later, Stockport found themselves on the receiving end of a defeat by a four-goal margin against Scunthorpe United. The game was Neil's 27th consecutive start for the Hatters since his debut against Chester, but it would prove to be his last competitive match for the club, and the final Football League game he ever featured in.

A week after that 4-0 defeat, on 20 March, the *Stockport Advertiser* linked Neil with becoming the next manager of Scunthorpe United. It was a rumour he denied, stating that he wanted to continue playing, but that he might be open to a player-coach role. The following week, he signed a new deal at Edgeley Park until the end of the season to do just that, becoming the first coach in the club's 66-year history. The same publication reported that Willie Moir felt the two 'think alike on tactics and soccer principles'.

Two days after that news was announced, Neil managed the Hatters away at Hartlepools United in the absence of Moir, and the team won their first away game in six months. He managed the reserves for the next couple of months, and in June 1958, it was reported that Neil had signed a twelve-month extension as player-coach. Ironically, despite having once been the best centre-half in the country and an undroppable England international, it was as a 36-year-old player-coach in the Third Division North with Stockport County that Neil was on his highest standard salary. In

1958, the maximum wage was raised to £20 a week, the last time it would go up before finally being abolished in January 1961. In his final season in the Football League, Franklin was paid £20 a week plus bonuses, compared to the £12 a week he received in his prime.

Coaching and management was the natural calling for a footballing obsessive like Neil, who had a strong belief in how the game ought to be played. After playing his final game for Stockport County on 28 April in a 5-0 friendly win against the now defunct Western Command of the British Army, Neil headed to the FA's Coaching School at Lilleshall in Shropshire. Neil's former England manager Walter Winterbottom was behind the founding of a new National Coaching Scheme and the summer coaching courses at Lilleshall.

From August onwards, Neil took full charge of Stockport's reserve team, whom he continued to play for as well. Stockport County Reserves had finished 19th in the Cheshire League the previous season, but they would be playing in the newly formed North Regional League for the 1958–59 season. They went undefeated in the first nine games of the season, which included a 5-0 win against Doncaster Rovers Reserves. The Hatters second string also won 5-0 against Hull City Reserves, Gateshead Reserves and Workington Reserves under Neil's stewardship, as he guided them to a much-improved seventh-placed finish, playing in 25 of the 36 North Regional League games that season himself.

It wasn't just the reserves though; he stood in for Willie Moir to manage the first team once more on 1 November 1958 in a 2-1 defeat to Mansfield. A couple of weeks earlier, he had spent two days coaching the RAF Command team, who played Stockport's first team in return for the favour on 24 November, a match which Stockport won 4-0.

All was not well that season at Edgeley Park, though. After a poor start to the season, County lost 8-2 away at Colchester United at the start of October. That match led to something of an inquest and a lot of in-house fighting. Colchester had only scored 17 goals in their first 11 games, yet they'd just put eight past County and it should have been more. That defeat left the Hatters four points off safety at an early stage, and goalkeeper Arthur Barnard, inside-forward Eddie Mulvey and centre-forward Bill Holden were all reportedly seeking transfers, although Mulvey denied that he was looking to move on.

Wholesale changes were made for the following week's match-up with Bournemouth and Boscombe Athletic, and the manager's shake-up paid off, with the Hatters recording a first win since August. One of the players who came in that day and made his debut was Alec Acton. A nineteen-year-old half-back, Acton had been signed from Stoke City on the advice of Franklin without having made an appearance for the Potters first team.

Injury prevented him from making an early impact, but despite positive reviews for his display against Bournemouth, it didn't seem like Willie Moir was much of a fan. Acton played only seven further games for County's first team that season, whilst he made seventeen appearances for Neil's reserves. Throughout the festive period, there were suggestions of differences between Moir and the board, all whilst County's only genuine goal threat Bill Holden was pushing for a move elsewhere, claiming Stockport were denying him from earning the maximum £20 a week.

Despite a convincing 4-0 win against Southampton in their final game of the season, Stockport were relegated in 21st place in their first season in the national Third Division. The fallout from the demotion, which had been bubbling away since that 8-2 defeat to Colchester in October, was sizeable. Three players were released, four were made available for transfers and Neil Franklin was sacked. A cloud hung over the future of Willie Moir, as it had done for some time, but Neil's fate was sealed.

Neil was both angry and confused. He was angry because the

board had taken the decision without even offering him the courtesy of a meeting. He was confused because he couldn't understand why he was being punished for the poor form of the first team; after all, he had no say on first-team matters, he managed the reserve team, and they had enjoyed a thoroughly decent campaign. On 7 May 1959, the *Stockport Advertiser* reported that Neil was 'fed up of being unfairly blamed for County's position'. The club claimed that Neil had 'shouted too soon', as they had only terminated his deal as a player and not as a coach. The same paper also reported that letters had been sent backing Neil as manager over Moir, but to no avail. Moir kept his job until the following season, when Stockport finished mid-table and the two parted company.

Aged thirty-seven and out of work, within a week of his dismissal Neil applied to become the next manager of Millwall. A Second Division side at the end of the war, they had dropped into the Fourth Division in 1958. They appointed Jimmy Seed as manager in January 1958, but having just spent twenty-three years in charge of Charlton Athletic, he lasted only a year and a half before resigning at the Old Den. Millwall were a club with good potential; they still got decent crowds for the Fourth Division, and they could call upon Neil's former Hull City teammate, the ever-prolific Alf Ackerman, up front. Neil was unsuccessful though, as the Millwall board sided with another former England international, Reg Smith, who also lasted only eighteen months with the club.

When the 1959–60 season kicked off, Neil Franklin was still unattached. It was the first time in twenty years a season had begun in which he was not contracted to a club, but that wouldn't last long. Having been linked with a shocking move to a Southern League club almost a decade earlier, now such a move would happen, although it was rather less sensational at this stage of his career.

Wellington Town of the Southern League Premier Division had just lost their second game of the season 1-0 away at Poole Town, with three of their first team players picking up injuries in the process. With a depleted squad and another game in only two days' time, their boss, Johnny Hancocks, reached out to Neil Franklin. A prolific outside-right who won both the First Division and the FA Cup with Wolverhampton Wanderers, Hancocks' international opportunities had been limited by the brilliance of Stanley Matthews and Tom Finney, but he did win three caps for England, and all came alongside Neil. Now aged forty, he was back in his native Shropshire. Below is an extract of the programme notes, written by Hancock, for their home game against Kettering a week later:

> After the match [vs Poole Town] we sent an S.O.S. for Neil Franklin to join us and he came down to Bournemouth on Friday in time for the match at Yeovil on the following day. This programme must go to press before the result of that game is known but the lads were determined to get some reward for the long trip from the two matches and with Bert Richards and his men working to get the casualties fit, we were hoping for at least a point on the famous Yeovil slope.

Neil did play, at half-back rather than centre-half, and Wellington lost 7-0. He agreed terms with his former international teammate as a player-coach, making his second start on 7 September 1959 in the second leg of a Southern League Cup tie against Kettering Town. A 3-3 draw, including a goal by his boss, who often played on the left wing by this time, saw Wellington progress 7-4 on aggregate. Neil was one of three new recruits for the injury-stricken Lilywhites, and all three earned positive reviews from the Bucks Head faithful. The Wellington programme for their next home game included some trivia, querying, 'Did you know that between Neil Franklin vacating the England centre-half position and Billy Wright taking over, no fewer than 11 players were tried as pivot without any lasting success?'

Their new signing certainly did. At this point, it's worth noting that I have seen it claimed in various places that Neil Franklin left England once more in 1959 and headed to New Zealand's capital of Wellington. For the purposes of this book, I could possibly wish that were true, as it would make for a great story, but sadly it is not. Presumably, the confusion comes down to Wellington Town FC having been renamed Telford United FC in 1969, following the creation of Telford in the mid- to late 1960s. Someone, somewhere, must have seen that Neil Franklin signed for Wellington Town and assumed they were a club in Wellington, New Zealand.

Alas, it was Salop not Australasia, and the Land of the Wrekin rather than the Long White Cloud. In fact, it was the even more modest surroundings of Wellington Town's reserves at times, as Just as had been the case at Stockport, Neil was tasked with helping out the Bucks second string. He inherited a reserve team that had begun the campaign with a 9-0 defeat to Aston Villa Reserves, so it is probably fair to say some defensive work needed to be done.

He stepped in on 12 September, deputising at centre-half and helping the young charges to a 4-1 win over Hednesford. It was a pleasing result, but Neil was soon back in the first team, including for Wellington's FA Cup First Round replay, which saw the club dumped out by Shropshire rivals Oswestry Town for the third consecutive season. Oswestry had a player-manager of their own— they were rather popular in the lower leagues during the 1950s you may have noticed—in the form of Neil's former Stoke teammate George Antonio, and he was the man of the match in the first match between the two at the Bucks Head stadium.

Another man in the Oswestry side that overcame Wellington was Ken Roberts. One of the youngest men I've spoken to who played with or against Neil, Ken was eighty-one, soon to turn eighty-two, when I spoke with him over the phone. His voice quickly perked up when I uttered the words 'Neil Franklin', suggesting either some vivid memories or just relief that I wasn't a cold-caller. The first thing Ken recalled about Neil was his 'piercing pale blue eyes,' but he soon moved on to footballing matters. Ken was twenty-three when he came up against Neil, and he found himself playing in the Southern League after five years in the First Division with Aston Villa, where he had sustained cruciate ligament damage which ended his career prematurely.

Prior to his move to Villa Park, Ken had become the joint youngest Football League player of all time, making his Wrexham debut aged 15 years and 158 days. The record, which he tied in 1951, wouldn't be beaten until Reuben Noble-Lazarus played four minutes of Championship football for Barnsley in 2008, at 113 days younger than when Ken first deputised. He considers Neil to be one of the finest players he ever shared a pitch with. 'He definitely should have been playing at a higher level, I couldn't believe it. When I found out he'd gone to Wellington, I relished the opportunity to play against him, he was an excellent player all-round.' When asked if Neil showed signs of having slowed down at the ripe old age of thirty-seven, Ken responded, 'I don't know about that. Put it this way, he did alright . . . and if he had slowed down, he made up for it in skill.'

It was high praise indeed, especially when you add in some context. Ken had joined Oswestry in an attempt to breathe new life into his career following his devastating injury at Aston Villa, and in the game against Wellington, Neil put in a full-blooded tackle on the number ten. It was a clean enough challenge, but Neil's full weight seemed to follow through with it. 'Neil, you've done me,' Ken told the former England international, to which he received a dismissive, 'No I haven't' in response. As it turns out, he had. Three broken ribs, in fact. Ken describes Neil as being very apologetic, and he certainly hasn't let the injury thwart the regard in which he holds him.

Ken raised a valid question though: What was Neil Franklin doing at Wellington Town? Well, there were a few reasons. Off the back of stints with Crewe and Stockport, he was hardly going to walk into a First Division side at his age, even if he wouldn't necessarily have looked out of place doing so. Geography also came into it once more, since Wellington's Bucks Head stadium was only a thirty-mile drive from the Bell & Bear pub in Shelton, where Neil was now licensee. Then there were the finances; as wild as it seems today, Southern League Premier Division clubs could offer their star men as much as top players in the First Division earned. Ken Roberts told me he was earning £15 a week during his time at Oswestry, when the Football League's maximum wage was £20 a week. Given Neil's status, it would be reasonable to think he was on similar or more than £20 a week. Add in the fact that he knew the Wellington boss Johnny Hancocks from their time together with England and having played against one and another in the First Division, along with Neil having a boyish love of the game regardless of the level or standard, it becomes easier to see how he ended up with the Bucks.

The fact that the role was as a player-coach served as further appeal to Neil, who had got his first taste of coaching at Stockport, and was well aware that his playing days were approaching an end. He worked alongside Johnny Hancocks on the coaching and tactical side of things, as well as taking a more hands-on approach with the reserves.

Hancocks was a man in trouble though, as the season went from bad to terrible in the early parts of the campaign. Things really began to fall apart in October, with the club losing three and drawing one of their four matches that month. At the end of the month, Hancocks was sacked, or 'released from his managerial duties', as the club's programme notes put it ahead of their next match against Cambridge City. That phraseology did make some sense actually; since Hancocks had been a player-manager, his sacking only terminated his contract as a manager, and he remained a member of the playing staff.

Hancocks had been the Wellington Town manager for the last three seasons, and for every home game during that period, he would head the programme notes. The opening page was titled 'Johnny Hancocks Notes', and it was signed off with the manager's signature. For the rest of the season though, the page would be headed, 'From the touchline . . .' and was signed off with the word, Onlooker.

Onlooker appears to have been a member of club staff, but the man who had been tasked with taking over coaching and management of the first team was Neil Franklin. Neil had only been at the club a little over two months, but in an unusual turn of events he was managing the man who had brought him to the club, with Johnny Hancocks now simply available to him as either an outside-left or an outside-right. It must have been an awkward situation, but Neil wasted little time mixing things up at Bucks Head.

The programme notes for the first game following Hancocks' dismissal reveals that, 'Player-coach Neil Franklin has introduced some changes in the training schedule and all players in the first team, except Alan Rogers, will train together at the Bucks Head on Tuesdays and Thursdays.' The fact that the programme notes weren't signed off by Neil is due to the fact he had not officially been appointed as Johnny Hancocks' successor; rather he had simply been handed the first-team reigns until further notice. In modern terms, the role would be described as one of an interim manager.

Initially, Neil's appointment was a double-whammy disaster. Not only did Wellington's form remain in the doldrums, but without his management, the club's one bright light—the reserves—began to fall apart as well. It took nine matches before the young boss recorded his first win with the first team, and it arrived in the form of a 3-1 win away at King's Lynn. That kick-started a good run between late November and late February, in which the club won six, lost two and drew two. It was a crucial purple patch for

Neil, with the Bucks at risk of being cut adrift in the relegation places prior to it.

The last victory of that run was one of the most impressive in a number of years for Wellington. They went away to Bath City, who were miles ahead at the top of the division and would go on to win 32 of their 42 games that season, finishing 13 points clear at the top of the league in an era when a win only secured 2 points. Wellington went to Twerton Park and beat the division's runaway leaders 5-1. In their next home game, the club boasted of having 'achieved one of their greatest successes in post-war football', describing the team's performance as 'stupendous'.

During that good run, a number of changes occurred at Bucks Head. In January, Johnny Hancocks unsurprisingly parted company with the club, dropping down to Division One of the Southern Football League and signing for Cambridge United. It seemed to be a rather bitter parting, with the club pointing out that Hancocks 'could not have picked a more awkward place for travelling' upon announcement of his departure, and they noted with glee that he had been dropped to Cambridge's reserves a couple of months later. Also in January, Bert Richards, who had played for Wellington in the 1920s, rejoined the club as a coach.

However, despite having just recorded back-to-back wins against Cambridge City and Kettering Town, the Wellington board decided to appoint a more experienced coach as their full-time manager in the second week of April 1960. The announcement confirmed that the new manager would 'take over the duties of Johnny Hancocks, for Neil Franklin who was engaged as a player-coach, despite the fact that he selected the team, was never elevated to the position held by Hancocks.'

The announcement revealed the name of their new boss as 'Reg. Lewin'. The good people of Wellington must have thought their board had gone for a real unknown candidate, since there was no one involved in the game of football who went by that name. As it happened, Wellington's unnamed onlooker had made a bit of a blunder, since their newly appointed manager was in fact 'Ron' Lewin. A post-war defender for both Fulham and Gillingham, Lewin was only a couple of years older than Neil, but he did have greater experience of managing in the game. He had spent two years as manager of the Norwegian national team, becoming only the second man to take charge of the country and guiding them to a famous win over Hungary in June 1957. After that, Lewin took charge of fellow Southern League outfit Cheltenham Town, where he had two and a half successful seasons and finished fourth in his best campaign.

Neil may no longer have been in charge of first-team matters, but with a new man in charge, he was recalled to the starting XI. Having been out of the team for almost four months since Boxing Day, he made three appearances in April, his last three for Wellington Town. Lewin wasn't the only man whose name caused the Wellington programme writers some trouble: from Lewin's arrival in April until the end of the season in May, Franklin was misspelt as 'Franklyn'.

Wellington won just one of their remaining eight league games under Lewin, but the back-to-back wins that immediately preceded his arrival were enough to ensure survival. Neil played his last game for the club in a 3-0 defeat away at Headington United, and left his role as player-coach after the season concluded with victory in the Shropshire Senior Cup.

Around the same time as Neil left Wellington, he also left the Bell & Bear, a beautiful Edwardian pub in Shelton. Within a couple of months, Neil had itchy feet. The football bug was well and truly in his blood, and he wasn't yet ready to turn his attention to coaching and his back on playing the game for good. Wellington's nearest club, Sankeys, their full name being 'Sankeys of Wellington', had moved from the Shropshire County League to the more professional Cheshire County League over the summer, and they asked

Neil if he would be interested in joining them for their first season at a higher level. Sankeys had brought in some decent players ahead of their debut Cheshire County campaign, including a couple of former First Division players.

One such player was Johnny Hancocks, the manager who had brought Neil to Wellington Town. If you suspect that his own signing then taking over selection and coaching duties must have created some sense of awkwardness between the two at Wellington, then one can only assume similar feelings lingered just a few miles down the road.

Sankey's were the works team of the automotive company GKN Sankeys, who opened a large plant in Wellington in the early 1900s. Whilst the team started playing league football in 1954 but were dissolved by 1988, the company, GKN, has enjoyed a rather different fate: it is currently a FTSE 100 constituent with a revenue in excess of £9.6 billion. Neil spent half a season with Sankeys, departing around Christmas time after more than twenty appearances and only missing one game. The club put in a respectable showing in their first Cheshire County League season, finishing 16th out of twenty two teams.

CHAPTER 16

A Favour for Frank

Neil Franklin played football across the globe, won international acclaim and set a world record fee for a defender; but one thing he had never managed to do was win a league title. That was true up until virtually his last chapter as a footballer. In January 1961, mid-way through the 1960–61 season, Neil left Sankeys to join Macclesfield Town.

Located between two of Neil's former clubs, Stockport County and Stoke City, Macclesfield was—and still is—a quaint market town in Cheshire that had come through the war unscathed. Said to be the only mill town that wasn't bombed throughout the war, Macclesfield's historic Moss Rose ground was a little over twenty miles north of Neil's home in Stoke-on-Trent. There was a bigger reason why Neil joined the Silkmen though, and that was their manager, Frank Bowyer.

A brilliant inside-forward who spent twenty-three years contracted to Stoke City, national service meant Bowyer didn't make his league debut until 1948, just a couple of months shy of his 26th birthday. He made amends, however, remaining in the Potters first team until the age of thirty-eight. In that time, he racked up 436 peacetime appearances, which is the ninth most of any player in Stoke City history, and scored 149 peacetime goals, putting him third in the clubs all-time scoring charts. He was Stoke City's seasonal top scorer for six separate campaigns, one in which he was tied with Johnny King, whilst he took the title outright for the other five. He was pretty prolific for an inside-forward then, and you can bet you'd be able to add a good few goals to that tally had Stanley Matthews not left the club a year before Bowyer made his league debut.

Less than three months and five miles separated when and where Franklin and Bowyer had been born, and they both came through the youth ranks at the Victoria Ground. Of course, Neil's ill-fated voyage to Bogotá meant the two players only got a couple of seasons together in Stoke's first-team ranks, but they still knew each other well and were great admirers of each other's ability. Neil considered Frank to be a hugely underrated player, which he put down in large part to his loyalty to Stoke. In his book, Neil described Frank as 'the best uncapped inside forward I have seen'. Frank had actually come close to a transfer to Bolton at one stage, but eventually decided against the move and remained at the Vic.

Until 1960 that is, when—at the age of thirty-eight—he left Stoke to become player-manager at Macclesfield Town. At Moss Rose, Bowyer quickly began bringing in some experienced heads from his time in the top two tiers. In fact, at a glance you could be forgiven for thinking the Macclesfield side was some kind of Football League veterans' team. As well as Bowyer, who had an elegance on a football pitch which he could contrast with a ferocious shot in the blink of an eye, there were eight other former Football League players.

At right-back there was Keith Bannister, who had given eight years of post-war service to Sheffield Wednesday, much of which had been interrupted by injury. On the wing, they had John 'Dickie' Cunliffe, a Port Vale legend who won two titles with the Valiants, joining Macclesfield off the back of a single season at Stoke City, and aged thirty he was hardly long over-the-hill. Alongside Bowyer at inside-forward was Bill Finney, no relation to the Preston and England star, who had partnered Bowyer in that position for five years at Stoke City. Then there was Ken Griffiths, also aged 30, who had scored 52 goals in 179 league games for Port Vale as a forward, and Derek Tomkinson, another inside-forward formerly of Port Vale and Crewe.

Albert Leake and Stan Smith were another couple of ex-Vale players who were instrumental in Bowyer's Macclesfield side. Leake had come through the youth ranks with Stoke, before racking up more than 250 league appearances with Port Vale; he would go on to replace Bowyer as Macclesfield's player-manager. Smith, meanwhile, who was another product of Stoke's youth setup, had less than 100 Football League appearances to his name, but would prove to be an inspired signing for Frank Bowyer.

The team looked to be rather stacked for playing in the Cheshire County League, and so it proved. Stan Smith's speed and powerful shooting yielded 38 goals from 33 appearances, former Manchester City youth player Rex Grey scored 35, Dickie Cunliffe notched 15 from the left wing, and the boss himself Frank Bowyer showed that his goal-scoring exploits had not yet deserted him, managing 32 goals for the season.

Neil made his Macclesfield Town debut on 21 January for a home league game against struggling Rhyl. He came into the team for former Manchester United trainee Roger Wood, who was in his eighth and final season at Moss Rose. In front of a 2,184-strong crowd, Neil put in an assured display, anchoring a defence which kept a clean sheet as the Silkmen blew their Welsh opposition away. Stan Smith bagged a hat-trick in a 5-0 win. The *County Express* newspaper gave the following account of the match:

> With the half back line strengthened by the inclusion of Neil Franklin former England and Stoke City player and Albert Leake Port Vale star, signed the previous day, Macclesfield looked Championship class when they beat Rhyl 5-0 on the Moss Rose ground on Saturday writes Silkman [pen name of the *County Express* sports reporter].

A FAVOUR FOR FRANK

A supporter who stopped me as I passed my way through the crowd of delighted supporters at the close summed up the view of the majority when he commented, 'Now it looks a really good side.'

In only Neil's third game for Macclesfield he faced one of his former clubs, Crewe Alexandra. The Alex had got their act together a bit by this point, and instead of perennially propping up the rest of the league, they were enjoying the dizzying heights of sixth place in the Fourth Division when they travelled to Moss Rose. A crowd of almost 4,000 turned out to witness the Cheshire Senior Cup match between the two clubs, in which Crewe emerged as narrow 1-0 winners. It was the only cup appearance Neil ever made for Macclesfield.

From his debut onwards, Neil made ten consecutive starts for the Silkmen, which included the ninth and final club goal of his career. It came on 4 March away at Wrexham Reserves, and it was Macclesfield's second in a game which ended in a 3-3 draw. *County Express* newspaper covered the goal, writing, 'The half however was 26 minutes old when following a well placed corner by Cunliffe, Franklin who had rushed up into the goal mouth headed into the net.'

A couple of weeks later, Neil faced another former club—the team where he had started the season—Sankeys. It was something of a demolition job at Moss Rose, as player-manager Frank Bowyer claimed the match ball this time in a 7-1 win.

Neil missed the end of March and the start of April, but returned for wins against Tranmere Rovers Reserves, Ellesmere Port Town and Bangor City. His last game for Macclesfield against Bangor was witnessed by more than 3,000 fans, and for the first time in his career he had won a league title. Although Macclesfield had secured the title a couple of weeks earlier, it was their first home game as champions, and perhaps a fitting yet poignant note to go out on for a player whose trophy cabinet really did not align with his talents.

Macclesfield Town fan Mike Clark was just a 19-year-old at the time of Neil's brief stint at Moss Rose, but he has vivid memories of watching the classy centre-half. He may only have played 14 games for the club, but Mike pointed out the fact that the club were fourth when he arrived and champions when he departed, and he's happy to label Neil as Macclesfield's 'greatest ever player'. A lifelong fan who occasionally used to write guest articles for the Macclesfield programme, Mike still attends games at Moss Rose, and he kindly shared some of his memories of watching Franklin in action.

'He was without doubt a genius, and he stood out in non-league because he was a footballer. To have Frank Bowyer, England's finest uncapped inside-forward, and Neil Franklin playing for the Macc at the same time, we felt very lucky. There was one game where we were really hanging on, and Neil was basically just keeping them out on his own.'

It's a sentiment echoed by former Macclesfield player and manager Keith Goalen, who made 441 appearances over 13 years with the Silkmen. Only three men have played more games for Macclesfield Town than Goalen, who also guided the club to promotion as manager and a famous FA Cup Third Round win over Fulham, all whilst working as a solicitor. Keith was also the first non-league player to win the *London Evening Standard*'s 'Footballer of the Month' award. It all sounds rather impressive, yet Goalen is as humble as they come. Of his 441 appearances for the Macc, 12 came alongside Neil Franklin, and he shared those happy memories from almost six decades ago with me.

'He was a footballer before his time. Neil came along and actually played football, it was unheard of for a centre-half, managers didn't really stand for it. I think he got away with it because he'd played for England. He was the best footballer I have ever played with; his only fault was that he thought everyone was as good as he was, which they weren't.'

Keith recalled Neil's classic trick of carrying the ball out of defence before slipping it off with a sharp pass to a teammate at the final second. 'I can picture it now,' he said. 'He'd play me a little slide pass and I'd just whack it.' Keith was playing as a left-half at that time, and often found himself being used as an outlet. Neil could grow frustrated at Keith and others for not sharing his comfort and composure on the ball, but this was non-league football, and Neil ended up getting on well with his Macclesfield teammates, later returning to Moss Rose to play in Keith's testimonial.

Keith described Neil as 'the first defender I ever saw who could play football', which perhaps says more about both the English and non-league game than it does Neil Franklin, but it's certainly true that Franklin still stood out a mile in the final spell of his career. 'You wouldn't have put him at thirty-nine,' Keith told me. When asked if he was surprised Neil didn't stay on beyond his single half-season with the Silkmen, Keith said, 'I felt he could have played another couple of seasons, it's difficult to tell with players like that, because they don't need to go running about everywhere anyway.'

I asked Keith if he would liken Neil's style to any players he has watched in the fifty-seven years that have followed their time together, to which he replied, 'The majority of defenders have his style now, they just don't have his ability to hold onto the ball until the last second.' It's a question I've asked a number of people who either played with or watched Franklin in action, and it's one they almost universally hesitate to answer. Bobby Moore's name has cropped up a couple of times, as have Roy McFarland's and Paul McGrath's on one or two occasions, but for the most part, those I've spoken to struggle to find a genuine like-for-like comparison.

After leaving Macclesfield, Neil returned to Sankeys of Wellington for one last hurrah. He took over as player-manager in

May 1961, and left by mutual agreement in August 1962. In his single season in charge, he guided the club to a 12th placed finish, four places and three points better than their previous seasons efforts. The club managed to record a 1-1 draw against Macclesfield, who finished second that season, as Ellesmere Port Town claimed the title. It was Neil Franklin's last as a professional footballer.

CHAPTER 17

The Franklin Dream Team

Fantasy football is a common pastime among casual football fans in the twenty-first century, but don't think fans and players of yesteryear didn't put together dream teams of their own. Pick up the autobiography of any football star from the 1940s or 50s, and you can pretty much guarantee that they will have set aside a chapter or some portion of the book to their fantasy XI. Neil Franklin was no exception, and his dream team emphasises the sheer quality he played with and against during a golden era for the English game.

Neil restricted his XI to British players only, ruling out some of the great continental stars he had come up against with England. He reserved high praise for the likes of French goalkeeper Julien Darui, Swedish centre-forward Gunnar Nordahl and Hungarian talisman Ferenc Puskás, but limited the dream team to Football League players as he had played with, against or watched them more closely and frequently. It's worth noting also that the XI was drawn up in 1955, so naturally it deals only with players of Neil's generation, not that there were slim pickings.

Between the sticks, honourable mentions went to the likes of Sam Bartram, Bert Williams and Bert Trautmann, but the number-one shirt is handed to Frank Swift. Stoke City goalkeeper Dennis Herod was Neil's closest friend in the game, both whilst they were teammates and for many years after that. The duos close bond off the pitch undoubtedly helped Stoke City once they crossed the white line. Any defender will tell you the importance of having a good understanding with your goalkeeper, and vice versa, and the pair shared a brilliant rapport at the Victoria Ground.

Like all relationships though, it wasn't perfect, and a breakdown came one Saturday away at Derby County when a fierce strike downfield by Dennis didn't travel very far before whacking Neil on the back of the head. The Stoke City number one was 'panic-stricken', not because his teammate and close pal lay strewn on the grass, but because the ball was heading towards goal. Fortunately for the Potters, the ball dropped wide of the right-hand post, but Dennis wasn't impressed. 'Why don't you keep your big head out of the way?' he barked. One breakdown in more than 100 games together isn't bad going, however, and as well as sharing a pitch, the two shared a passion for horse racing. They could often be found having a flutter at the local bookies, and Dennis would remain a close friend of Neil's until the end.

Herod was a fine servant to Stoke City and a good pal, but there's no room for sentiment in the Franklin XI, and Dennis was never a goalkeeper of international class. Frank Swift most certainly was, and he too was a brilliant character. A giant presence on the pitch and an even larger one in the England and Manchester City dressing room, 'Swifty'—as he was known—was England's resident prankster. A happy-go-lucky character who had a knack for removing any pre-game stresses or anxieties among his teammates, Neil described him as being 'worth a goal to any side which had him'.

Frank Swift combined smart anticipation with hands safer than Fort Knox. There was another reason Neil Franklin was a big fan of his though: his distribution. Don't be fooled into thinking the ball-playing goalkeeper is a modern phenomenon created by Pep Guardiola. Frank Swift was happy to play it long or short, but crucially, he would kick or throw the ball with remarkable accuracy. It's easy to see why the Man City legend would appeal to Neil then, and he summed it up by writing, 'So Frank Swift is a certainty for my team . . . otherwise the opponents might pick him, and I would much rather have Frank Swift with me than against me.'

Swift made 14 wartime appearances and won 19 peacetime caps for England, picking up the nickname 'frying pan hands' thanks to his supposed 29.8cm finger span. He spent his entire sixteen-year career at Manchester City, before becoming a sports journalist with the *News of the World*. He was aboard the British European Airways Flight 609 which crashed on its third attempt to take off at Munich-Riem Airport after reporting on Manchester United's European Cup win over Red Star Belgrade. Swift was still alive when ambulances arrived at the wreckage, but his aorta had been severed by his seat belt, and he died during the journey to the hospital, aged forty-four. A beloved figure, half a century on from his death Manchester City faced Manchester United on the 50th anniversary of the Munich air disaster. Five minutes from the end of the game, the Man City fans began a chanting, 'One Frank Swift, there's only one Frank Swift.' All four corners of Old Trafford responded in applause for one of England's all-time greats.

So goalkeeper is a sure-fire thing, and there wasn't much doubt in Neil Franklin's mind when it came to the full-backs either. One might point out that Neil unsurprisingly employed the W-M formation that dominated English football throughout his career. He went for two full-backs who knew Swifty and each other very well: George Hardwick and Laurie Scott. Both players were playing for England when Neil broke into the national team setup during the war, and he slotted in between them at centre-half.

Hardwick is a Middlesbrough legend whose statue can be found outside Boro's Riverside Stadium today. A fierce but fair tackler, taking a whack from Hardwick was likened to being hit by a train. England's standout post-war left-back, he had shrugged off shrapnel injuries to both legs during the war, but found a knee injury in 1948 more difficult to bounce back from. He maintained his place in the Middlesbrough side, and later joined Oldham Athletic, but it cut his international career short. The injury restricted him to only 13 caps for England, and he captained his country in all 13 games.

Scott's caps tally of 17 seems equally miserly for a player of such outstanding talent, although that owed more to the fact that he was already twenty-nine when peacetime football returned to Britain, rather than to any injuries he sustained. Deceptively quick in his younger days, he too suffered setbacks in 1948: first appendicitis and then a knee injury of his own. Scott returned to the England setup for the 1950 World Cup in Brazil, having just won the FA Cup with Arsenal; but aged thirty-three, he was backup to Alf Ramsey at the tournament. Neil described both Hardwick and Scott as 'masters of positional play'.

Manchester United's great utility man Johnny Carey was another player Neil admired. Having broken into the Manchester United team as an inside-forward, Ireland international Carey later became a half-back and eventually settled as a full-back, having been one of United's star players in all three roles. 'There can have been few cooler or more classical players,' Neil wrote of the 1949 FWA Footballer of the Year, who he faced at both club and international level. Carey may well have had a shot at the full-back spots in the 'Franklin XI' were it not for Neil's British-only rule.

Next up is the centre-half spot, where there are many outstanding candidates. One of them was Wolves legend Stan Cullis, who Neil described as a 'truly fine player'. Neil replaced Cullis as England's centre-half, with the future Wolves boss ending his career just one season after the war. Then there were Scotland's star defenders, Willie Woodburn (centre-half) and George Young (full-back and later centre-half), both of whom starred for Rangers and

Scotland, and were very highly thought of by Neil. Actually, Neil rated all of the Scotland teams he faced very highly, considering them to be technically equal to—if not better—than England. Neil felt that the Scots ill-discipline and occasional tendency to let their tempers get the better of them was the only reason they didn't have a better record against England.

The player who takes the centre-half place in the Franklin Dream Team though, is the one and only John Charles. Neil faced Charles as a teenage centre-forward when he had just broken through at Leeds United, and he watched and admired from afar as he matured into one of the finest centre-forwards or centre-halves in the game. Neil ran out of superlatives for the Welsh great, who was among the most complete footballers in the history of the game. Stanley Matthews is the only player Neil Franklin rated higher than Charles, and that is some praise. Neil modestly left himself out of his 'Franklin XI', unlike some, but he would not have ranked himself higher than the Welshman regardless. Charles was the only player Neil felt he could not beat to an aerial ball, and he eventually decided his efforts were better placed letting him lay the ball off and then pressing. Neil put simply, 'Any selector who had John Charles available and didn't pick him would be out of his mind.' There was of course another reason why Neil Franklin was an enormous John Charles fan, and that was because he was a ball-playing defender just like himself. He described Charles as the 'perfect footballing centre-half', and greatly admired his clean approach to the game and unyielding determination to rely on his talents as a footballer before his imposing size and stature. He wasn't called 'The Gentle Giant' for nothing.

If it wasn't for the genius of Charles, then the centre-half position probably would have gone to Tommy 'T G' Jones. The 'Prince of Wales' as some called him, Jones spent fourteen years contracted to Everton, but lost his prime years to the war. His days as an international ended at thirty three, just as an 18-year-old

John Charles was breaking into the Welsh setup. The two never played for Wales together. Jones was five years Neil's senior, and he described the adopted Evertonian as an 'idol' while he was coming through the ranks at Stoke City, as well as calling him 'the complete centre-half.'

In front of the back three, Neil opted for Matt Busby and Frank Soo as his half-backs, or central and holding midfielders as we would call them today. At right-half, Busby was a man who Neil looked up to, and the pair shared a footballing philosophy. He may be better remembered for his time as Manchester United manager now, but make no mistake, Matt Busby was a fine footballer. Busby was some thirteen years older than Neil, but the two faced each other in both wartime representative and international fixtures, as well as playing alongside one and another for a couple of exhibition games in Belgium that were put on as entertainment for the troops.

It was during that latter trip that Sir Matt, as he would later be titled, had a lasting effect on a young Neil Franklin. Just before the two teams took to the field, Busby, then of Liverpool, turned to Neil and said, 'Just remember, Neil, keep playing football at all times and you'll never go far wrong.' They won the game 8-1. It was an ethos already well-held by Neil, but hearing it from such an established professional gave him great belief going forward, and it was a mentality he stuck to throughout his career. Busby was well into his thirties when Neil first shared a football pitch with him, but Neil still felt his talents stood out a mile, writing, 'I didn't play with Matt at the height of his fame, but I saw enough of him to realize that they don't come any better.' Neil called Matt 'the perfect footballer, cool, calculating and careful', adding that he 'passed a ball as delicately as a painter treats his canvas'. From what he saw of him as a player, Busby's extraordinary success as a manager came as little surprise to Neil.

THE FRANKLIN DREAM TEAM

The man partnering Busby in the middle of the park is someone who is rather less well known to modern football fans. A hugely underrated footballer, Frank Soo was the first non-white player to represent England, and he remains the only player of Asian descent to have done so. Even in his own time, Neil wrote that, 'Frank was always a better player than he was given credit for, and in my early days he helped me a lot.' A quick and thoughtful player, Soo was a tireless runner who was technically very astute, confident in possession and a brilliant passer of the ball. Neil described him as 'one of the grandest wing-halves and greatest fellows you could wish to meet', and backed that up by picking him over truly great half-backs like Joe Mercer and Henry Cockburn.

There are a few reasons why Soo doesn't have the legacy he probably ought to today. There's the fact that he really did lose the best years of his career to the Second World War, which in turn meant that all nine of his England appearances were in wartime fixtures not met with official caps. The best years of his career were spent with Stoke City, whose history is not nearly as celebrated internationally or even nationally as many other English clubs, and he never won a trophy as a player. He left Stoke immediately after the war, by which time he was thirty-two, and played his last meaningful football for Luton Town in the Second Division. Stan Mortensen described Soo as being 'incapable of a clumsy moment', so whilst his name may look out of place in this XI, rest assured that Frank Soo would not have looked out of place in any side.

One perhaps somewhat notable omission from this XI, either as a wing-half or as a centre-half, is Billy Wright. Neil admired Wright, who featured in every one of his 27 England caps, but more for his mentality and attitude than sheer ability. That is not to say he didn't think Wright was a good player, far from it, just not quite in that very top bracket. As Neil put it, 'I cannot rank Billy with greats like Busby, Mercer or Charles.' It was often said that if Neil hadn't gone to Colombia, it would have been him and not Wright who became the first player to reach 100 caps, and Wright would rarely have played for England.

It wasn't a sentiment that Neil got on board with. Although he would obviously have kept his place at centre-half, Billy Wright was a half-back when Neil left for Bogotá, so Neil logically pointed out that Wright would simply have stayed at right-half rather than moving to centre-half, and the two would have continued playing for England together. Wright himself did include Neil in his 'England Dream Team', selected during the 1960s, describing Neil as 'a superb stylist with an instinctive positional sense'.

The inside-forward position, which is next up, is one that has enjoyed something of a renaissance in recent years, albeit with that nomenclature rarely used. In the W-M formation, the dominant formation of Neil's era, a team has an inside-left and an inside-right. The position began to die out in the late 1950s and early 1960s when teams increasingly began to favour a back four over a back three, particularly the 4-2-4 formation that was seemingly perfected by the Brazilians. In more recent times, however, the 4-2-3-1 formation has become very popular among top teams. The two wide players in a 4-2-3-1 are often not what we might call 'true wingers', with offensive full-backs typically providing greater width, whilst all three players playing behind the forward will look to pick up pockets of space. It could be argued then, that what we see today is a return of the old inside-forwards: attacking midfield schemers who play in the 'hole' behind the centre-forward, using slick movement, good ball skills and vision to unpick the opposition's defence. In a sense, the 4-2-3-1, and formations similar to it, deploys three inside-forwards, and counteracting a trio of players who play those roles well has proved tricky.

THE FRANKLIN DREAM TEAM

Many of the most celebrated players of Neil's era were inside-forwards, and the position was a magnet for mavericks and entertainers. In that category, there can be few finer candidates than Len Shackleton. One of the most technically gifted players this country has ever produced, readers of this book will remember that Len was the man—or boy rather—who prevented Neil from winning schoolboy representative honours with his virtuoso display in a Midland vs the North game when the two were only fifteen years old. Shack went on to have a remarkable career, just as his talents suggested he would, but it could have been even better. He enhanced his reputation with Bradford Park Avenue before the war, and became the second-most expensive player in the history of British football when he joined Newcastle United, only to score a double hat-trick on his debut.

Of Len's talents, there could be no doubts, but his maverick personality and unique approach to the game didn't win everyone over. Neil may have regarded himself 'purely and simply as a public entertainer', but Shackleton took that to another level. It was entertainment above all else, and that included winning. Shackleton never won a trophy during his career and was capped only five times by England, three of those coming alongside Neil. 'The Clown Prince of Soccer', as many referred to him, tended to divide opinion. Many of his antics, such as sitting on the ball, playing one-twos with the corner flag and pretending to comb his hair whilst on the ball, were not remotely beneficial to his team, but that ought not detract from Shackleton's genuine ability. He had incredibly close control, laser-like accuracy when passing or shooting, and the ability to send defenders one way or another with the subtlest of shimmies.

One of the reasons why the FA could afford to restrict a maverick like Shackleton to only five caps is because they weren't exactly short of quality inside-forwards, and just as the England selectors tended to do, Neil didn't include Shackleton in his final

XI. Shack may miss out, but another Sunderland legend does not. At inside-right Neil went for the silver-haired genius that was Raich Carter. The only footballer to win an FA Cup before and after the war, Raich lost his best years to WWII, but the country saw more than enough of him to know they had witnessed a special talent.

Carter was also an entertainer who loved to play up to the crowd. During his time at Hull City, he once left the field and sat in the stands momentarily after the referee made what he deemed to be an unjust decision. However, Carter was also ruthlessly efficient when it mattered, and he captained Sunderland to a First Division title at the age of twenty-three. Stanley Matthews described Raich as his 'ideal partner', and the partnership of Carter at inside-right and Matthews at outside-right would strike fear into any opposition. Raich was a supremely intelligent footballer whose movement and dribbling prowess beguiled defenders. His understanding and technique were second to none; every move was thoughtful, measured and precise, which would be the blueprint were Neil Franklin creating a perfect footballer.

Partnering the great Raich Carter at inside-forward is Wilf Mannion. Matthews described Mannion as 'the Mozart of football', and just as it was with a young Wolfgang, young Wilf's talent were obvious from an early age. He looked as though he had been born with a ball at his feet, as he beat players with such grace and skill. They called him 'Golden Boy' for more than just his distinctive blond hair, and it is testament to his ability that Neil left out the likes of Don Revie, Stan Mortensen, Jimmy Hagan and Peter Doherty, all of whom he regarded as top-class players, in favour of Mannion.

The wingers are rather more straightforward, although we ought to mention Scotland's wide stars Willie Waddell and Billy Liddell, both of whom Neil was quick to praise. However, he thought even more highly of their English counterparts. The right-wing spot is the most predictable inclusion in the 'Franklin XI', naturally going to Stanley Matthews. Stan requires little intro-duction, since we have already discussed Neil's opinion of him as both a player and a person at length. To quote Neil, 'Unreservedly, I say that Stanley Matthews is the greatest player I have ever seen. His inclusion in this team is as guaranteed as it is that the oppo-sition's left-back wouldn't be getting any sleep the night before playing us.'

On the left flank is another legend of the game, Sir Tom Finney. Some felt that Finney was an even finer footballer than Matthews, but whilst Neil would have none of that, he still con-sidered him to be the second-best wide player he ever came across. Finney was of course an outside-right for Preston North End, where he enjoys near-mythical status, but the presence of Stanley Matthews saw him spend the majority of his England career on the left, and that's the case once more here. Neil described Finney as a 'serious sort of footballer', who was 'equally capable on either flank'. A brilliant dribbler who knew where the back of the net was, Neil wrote that, 'Tom in his prime was too good a player to leave out.'

Finney played in the 1950, 1954 and 1958 World Cup finals with England, scoring 30 goals from 76 caps for his country. There are few clubs so synonymous with a single player as Preston North End are with Tom Finney. Having helped the club win a Second Division title in 1951, they were never relegated from that point on with Finney in the side, finishing second twice, third once, and reaching the final of an FA Cup. He retired at the age of 38, hav-ing scored 21 goals in his final season. Preston were relegated in their first campaign without him. It's difficult to overestimate his influence at Deepdale.

So the wingers were always a pretty sure-fire thing, but the real headaches arrive with the last spot in this XI . . . the centre-forward. Whoever was at the apex of this side should get chances aplenty, and Neil played both with and against a number of strikers who knew how to put the ball in the back of the net. When he first came through at the Victoria Ground, Stoke had a very special centre-forward of their own—Freddie Steele. An explosive centre-forward, Steele had a frightening burst of pace over short distances, a tremendous leap and a bullet of a header. Stanley Matthews described him as 'lethal, clinical and merciless' in the penalty box, and he scored eight goals from six caps for England. That's not enough to make the 'Franklin XI' though, such was the plethora of options at Neil's disposal.

We start with some of the less well-known strikers who Neil held in high regard, and there is no finer example of such a player than Roy Swinbourne. A one-club man, Swinbourne spent his entire career, which ended prematurely due to injury at twenty-eight, playing for Wolverhampton Wanderers in the First Division. Neil's own bio of Swinbourne stated that, 'He is tall, beautifully built and he moves with the speed and grace of a gazelle', adding, 'On top of that he is as good a goal maker as a goal taker.' He scored 107 goals in 211 top-flight games for Wolves, but never won a full cap for England. No stat better displays England's strength in attack at the time than that.

A fellow star of the West Midlands who won little international recognition was Ronnie Allen. A daintier forward, Neil likened Allen to the prolific Scot Lawrie Reilly. Both players were not so much out-and-out centre-forwards, with Allen even known to play on the wing at times, but both had goal-scoring records that were the envy of front men up and down the country. Whether Neil was facing Allen against West Brom in the First Division or Reilly against Scotland in an international, he considered both players to be tricky customers who were difficult to pick up.

THE FRANKLIN DREAM TEAM

Franklin had similar praise for Roy Bentley, who was arguably better at inside-forward than he was at centre-forward. Bentley was tidy on the ball, had a cannon of a shot and a gigantic leap. Those type of centre-forwards, like Allen and Bentley, who relied more on speed of mind and feet, were far from typical in Neil's day. The predominant style of centre-forward was a big, bustling menace who could hit and head a ball a ball with power and accuracy, never giving his opponent a minute's rest.

In that discipline, there are few finer examples than Jock Dodds. You'll remember Dodds from his wartime appearances for Scotland or perhaps his work as an agent of Millonarios in Bogotá earlier in this book, but we are yet to deal with his talents as a player. A pre-war sensation who was thirty-one when the conflict came to an end, he was still prolific with Everton and Lincoln City in the mid–late 1940s. Dodds was not the most graceful of forwards, but you'd always rather have him in your team than playing against you.

He was the first centre-forward Neil faced as England's centre-half, and you could barely wish for a more brutal baptism of fire. As Neil put it, 'Dodds was three stones heavier than I was, and he loved to use his weight, although, and let me emphasize this, he used it fairly.' Neil described Dodds as 'the fiercest-looking centre-forward I have ever known.' Some described Dodds as a dirty player, but it wasn't a sentiment Neil agreed with, and although he may not have fitted the purist Franklin philosophy, Neil made certain allowances for centre-forwards who averaged better than a goal every other game.

Another prolific centre-forward in the Dodds-mould was Nat Lofthouse. A few years younger than Neil, Nat was only twenty when he played against Franklin in that fateful 1946 FA Cup replay that ended in tragedy at Burnden Park. He made his England debut four years later, and went on to score 30 goals from 33 caps for the Three Lions. Going up against Nat Lofthouse was like going into battle, and you knew you were in for ninety minutes of restless, rumbustious 'fun'. Neil described Lofthouse as 'the hardest centre-forward to play against', and there can be little higher praise of a forward than that. Lofthouse was fast, strong, brilliant in the air and smart with his movement, but below is Neil Franklin's take on Nat Lofthouse's 'secret weapon' that set him apart from other centre-forwards.

'His [Lofthouse's] early upbringing was lacking in one department. Nobody ever told him how to tell when he was beaten, and to this very day Nat Lofthouse has gone through life completely incapable of seeing when someone has got the better of him. Maybe it is too late to complete his education now, but I wish someone would try.

'You take the ball off Nat, or intercept a pass meant for him, and justifiably you feel proud. But the next second, there is Nat challenging you. You can brush some players who challenge you off like a fly, but not Nat Lofthouse. He is tough and tenacious.

'If you do succeed in beating him a second time, you still cannot feel safe, because he will come at you again. And so it goes on. Nat Lofthouse never stops working and worrying, never lets you relax for a second.

'This is a great bogey for defenders, who, just like everyone else, like that extra split second to gather their wits. But Nat Lafthouse never gives you any time at all. He is always there, always working, always harrying. There isn't a centre-forward in the business who can worry so many defenders into so many errors as Nat Lofthouse.'

Nat Lofthouse is to Bolton Wanderers what Tom Finney is to Preston North End. To this day, he remains the club's all-time leading scorer, having bagged 285 goals in 503 appearances. He is England's sixth-highest scorer of all time, and everyone who has scored more than him racked up at least half a century of caps, compared to his thirty three. Lofthouse undoubtedly came close to making the 'Franklin XI', whilst fellow physical centre-forward Trevor Ford also warrants a mention, as does Newcastle United great Jackie Milburn, but neither quite make the cut.

One man who stands out in terms of his goal scoring even among the pantheon of greats we have just reeled off is Derek Dooley. Largely forgotten outside of his hometown of Sheffield, Dooley was a goal-getter almost without peer, and one of few men adored by the fans of both Sheffield clubs. Never afraid to put his body on the line in the pursuit of scoring yet another goal, it was that relentless appetite to score goals that cut his career so short. In a match away at Preston, Dooley suffered a leg break after colliding with the Preston goalkeeper George Thompson. Gangrene set in, and whilst he survived after his life had appeared to be in serious danger, his leg had to be amputated and his career was ended shortly after his 23rd birthday.

The season before his injury, Dooley had scored 46 goals in 30 league games for Sheffield Wednesday, inspiring them to a Second Division title. The goals showed no signs of drying up in the First Division prior to his career-ending injury, and he retired prematurely with a record of 62 goals from 61 league games. The red-haired forward, who the press nicknamed 'Deadshot Derek', scored every type of goal. Neil Franklin even felt he could have been the man to break Dixie Dean's record for the most goals in a top-flight season. We are now ninety years on from Dean's record-breaking campaign, and no one has done what Neil felt Derek was capable of. Dooley went on to manage Sheffield Wednesday before holding a number of roles at Sheffield United.

There is a reason why technicians like Reilly, grafters like Lofthouse and goal-scoring machines like Dooley all missed out on the 'Franklin XI', and that is because Neil felt one man combined the roles of all three. That man was Tommy Lawton, formerly of

Everton, Chelsea and England, among others. Lawton was a football all-rounder. He had all the classical traits of a centre-forward: he was big and tough, had a belting shot with either foot and was a menace in the air. What set Tommy apart was the way he twinned those skills with fantastic close control and the ability to create goals as well as simply scoring them, whether that be for himself or his teammates.

Lawton began his career with Burnley, where he became the youngest forward in Football League history aged 16 and 174 days when he made his debut. His extraordinary promise prompted the Everton committee to bring him to Goodison Park, where he had an ageing Dixie Dean to tutor him. When Dean left the club in 1937, Lawton proved himself to be a more than adequate replacement, averaging a little under a goal a game and helping the Toffees win the last pre-war First Division title.

He became Britain's first £20,000 footballer in 1947, aged twenty-eight, when he left Chelsea for Third Division South side Notts County. He led the line for England when the national team reached the pinnacle of its powers in 1948, but that was also his final year as an England international, bowing out with a record of 22 goals from 23 caps. Put simply, Tommy was a player Neil held in the highest regard. He wrote of his former England teammate, 'Even in the best of players you can usually spot a flaw, but Tommy Lawton baffles me in that respect as effectively as he has baffled me on the field.' The thinking man's centre-forward, it's little wonder Neil plumped for Lawton up top. Tommy was an intelligent footballer, whose cunning movement and supreme ability both to feet and aerially, made him a constant thorn in defender's sides. Below is a more comprehensive summary of Tommy Lawton by Neil Franklin:

'Lawton was lucky enough to have everything a centre-forward needs. He had the height, the physique and the football brain. When you watched him play you could almost see him thinking.

He has lived for the game, studied it carefully, and is a master tactician. He was always the true leader of any attack, probing the weak spots in the opposing defence, and once he had found them, attacking them with all the skill and ferocity he could summon.'

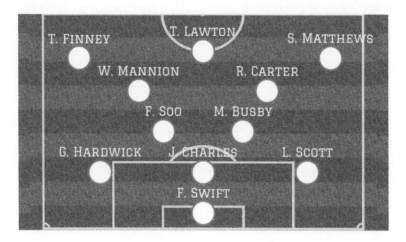

CHAPTER 18

Success and Conflict in Cyprus

Neil Franklin's career and armed conflict are inextricably intertwined. His early career was defined by the Second World War, robbing him of six years in the Football League but fast-tracking his first-team opportunities. His route to Colombia was paved by a brutal and bloody civil war which made living in the country a real struggle. Now, as we come to Neil's transition from player to manager, he would still find the irrepressible force of conflict lurking around the corner.

Having ended his career at Sankeys in 1962, aged forty, management seemed like the logical next step for Neil Franklin. He had gained managerial experience at Stockport, Wellington and Sankeys, managing at both first-team and reserve-team level, and his love of the game was undying. However, a transition into management, at a decent level at least, would not be easy. Although Neil was a former England international whose play had attracted particular praise for his intelligence and understanding on the pitch, he still had a blotted copybook. It may have been more than a decade since his misbegotten two-month stay in Bogotá, but no one in football had forgotten about it. It's difficult to stress just how big a story it was at the time, and Neil Franklin was not just going to walk into a Second Division job as Raich Carter had done at Hull City.

By the early 1960s, Neil had ended his association with the Bell & Bear public house in Shelton, and was looking for permanent work in football management. In May 1959, with tensions flaring at Stockport and Neil's time with the club drawing to a close, the *Daily Herald* newspaper reported that he had applied for the managerial post at Leeds United. The job went to Jack Taylor though, and over the next few years no Football League clubs approached Franklin.

In February 1963, however, an interesting proposal arrived at the door of Neil Franklin. It came from APOEL of Nicosia in Cyprus. APOEL were an amateur club, but they had just finished second in the Cypriot First Division, and had some rather illustrious former managers. Head coaches didn't tend to hang around long at APOEL; they had been through nine in the previous ten years before approaching Neil, which may seem like the norm today, but it would have been highly irregular for a club to have done that in England in the 1950s or 60s.

Those nine included a couple of big names though, like Béla Guttmann, the great Hungarian head coach who would go on to lead Benfica to consecutive European Cup triumphs in the 1960s. Another was Jesse Carver, the most recent incumbent of the role before they came knocking for Franklin. Carver was an Englishman, born in Liverpool, and he turned out for Blackburn and Newcastle in his playing days. His managerial career took him across the continent, earning him many plaudits, lucrative salaries and jobs at some of Europe's top clubs. APOEL were the last club Carver managed, arriving in Nicosia with the experience of having managed the likes of Inter Milan, Juventus and the Netherlands national team.

The omens were good, but the last time an unusual overseas proposal arrived at Neil Franklin's home in Staffordshire, things hadn't quite panned out as he would have hoped. A little older and a little wiser, this time Franklin flew over to the Cypriot capital before signing on any dotted lines. He travelled to the historic

Hellenic city on his own and was suitably convinced that this wouldn't be a repeat of Bogotá, and he agreed terms with the club.

Football in Cyprus, even at the highest level, remained largely amateur up until the 1990s, and Neil would find the standard of training and 'professionalism' to be far poorer than in the English non-league game. He was, however, pleasantly surprised by the technical ability of many of the players he inherited. If their fitness and commitment could be improved, it seemed he had a talented group at his disposal.

Neil had arrived at an exciting time for Cypriot football. Despite having been founded in 1948, the Cyprus Football Association only became UEFA-affiliated in 1962. As a result, the 1963–64 season was the first in which Cypriot clubs would be admitted to European competitions. In the previous season, under Jesse Carver, APOEL had finished as runners-up, so title winners Anorthosis Famagusta would be entered into the European Cup, whilst APOEL would go into the European Cup Winners' Cup thanks to their success in the Cypriot Cup.

The tournament was in its infancy, this being just its fourth edition, but the quality was very high. Spain would be represented by Barcelona, Germany by Hamburg, Scotland by Celtic, and England by Manchester United. Thankfully for Neil, they dodged those giants in the First Round, instead being drawn against Norwegian outfit SK Gjøvik-Lyn. They too were making their European football debut, although, unlike Cyprus, other Norwegian clubs like Fredrikstad and Lyn had previously competed. With that being said, those Norwegian teams had played four games between them, losing on every occasion by at least a four-goal margin.

The first leg took place on 8 September 1963, and on a hot Sunday afternoon at the GSP Stadium, APOEL put the Norwegians to the sword. Takis Chailis hit a hat-trick, with Nikos Agathokleous, Marios Papallos and Nikos Kantzilieris also getting themselves on the scoresheet. It was a day of firsts, and victory had been achieved in emphatic fashion. Since the title winners Anorthosis Famagusta didn't play their first game until three days later, APOEL became the first Cypriot team to play in a European competition. Naturally, they also became the first Cypriot team to win in a European competition, a feat that wouldn't be repeated until Omonia beat Waterford of Ireland in 1972. What's more, since no Greek team had ever won a European Cup Winners' Cup game, Neil Franklin had also guided APOEL to the first win in the competition for any Hellenic side.

Three weeks later, APOEL headed to the town of Gjøvik for the return leg. Defender Savvas Partakis scored the only goal of the game, giving APOEL a resounding 7-0 aggregate lead. It was a great moment for Neil and his players, but the Second Round promised to be an entirely different proposition. The minnows had been dumped out in the First Round, and APOEL were now drawn against Sporting Clube de Portugal. One of Portugal's so-called 'big three', they had won the Taça de Portugal to qualify for the European Cup Winners' Cup the previous season.

The Portuguese game had come a long way in the very short space of time since Neil had beaten their national team 10-0 with England in 1948. Inspired by Eusébio, who was arguably the best player in Europe at the time, Benfica had put an end to Real Madrid's dominance in the European Cup with back-to-back wins, as well as reaching three consecutive finals.

It looked to be an absolute mismatch between APOEL's amateurs and Sporting's highly regarded stars, and that's exactly how it turned out. Neil likened taking his APOEL players to Lisbon to 'taking children on a school trip'. They were all very giddy and excitable, and within seven minutes they were 2-0 down. Neil got no favours off the English referee James Finney, and by the time the rout was over, Angolan forward Mascarenhas had six, his strike partner Ernesto Figueredo had three, and Sporting had sixteen. Midfielder Solis Andreou got one back for APOEL, but the final score of 16-1 was pretty disheartening, especially since it came two years before UEFA introduced the 'Away Goals Rule' in the competition . . .

APOEL put up a bit of a braver fight in the second leg, only losing 2-0 this time, although one wonders whether the opposition began to take pity on them. The final score on aggregate was 18-1, and at the time of writing, it remains the heaviest defeat inflicted on a team in the history of European competition. In just a few months, Neil Franklin had set numerous firsts and records. Whether they were for good or bad, yet again things were rarely dull for Neil Franklin. If it were any consolation, Sporting went on to thump a Manchester United team containing George Best, Bobby Charlton and Denis Law 5-0 in the next round (6-4 on aggregate), beat Lyon in the semi-finals and MTK Budapest in the final to win that year's competition.

Gratefully, APOEL faced rather more modest opposition in the league, which had started pretty well for Neil. His first seven games had yielded five wins, one draw and one defeat. The club sat second in the league, one point behind the unbeaten leaders, AC Omonia. All Neil's hard work was to be in vain though, since a crisis in the region was on the horizon.

Cyprus had been invaded by the Ottoman Empire in 1570, and by 1571 they had conquered the island from the Venetians. The country lies just over 40 miles south of Turkey, and the Ottomans remained in control for the next 307 years, during which time more than 30,000 Turkish mainlanders settled there. That created two distinct ethnicities on the island: the Turkish-Cypriots and the Greek-Cypriots. Britain had annexed Cyprus from Turkey in 1914, but in 1960, the occupation ended and the Republic of Cyprus was proclaimed. By this time, tensions between Turkish-Cypriots and Greek-Cypriots had already begun to rise. In June 1958, there had been a bombing at the Turkish Embassy in Nicosia. Although the explosion was later reported to have been carried out by the Turks themselves in order to accelerate tensions, that's exactly what happened, as Turkish-Cypriots began rioting and people on both sides began selling their homes, creating de facto segregation between the two ethnic groups.

The new constitution of the Republic of Cyprus had guaranteed the Turkish-Cypriots would get vice-presidency, three out of ten ministerial posts and 30 per cent of jobs in the public sector, as well as an equal number of judges in the Supreme Court. A number of Greek-Cypriots took a poor view of the constitution, since Turkish-Cypriots made up only 18 per cent of the population, and Greek-Cypriots contributed more than 90 per cent of all taxes.

He may not have known it, but when Neil Franklin arrived in Nicosia in 1963, the tensions in Cyprus were just about at boiling point. In November 1963, the President of the Republic of Cyprus, Archbishop Makarios III, proposed thirteen amendments to the constitution, which would reduce Turkish-Cypriot voting power and presence in judicial, military and civil service positions. Naturally, the alterations weren't universally popular, and they brought the two already polarised factions closer to conflict.

Although violence is generally considered to have begun on the night of 20 December 1963, in truth, it had started shortly after Makarios's proposals. It was on that night, however, that the violence reached a crescendo. In the early hours of 21 December, a Greek-Cypriot police officer shot and killed a Turkish-Cypriot man and woman who had refused to present their identification papers having been stopped in their cars. Almost forty-eight hours passed without further incident, but on the night of the 22nd, gunshots rang out in Nicosia. It was the beginning of months of violence on the island. Some Turkish-Cypriot mosques were desecrated, whilst others were used to fire machine guns from. Mass graves containing the corpses of Turkish-Cypriots who had been declared missing and presumed dead over this period were later discovered. More than 500 people are believed to have been killed in the multiple conflicts in total, with Turkish-Cypriots suffering the most casualties and fatalities on this occasion, with a further 25,000 forced into abandoning their homes.

The events of 20–21 December 1963 and the days that followed became known as 'Bloody Christmas', but Neil Franklin had left Nicosia prior to that eruption of violence. When Makarios had put forward his proposals, conflict seemed inevitable, and tremors could already be felt around the country. APOEL advised Neil that it might not be safe for him to stay in Cyprus. The club were no strangers to the island's social and political upheaval. Back in the mid-1950s, APOEL had gone from finishing second to finishing last in the Cypriot First Division, as so many of their players were unavailable due to being active members of the nationalist guerrilla organisation EOKA.

Thankfully, Neil heeded the club's advice, and his contract was terminated at APOEL. The league season was suspended after seven games, with the club in second place. He left having made history, for both good and bad results, but he had also won his first piece of silverware in management. In the Pakkos Shield, now known as the Cypriot Super Cup and the Cypriot equivalent of the FA Community Shield, Neil guided APOEL to a 1-0 victory over reigning champions Anorthosis Famagusta. It was APOEL's third appearance in the Pakkos Shield, but the first from which they emerged victorious.

Conflict continued in Cyprus, as Turkey intervened in 1964 and eventually launched a full-scale invasion in 1974. After around a month of fighting, a ceasefire was declared with Turkish forces having taken control of approximately 36 per cent of Cyprus. To this day, the island remains divided, with a so-called 'Green Line' guarded by UN forces separating Northern Cyprus from the rest of the island. Football resumed as normal the following season, and APOEL won the league title. The following year, Gyula Zsengellér, the famous Hungarian centre-forward who had been one of the

European success stories of the El Dorado era in Colombia, took over as first-team manager. As I write, APOEL are ranked 50th by UEFA's club coefficients, ahead of Feyenoord, Valencia and both AC Milan and Inter Milan. In 2012, the club reached the quarter-finals of the Champions League, where it took Real Madrid to halt their European dreams.

Whilst Neil had been managing in Cyprus, the *Stockport Advertiser* reported that he had been contacted by his former club Stockport County regarding their managerial vacancy. Neil remained in Nicosia up until the end of November, though. His former Hull City teammate Trevor Porteous got the manager's job at Edgeley Park, but it wouldn't take long for Neil to take up his first official managerial post in the Football League.

Upon his return from the Mediterranean island, Franklin featured in a brief interview in the *Daily Mirror*, when he was quoted as saying, 'It's great out there,' adding, 'Whisky at 14s a bottle, sunshine all day, tax-free cars and plenty of bathing. But the thousands of British soldiers all miss the same thing—Soccer on a Saturday afternoon. Without it, they're lost.'

Clearly Neil found the weather and locals to be more hospitable in Nicosia than Bogotá, but his experiences would have been very different had he stuck around for another month. Despite finding them to be ill-disciplined and frustrating at times, Neil did develop a rapport with the APOEL players during his time there, and he would later return to Nicosia to catch up with his former charges, although he never returned in a professional capacity.

CHAPTER 19

Yo-Yoing with the U's

Neil barely had time to unpack his suitcase in Stoke-on-Trent before being on the move once more. During the final days of October 1963, Benny Fenton had left Colchester United to join Leyton Orient. Following Fenton's departure from Layer Road, the U's were on the lookout for a new manager, and Neil's return from Nicosia proved to be excellent timing.

By the last week of November, newspapers were reporting that Neil Franklin would be the next Colchester United manager. On 5 December 1963, speculation turned to confirmation, with Neil appointed as manager by long-time club chairman Bill Allen. Colchester had offered Neil a salary of £1,650, along with a Ford Corsair to help him get about and a clubhouse for him to live in; as well as generously offering to reimburse the roughly £90 airfare Neil had spent to get back to England from Cyprus. For the first time in Neil's life, he was employed by an English club that was south of Leicester. He arrived at a well-placed Colchester side who were sat 10th in the Third Division, level on points—albeit having played two extra games—with his former club Hull City.

In Bobby Hunt and Martyn King, the club had two prolific centre-forwards whose goal-scoring form ought to have ensured there were no fears of relegation at Layer Road at the very least. The Essex-based outfit were playing at the highest level in their history, and averaging just over 5,000 through the turnstiles for home games. They had finished the previous season in 12th place, although it had been a particularly congested bottom half of the table. Despite their commendable position in the table, only two teams had conceded more goals than them in the entire league, and no one outside of the relegation places had a worse goal difference.

It would be fair to say then, that the U's were something of a mixed bag, but it was a good platform for Neil Franklin's first managerial position in the Football League. A bumper crowd of 6,481 turned out as he made his managerial bow at Layer Road for an FA Cup Second Round tie against Queens Park Rangers. Franklin only met his players on the day of the game, and with little time for direction from their new boss, the U's were beaten 1-0.

Neil's first league game was a trip to Oakwell, where the team drew 1-1. A week later, a Bobby Hunt penalty secured a second consecutive 1-1 draw, this time at home to Hull City. In the programme notes for that game, Neil opened with a paragraph reading, 'COLCHESTER for promotion—why not? Football is a strange and fascinating game, and while you cannot command success, 100 per cent effort goes a long way towards progress.'

On Boxing Day 1963, Colchester made it three unbeaten and Neil oversaw his first win as U's manager, as trusty forwards Hunt and King both found the back of the net in a 2-1 win against Reading. Neil's first league defeat came in the final game of 1963, and it was a real corker for the neutral. In the U's second game in three days against Reading, a veritable goal glut ensued at Elm Park. Colchester could have drawn the game, but two own goals courtesy of John Fowler and Keith Rutter saw Reading win 5-3.

It was early days, but Neil was already seeing why Colchester's front three were so celebrated in the historic market town. Bobby Hunt was arguably the pick of the bunch. Colchester-born, he had joined the club as an apprentice before being handed his debut in March 1960 as a 17-year-old. He started the game and scored at home to York City, and that set the tone, averaging better than a goal every other game in the club's blue and white stripes. Hunt hit 40 goals in 47 games as an 18-year-old, and like all fans, the

Colchester United faithful were overjoyed to be witnessing a local lad doing so well.

Picture their shock then, when three months into his new job, Neil Franklin sells their star man to Northampton Town. That's exactly what happened in March 1964, with Hunt having scored 23 goals in 38 games in the season at that point. The fee was reported to be at least £15,000, possibly close to £20,000, but that was little consolation to the U's fans. It was a sign of things to come, as Neil Franklin wasted no time ringing the changes at Layer Road.

The U's finished the season in 17th place, a run of just one win from their final 13 games seeing them finish four points worse off than the previous season. Bobby Hunt ended the season as the club's top scorer, despite having departed in March, although he would pick up a serious injury requiring a cartilage operation the following December, and was never quite the same player again.

The highlight of the season was probably a 4-0 win away at Neil's former club Crewe, which came just before Hunt's departure.

The following summer, Franklin took to the Colchester United squad like a bulldozer to a decrepit old building. Those fans who had been irked by Bobby Hunt's departure would be rubbing their eyes in disbelief in October 1964, when his strike partner Martyn King left for Wrexham. King hadn't been born in Colchester, but he did begin his professional career there. He was a well-rounded centre-forward who was a real natural in front of goal, and despite being the club's standout player following Hunt's departure, King was one of only a few part-time first-team players at Layer Road. With 132 goals from 212 league outings, King still stands to this day as the U's all-time leading scorer in the league.

He was sold to Wrexham for just £3,000, although former Welsh youth international Tecwyn Jones joined Colchester as part of that deal. Supporters were also aghast when Colchester United legend and fan favourite Peter Wright wasn't retained, aged thirty, with the same fate also befalling experienced wing-half

Roy McCrohan. Keith Rutter, who had been brought in for £4,000 and appointed club captain by former boss Benny Fenton, didn't get on with Neil, so he joined Romford on a free transfer. The U's reportedly turned down a £4,500 mid-season bid from Nottingham Forest for goalkeeper George Ramage, only for the player to be released two months later. All in all, eleven players departed Layer Road that season, in addition to the duo of Bobby Hunt and Pat Woods who had been sold in Neil's first half season.

We are used to wholesale changes at football clubs today, with managers coming and going so regularly and all wanting to bring in their own men and implement their own ideas. Even today though, twelve signings and eleven departures in your first full season would be shocking. Back in the 1960s, with significantly thinner squads and far greater consistency and longevity, it was practically unheard of.

Replacing the club's two star centre-forwards and a fan favourite who would later be celebrated with a statue at the ground was not going to be a simple task. For one thing, it cost Neil an awful lot of goodwill from supporters, and that would be reflected in the gate receipts. Franklin wanted to bring in footballers who could play the game the way he felt it ought to be played. Colchester may have been in the Third Division, but Neil didn't see that as an excuse not to play football. With that being said, quality ball-players were not available in abundance in England in the 1960s, especially for the boss of a Third Division club operating on a shoestring budget.

It should be noted that in his first season and a half at Layer Road, Neil Franklin brought in £21,000 in player sales, yet the club only re-invested a little over £3,000 on bringing players in during the same period. A struggle, perhaps, was inevitable. Still, Neil soon set about bringing in players. He had made just one signing in his first half season, Derek Trevis on a free transfer from Aston Villa, who proved to be a shrewd signing over the next five years.

During the summer, Neil brought in centre-forward Pat Connolly in an attempt to compensate for the goal-scoring prowess that had left the club. Pat was Staffordshire-born, had come through the youth ranks at Crewe and made a name for himself as a prolific scorer at non-league level with Macclesfield. Neil's son Gary was on the books at Macclesfield from 1963 to 1965, so Neil could get a good second opinion on Connolly's talents.

In one phone call we had, Gary fondly recalled a disgruntled Connolly half-jokingly telling him after being put through the rigours of pre-season training that his dad was a bastard. As well as Connolly, who Gary saw up close and personal at Macclesfield, Neil also had him take a look at a few other players for him. It was a family affair in the ersatz Colchester scouting network, which also included Neil's half-brother Len, who apparently had a good eye for a player despite not having played the game himself.

One notable arrival was Barrie Aitchison from Tottenham Hotspur. Aitchison was born in Colchester and came through the U's youth ranks before a move to Spurs. He spent ten years at Tottenham, but never made a single first-team appearance. He did enjoy success with the reserve side though, and a decade playing under Bill Nicholson ought to have ensured that he was more than just a bruiser.

The most expensive arrival was Arthur Longbottom, later known as Arthur Langley. A veteran inside-forward best known for his time with Queens Park Rangers, Longbottom had been top scorer at three different clubs, and he arrived from Oxford United for a fee of £1,500.

The season had begun in pretty miserable fashion, with only two wins from Colchester's opening sixteen matches. Furthermore, both those wins had come away from home, one against Port Vale and the other at Mansfield. Already disgruntled home supporters weren't getting a lot for their money then, and when Martyn King was sold at the start of October, the club occupied the relegation places, had yet to win a home game and had scored only three goals in six outings at Layer Road.

The end of September had been a really tough period for Neil. Forwards Mike Grice, Gareth Salisbury, Billy Stark and Barrie Aitchison were all sidelined at the same time, an injury crisis which prompted Franklin to look towards the transfer market. Funds were not freely available, so Ipswich Town wide man Noel Kearney arrived on trial. Kearney had had an impressive youth career at Ipswich Town, but never broke into the first team squad at Portman Road. He played three games for Colchester, and the club lost every one.

The first home win of the season did arrive in the second half of October against Bournemouth & Boscombe Athletic, but there were just 3,454 fans in attendance. Attendances were at an all-time low for the club since their admittance to the Football League in 1950. Having averaged more than 10,000 spectators in their very first campaign, their previous lowest turnouts had come in the 1960–61 season, when an average of just 4,962 turned up to watch the club's first relegation. Despite Neil Franklin's attempts to bring more considered and possession-based football to Essex, that record would be well-beaten in the 1964–65 season, the average figure at the end of the season standing at just 3,655. That wasn't much more than Macclesfield Town had been getting in the non-league game during Neil's time there, when the Silkmen averaged more than 3,000 in the 1960–61 season, with a seasonal record of 7,766 for an FA Cup game against Southport.

Gary recalls that Neil used to joke that people in Colchester had 'more interest in farming than football', and he could sometimes be found practically pleading fans to attend games and support the team in his programme notes. He was similarly unsubtle with the national press. In a September 1964 interview with the *Daily Mirror* regarding the contrast between the club's form at home and away, Neil was quoted as saying, 'The boys say they like playing away. They get a bit of atmosphere from the crowd—something that doesn't happen when we're at home.' Neil may have wanted fans to turn up in their droves, but in truth, everyone wants to watch a winning team, and Colchester weren't delivering on that front.

The goals had inevitably dried up following the departures of the club's centre-forwards, and a virtually brand-new set of players were trying to adjust to playing with one another and under a footballing philosophy that was alien to most of them. A footballing purist in the mould of a Cruyff or Guardiola, Franklin had Colchester players rather than Barcelona players at his disposal, and whilst he tried to implement his philosophy in phases, it was clearly a struggle for some of them. Just as Keith Goalen had said, one of Neil's great faults was assuming that everyone was as capable and composed as he was. It would have been fascinating to see how Neil Franklin would have got on with a top-class team, but in the Third Division with little investment, his approach could be accused of being idealistic.

He stuck to his guns, and over the festive period there were signs of improvement. Four wins from seven games brought the team to just one point from safety and provided cause for optimism. In the absence of Hunt and King, the duty of scoring goals fell largely on Billy Stark and Arthur Langley. Both players hit double figures, but neither threatened the division's top scorers chart in the way the aforementioned duo had done. Pat Connolly, having been brought in as King's replacement, managed only 7 goals from 21 outings before getting homesick and returning to the North West. From 70 goals scored in the 1963–64 season, Colchester managed a measly 50 in 1964–65, the second fewest in the division.

By the end of February, Colchester were one of five teams who had been cut adrift at the bottom of the Third Division, and four would be relegated. The club went unbeaten throughout March, going on a run of five games without defeat and winning three on the bounce. Unfortunately, fellow strugglers Walsall not only matched but bettered that form, going eight games without defeat and winning six. One of those wins came against Franklin's men, and that really knocked the wind out of the U's sails. They went on to lose their final five games, and their relegation to the Fourth Division was confirmed in Neil Franklin's first full season in charge of the club.

There was some respite for the Colchester United manager just a week after the season ended when he was invited to take part in a testimonial game. Over the years, Franklin featured in a whole host of benefit, testimonial and even mere Sunday league games. In fact, I'm not sure if he ever turned down the opportunity to put his boots back on 'one last time'. April 1965 was the most high-profile exhibition game he was ever involved in, however, as the great Stanley Matthews had finally decided to call time on his 33-year love affair with the game at the age of fifty. Incredibly, he was still playing in the top flight, having helped Stoke City to promotion from the Second Division two years earlier.

A sell-out crowd at the Victoria Ground was treated to a fantastic festival of football, as some of the game's greatest players of past and present, as well as the world's most august sports journalists, flocked to Staffordshire. Sir Stanley had arranged for two games to take place, one billed as the 'Post-War Favourites', featuring a who's who of Britain's finest retired players, and the other made up of current stars, advertised as 'Stan's XI vs an International XI'. Five of the International XI were Ballon d'Or winners, as were a couple of Stan's XI, including Matthews himself of course. The International XI boasted the likes of Lev Yashin, Alfredo Di Stéfano and Eusébio, whilst Stan's XI could call upon the many talents of Denis Law, Bobby Charlton and Jimmy Greaves.

The Post-War Favourites' match, which included many players far younger than Stan, highlighting his mind-boggling longevity within the game, boasted some equally illustrious names. Alongside Neil Franklin were the likes of Bert Trautmann, George

Hardwick, Nat Lofthouse, Don Revie and Tom Finney. Facing them would be the eclectic talents of Danny Blanchflower, Jimmy Dickinson and Jackie Milburn. Also playing for the opposition, who were marshalled by Walley Barnes, was that familiar face of Jock Dodds. Now aged forty-nine, the pace had deserted Dodds, but the battle certainly hadn't, and Neil Franklin would be tasked with containing the burly Scot for one last time.

Each team had just one reserve player who could be introduced at half-time, and in Neil's side it was his former Stoke and Macclesfield teammate Frank Bowyer. When the two teams adjourned to their dressing rooms at half-time, Bowyer asked if anyone was feeling the pace and could do with a break, a question which was met by eleven hands going up in the air! Time can be a cruel mistress to footballers, especially since this supporting act ahead of the afternoon's main event was only twenty minutes a half. The whole testimonial was watched live by 35,000 people at the Victoria Ground with more than 112 million tuning in via either TV or radio. Football's ultimate crowd-puller had done the trick once more in his final game.

After that though, it was back to Essex and back to reality for Neil Franklin. The following summer brought upheaval once more, and the money raised via player sales would never find its way into Neil's transfer coffers. He was still feeding off scraps in the transfer market, as eleven players were brought into the first team, only one of which required a fee. That one was John Hornsby, who arrived from non-league Evenwood Town with a hefty price tag of £25 and 5 shillings. The winger spent just a single season at Layer Road, during which time he made eleven appearances.

Neil's son, Gary, was once again able to offer his father some advice, this time regarding Peter Bullock, an inside-forward playing for Southend United. Born in Stoke-on-Trent, Bullock had been very highly regarded as a youngster. In 1958, he became Stoke

City's youngest-ever debutant and goal scorer in the same match, aged 16 years and 163 days, both are records which still stand. He went on to make 48 appearances, in which he scored 16 goals from inside-forward for the Potters, before the Second Division outfit cashed in and sold him to top flight Birmingham City for £10,000. In more than two seasons with Birmingham, Bullock made less than thirty appearances, eventually dropping down to the Third Division with Southend. Gary had gone to school with Peter, and he described him as a 'good ball-player'. Those three words were music to the ears of Neil Franklin, and he promptly brought Bullock to the club. It would prove to be an inspired signing. Bullock was still only twenty-three when he joined the club, and the former England youth international would display some of the form which had made him such a prospect during his early days in Staffordshire.

One signing which was of great disappointment to Neil Franklin was Jackie Bell. Neil went to great lengths to bring the former Newcastle United half-back to Layer Road. Bell had become one of the most expensive players in British football when he joined Norwich from Newcastle for £100,000 in 1962, so his arrival at Colchester in 1965 was seen as something of a coup. Through no fault of his own though, Bell's time with the U's was almost over before it had begun, with the midfielder discovering that he had diabetes and taking an early retirement on medical advice after just seven games.

In terms of outgoings, Billy Stark, who had formed Colchester's holy trinity alongside Martyn King and Bobby Hunt a couple of years earlier, became the last of the trio to depart. Stark had been the club's top scorer with 14 goals as they were relegated the previous season, but he would retain his Third Division status with a move to Luton Town, which involved the payment of £1,000 along with veteran forward Ted Phillips acting as a makeweight. The club's second-top scorer the previous season had been one of Neil's own signings, Arthur Longbottom, who scored 13 goals in all competitions. He also left the U's though, with Neil granting him permission to join Scarborough on a free transfer.

Thankfully, Colchester's third-top scorer from the previous season did remain with the club over the summer, although even that was a close-run thing! Derek Trevis's seven-goal haul from midfield was third only to Stark and Longbottom, and the U's had to rebuff interest from Second Division clubs following his impressive form. Trevis wasn't the only one: there were vultures circling around Mick Loughton following the club's relegation as well, with the defender having been transformed as a player under Neil Franklin.

Loughton was born in Colchester and he had been playing as an inside-forward in the club's youth ranks. Neil saw something in the youngster though, and he brought him into the first-team setup in 1964 and moved him to centre-half. It was a match made in heaven. Loughton became a regular in the U's defence, and Neil had himself something akin to a ball-playing centre-half. It's worth noting that Loughton went from being a first-team regular to being sold to non-league Brentwood Town the same year that Neil left the club.

This presented what some managers might have considered a selection dilemma for Neil Franklin, as one of his most accomplished and talented players was also a centre-half. The W-M formation had reigned supreme for so long in England, and although its dominance was just beginning to crack, it was still the prevailing system of Football League clubs. With Forbes and Loughton though, Neil Franklin began playing a back four with two centre-halves—or centre-backs—rather than one.

The back four was first introduced in the form of the 4-2-4 formation. The invention of the 4-2-4 can be credited to Hungary, Brazil or Russia, but even the success of the Brazilian national team at both the 1958 and 1962 World Cups with the system wasn't enough to convince everyone back in Blighty. Alf Ramsey was one of the first to adopt such an approach, and he had enjoyed much success with a type of 4-2-4, albeit far removed from Brazil's, at Ipswich Town.

Neil and Alf had played together in England's defence for a couple of years, and they were good friends. Gary recalled Neil staying in Alf's holiday home in Spain, and during their playing days, the pair shared similar footballing philosophies. Despite their similarities, there was one significant difference between Ramsey and Franklin. Ramsey was a pragmatist, whilst Franklin was an idealist, and Ramsey's pragmatism would become increasingly evident as his managerial career progressed and eventually when he became England manager.

Although Ramsey had certain ideas of how the game should be played, coming from a Tottenham family built on the philosophies of Peter McWilliam, Arthur Rowe and Bill Nicholson, he realised that playing that way in the Third Division South with third-tier players at Ipswich Town was unrealistic. That was where he began his managerial career back in 1955, and unlike Neil, he introduced his ideas very gradually. In the end, Ipswich never became a passing side akin to the Spurs environment that Ramsey had been brought up in. Instead, they were a highly efficient machine in which the whole was always greater than the sum of its parts.

Sir Alf guided the club to promotion from the Third Division South, promotion from the Second Division, and a First Division title in the club's first season at that level. He took over as England manager in 1963, and three years later, the country had won their first World Cup. Despite those incredible successes, England stumbled at subsequent tournaments; Ramsey's tactics were criticised at the 1970 World Cup and described as 'joyless' by well-known sports journalist Hugh McIlvanney at the 1972 European Championships, with England getting knocked out by West

Germany at both tournaments. He was sacked after England failed to qualify for the 1974 World Cup.

So although there were similarities in their early years, Ramsey's football went on to become everything Neil's was not. Alf's belief that it should only take three passes before your team was having a shot on goal, or his decision to play without wingers as they didn't contribute to enough phases of play, were utterly at odds with Neil's views on the game.

Not only did Neil play a back four, he encouraged his full-backs to bomb forward at every opportunity. Of course, this wasn't revolutionary in a global sense, but it was absolutely bizarre in England's fourth tier. Gary Franklin didn't manage to get down to Colchester to watch his dad's team play all that often, but when he did, he recalls opponents and spectators being baffled at the sight of essentially two attack-minded wing-backs playing in a back four. They ought not to have been so outraged: Brazil had just won consecutive World Cups with Nilton Santos and Djalma Santos doing just that. Okay, this wasn't Brazil, or the World Cup, it was Colchester United and the Fourth Division, but nowadays, virtually every full-back is required to have attacking attributes. In many cases, full-backs are little more than converted wingers who are occasionally asked to do a little bit of defending. That seems normal now, but when Neil was playing—and indeed, managing—the idea of a winger playing at full-back was almost as absurd as playing a centre-forward in net.

It took a long time for English football to accept that the game was changing, and latterly, had changed. For a long time, England programmes would do their utmost to somehow arrange the players Alf Ramsey had selected into a W-M formation, despite that bearing no resemblance to what the fans would see on the pitch. It was a similar story in the Football League. Below is an example of what I'm referring to, taken from a Doncaster Rovers' programme when they hosted the U's in December 1965, showing how they had Neil's team lining up:

Hornsby	Phillips	Stratton	Blackwood	Kaye
	Trevis	Loughton	Raine	
	Hall		Forbes	
		Buck		

As you can see, the programme lineups had Colchester playing a classic W-M, but you most likely already noticed some anomalies. They have Mick Loughton in his natural position of centre-half, but fellow centre-half Duncan Forbes appears to be playing at right-back. David Raine, who is displayed as a right-half, was in fact a right-back. If you drop him in at right-back and move Forbes infield alongside Loughton, it quickly becomes clear that it is a back four.

What was being described as the old W-M was far from it. In actuality, it was a very early 4-2-3-1, inasmuch as there was a back four, two half-backs or central midfielders, two wingers, one attacking midfielder and one centre-forward. However, even Neil himself would never have acknowledged that he was playing a 4-2-3-1. That system being recognised and referred to by that term didn't occur until the late 1980s at the very earliest, and most probably sometime later in Britain.

Whether it was the formation, the extra twelve months of getting his ideas across, the recruitment of his own players or just the drop in quality that follows a relegation, Franklin and his charges made a good start to the 1965–66 campaign. Following defeat on the opening day in Stoke-on-Trent against Port Vale, the club went six games unbeaten, a run which put them in the early promotion running.

Ted Phillips, who had arrived as part of Billy Stark's transfer to Luton Town, really hit the ground running at Layer Road. In his debut at home to Barnsley, the inside-forward bagged a hat-trick in a 4-0 win, with every one of his goals coming via his forehead. Phillips had formed one half of a formidable strike partnership under Alf Ramsey at Ipswich Town. Together with Ray Crawford, the duo had scored 33 and 28 goals respectively the season that the Tractor Boys won the First Division. Phillips wasn't the most complete of centre-forwards, but he knew how to hit a ball cleanly, firmly and accurately every time. Former teammate Jimmy Leadbetter said of him, 'He [Phillips] needed space, but if you could give him that and the ball, it was in the back of the net.' The 32-year-old had no trouble finding the back of the net in Essex either, scoring 8 goals in 12 games, before falling out with Neil and heading to Malta, where he briefly served as player-manager of Floriana FC.

Fortunately for Franklin, Phillips wasn't the only Colchester forward among the goals. Fellow summer signing Reg Stratton was proving a smart piece of business having arrived on a free transfer from Fulham. Stratton had a very impressive non-league career with Woking, where he scored and was on the winning team in front of 71,000 fans for an FA Amateur Cup final at Wembley. Capped by England amateurs, he was signed by Fulham in 1959, but he barely featured and scored only once in six years at Craven Cottage. His form at Colchester was similar to his non-league days though, bagging 21 goals in his debut season, 18 of which came in the league.

The U's went on another good run before Christmas, and they spent the festive period in the promotion places. Their home form that had been so disastrous the previous season, with Neil often coming to blows with the Colchester faithful, was the rock that their promotion push was being built upon. It took until the second half of February for the U's to lose their first home game, and slowly but surely, those disgruntled supporters were returning to Layer Road. From 3,634 the previous season, the average attendance rose to 5,225 for the 1965–66 campaign, with a season high of more than 10,000 turning out for a home game against Luton Town in April.

The 1965–66 season was a notable one as it was the first in which the Football League had sanctioned substitutions. At this time, however, a substitute could only be introduced if a player was injured and unable to continue. On 21 August 1965, Charlton Athletic stalwart Keith Peacock made history as the first Football League substitution, replacing the Addicks' injured goalkeeper Mike Rose after eleven minutes away at Bolton. The first official substitute in Colchester United history was full-back Ray Price, who Neil introduced following an injury to Ted Phillips.

Although the common consensus had been growing at such a rate that the eventual sanctioning of substitutions seemed inevitable, Neil Franklin had always been something of a sceptic—to put it mildly. He once wrote, 'Every so often the question of substitutes rears its ugly head, and I only wish that the next time such a thing happens someone chops off the head. For the people who are campaigning for substitutes are barking up the wrong tree. Yes, I know it is hard on a team that has a player injured during a game, but if you check up on these hard-luck stories you will find that the luck evens itself out during a season.' One of the reasons Neil resented the idea of substitutes was because he viewed being reduced to ten or even nine men as a challenge, and one which the game would be poorer without. His primary concern though, was the misuse of substitutes, which he himself had witnessed first-hand.

'In all the international games where no competition is at stake, substitution for injury is allowed, and I have seen the concession abused in a disgraceful manner. But who is to stop the abuse? Who can really say when a player is injured or when he has taken a dive on the order of the team manager? Surely we have not forgotten the comedy of the goalkeeper change when F.I.F.A. came to Wembley and drew 4-4 with England? Or when Hungary changed their goalkeeper for no apparent reason when leading 6-3 at Wembley? Or when they did the same thing when leading 7-1 in Budapest?'

Neil concluded by stating that, 'substitutes are as impossible as they are undesirable.' Whilst he may have been unusually conservative in his views on substitutions, he was quite right to spot the obvious dangers of managers misusing the rule for tactical reasons, and within a year the Football League had sanctioned tactical substitutions to avoid controversy. Today substitutes are as much a part of the game as goal kicks or injury time. The rules were expanded to allow two substitutes in 1987, and eventually on to the three substitutes from a seven-man bench that we are used to now, with FIFA currently experimenting with the option of a fourth substitute in a game that goes to extra time.

Having been sitting pretty just three points behind league leaders Tranmere Rovers with three games in hand on 25 December, there were some post-Christmas blues for the U's. Franklin's men went four games without a win, tasting defeat twice and slipping out of the promotion places. A Peter Bullock brace got the team back on track with a 2-1 win over Doncaster Rovers and an impressive run of form was to follow.

Eight wins from 11 games meant Colchester United occupied top spot in the Fourth Division when Harold Wilson came to power at the end of March. It was a run which included a 6-3 win over Bradford Park Avenue, a 3-0 win against Lincoln City, and a seasonal record attendance of over 10,000 at Layer Road for a 2-2 draw with Luton Town. Typically, though, Colchester saved their worst form for last, winning just three of their last twelve games. A return of just 13 points from a possible 36, including defeat on the final day away at Newport County, put the U's promotion hopes in doubt.

Neil must have been having flashbacks to Stoke's failed title bid of 1946–47 and the way in which it unravelled at Sheffield United. Colchester would have to wait fifteen minutes to discover their fate, with Luton Town only one point behind them, meaning a win for the Hatters against Chester would see Franklin's promotion plans foiled. After what was surely the longest quarter of an hour of Neil Franklin's life, the news came in from Cheshire: Chester and Luton had drawn 1-1, Colchester had been promoted on goal average. Their points tally of 56 had been matched by both Luton and Tranmere, but the U's had the best defensive record in the division, resulting in a superior goal average.

Brian Hall picked up the Player of the Year accolade at the club's end of season awards. Signed on a free transfer from Mansfield Town the previous year, Hall had spent the season playing as an attacking left-back. Talented and technical on the ball, Neil had encouraged Hall to get forward whenever possible, and his award could be seen as vindication of Neil Franklin's risky, ambitious and often criticised approach at Layer Road.

Over the summer, whilst Colchester United prepared for life back in the Third Division and Americans went ballistic at John Lennon's 'more popular than Jesus' quote, England were busy winning the World Cup under Neil's former teammate and pal Alf Ramsey. England's 'Wingless Wonders' won the tournament for the first time on home soil, defeating West Germany 4-2 in extratime in the final, as Geoff Hurst became the first man to score a hat-trick in a World Cup final. The country has neither won nor hosted a World Cup since. England met West Germany in the quarter-finals in 1970, but were this time beaten in extra-time, before failing to qualify for the finals four years later. As I've mentioned, England's absence from the 1974 tournament in West Germany cost Sir Alf Ramsey his job, and following his meteoric rise, he never held a permanent position within football management again.

It was a slightly less chaotic summer at Layer Road and for the first time on Neil Franklin's watch, the club spent more than they received in the transfer market. They still only made one substantial signing, and that was the arrival of Ken Hodgson from Bournemouth & Boscombe Athletic for £4,000. Ted Phillips departed for Malta, whilst Barrie Aitchison and Mike Grice were both released from their contracts. Experience arrived one month into the season in the form of Dennis Mochan, a Scottish full-back who had just racked up more than a century of top flight league appearances at Nottingham Forest. The only other signings that summer were two wingers, Johnny Martin from Aston Villa and Alan Shires from Southend United. Both players were still in their teens, and had played only one league game for their previous clubs.

Although the season started with a couple of disappointing and closely fought defeats to Middlesbrough and Shrewsbury, there was a feeling within the Colchester United camp that Franklin had assembled a good side, and they certainly didn't feel out of place in the Third Division. Results soon began to reflect this, as the club lost just one of their next ten games, a run which included a 5-0 win against Doncaster Rovers, who had won the Fourth Division title when the U's had been promoted the previous season. New signing Ken Hodgson was justifying his £4,000 fee, starting the season with 10 goals in 17 games. Hodgson wasn't the only one, both Reg Stratton and Peter Bullock regularly found themselves on the scoresheet, and for the first time since the departures of King and Hunt, Colchester were a team with goals in them.

Importantly, Franklin was also becoming more experienced as a manager. He still wanted to play good football, but he was becoming more conscious of players limitations and willing to tailor his tactics to their individual strengths. New signing Dennis Mochan told me, 'Neil never put you down, he'd just give you instructions, he was a great man manager,' adding, 'He was the best manager

I played under, he just loved to train with the ball, no silly messing about and running for no reason.'

One of the questions I was keen to ask Dennis, although he brought it up before I had time to ask it, was how involved Neil would be on the training ground. 'He always joined in training,' Dennis said. 'He had such strong legs, you could tell he played centre-half, and he'd always win any fifty fifties.' Derek Trevis had echoed such comments in an interview with the *Trinity Mirror* almost half a century earlier, telling the newspaper, 'While I never saw him [Franklin] at his peak for England and Stoke City, he was a marvellous centre-half. He used to join in our practice games and the way he used the ball was uncanny for a centre-half.'

Mochan painted a picture of Neil as a very personable and approachable manager who wasn't one to rant or rave regardless of how a game was going, in stark contrast to his successor. Of course, this fits in neatly with Neil's character anyway: he was a calm figure both on and off the pitch during his playing days, renowned for his composure and rarely losing his cool. The most agitated Neil got was when the game was in progress, since his inability to directly affect the pattern of play by actually pulling on a pair of boots and getting out there was a source of some frustration. In the dressing room though, he was a picture of calmness, always telling players how they could improve, rather than simply lambasting them for what they were doing wrong.

Colchester's form did waver a little after that good run, but they were still sitting pretty for a promoted side with incredibly limited resources, placed 13th in the league table at the start of the new year. Unfortunately, however, January and February were to bring the club's poorest form of the campaign. Six consecutive defeats dragged the club to within two points of the relegation zone, having played more games than all those below them, but still it seemed no panic set in, and the club somehow went the next six unbeaten, all but ensuring their safety by the end of March.

The league campaign may have been going well, but the U's were promptly dumped out of both cup competitions in rather emphatic style. Queens Park Rangers, who had put Neil's side out of the FA Cup with a 4-0 win in the First Round the previous season, were this time drawn against the U's in the First Round of the League Cup. A charismatic young centre-forward scored four goals on his own this time for Rangers, as they beat the U's 5-0 on this occasion. His name was Rodney Marsh, and although he didn't have his famous long blond hair at this time, he was well on his way to punk football stardom, scoring 44 goals in 53 games that season as QPR won both the Third Division and the League Cup.

Colchester's post-March form was a bit of a mixed bag as the season meandered to an end with no fears of relegation or hopes of promotion. It did at least end with a win, with a Peter Bullock hat-trick inspiring the team to a 3-2 success against Brighton. Those three goals took Bullock to 15 for the season, whilst Ken Hodgson bagged 16 and Reg Stratton was the U's top scorer with 24. Only seven teams scored more goals in the Third Division than Franklin's men, who ended the season 13th in what was considered to be an entertaining and successful campaign.

The mid-table finish was followed by a much quieter summer in terms of incomings and outgoing at Layer Road. Three of Neil's own signings, David Raine, Ray Price and South African goal-keeper Sandy Kennon were released, whilst the only other departure was Brian Westlake. The U's made a good profit on Westlake, who had joined the club only five months earlier, receiving a reported £5,000 fee from Belgian outfit Royal Daring Club de Bruxelles. It was four in and four out, with three players arriving on frees and one for a fee. Club legend John Fowler returned briefly to make three final appearances, Tommy McKechnie arrived from

Bournemouth to fill the attacking void vacated by Westlake, and Arsenal trainee Ernie Adams was brought in as Sandy Kennon's replacement. Colchester's sole transfer expenditure went on Terry Price, a diminutive winger who was signed from Leyton Orient for a fee of £2,000.

Away from football, it was also a significant summer for Neil Franklin. The summer of 1967 is often referred to as the 'Summer of Love', and it was for Neil, who married for the second time in September. It was on Braintree in Essex rather than the Haight-Ashbury district of San Francisco that Neil and his new wife Beryl descended when making their vows, but it was a summer of love nonetheless. Neil had separated from his first wife Vera around the time that he went to manage in Cyprus and met Beryl during his time in Essex.

The season began brightly, as the U's lost just two of their opening eleven games, with Peter Bullock getting among the goals once more. The club were swiftly dumped out of the League Cup however, losing 4-0 to divisional rivals Brighton & Hove Albion in August. The FA Cup started a little better, as the U's were once again paired with a fellow Third Division club. High-flying Torquay United were the opponents, and Franklin's men ended their cup dreams in a replay at Layer Road, with Derek Trevis scoring both goals in a 2-1 win.

On Christmas Day, Colchester were slap bang in the middle of the Third Division table, occupying 12th place. It looked like another season of consolidation, but the second half of the campaign was to bring joy in one competition but despair in another. The FA Cup Second Round brought about an all-Essex tie, as Colchester United were drawn against Chelmsford City. Chelmsford had applied to join the Football League nine times but had seen their applications rejected on each occasion, so they competed in the Southern League. They were among the most accomplished sides in the non-league game though, and a crowd of over

16,000 turned out at the New Writtle Street stadium for the match, which Colchester won 2-0.

The next round would be the biggest match of Neil Franklin's Colchester United tenure. The U's were handed a home tie against First Division side West Bromwich Albion. Spearheaded by the goals of Jeff Astle, the Baggies had reached Wembley finals in each of the past two seasons. Astle had been the prodigy of Neil's old England buddy Tommy Lawton at Notts County, before making a £25,000 move to the Hawthorns. Much like Lawton, Astle had a phenomenal ability when it came to heading a football, and although his international career never really took off, he became one of the greatest players and most prolific scorers in the history of West Bromwich Albion.

Colchester knew that man for man West Brom were a far superior outfit, but Neil Franklin had a plan to try and level out the gulf in class. Dennis Mochan recalls his manager telling the players, 'Don't give them time, they're used to having time.' That was Neil's game plan, he wanted to make use of the small pitch at Layer Road and constantly harry the West Brom players.

This attempt to unsettle their First Division opposition worked a treat, and Reg Stratton gave the U's a shock lead. Future England international Tony 'Bomber' Brown gave West Brom their equaliser, but Colchester nicked it in the final seconds . . . or so they thought. The U's last-gasp winner in the dying embers of the game looked to have confirmed a memorable cup upset, and Baggies centre-half John Talbut whacked the ball out of the ground in frustration. Amidst the celebrations though, the referee had spotted something he didn't like. He blew his whistle and the goal was disallowed. To this day, surviving players from both sides have no idea why the goal didn't stand.

In the replay four days later, the Colchester players were unable to replicate their first leg success. A combination of the larger pitch at the Hawthorns, the fact the Baggies now knew what to expect and Colchester's inevitably tired legs resulted in a comfortable 4-0 win for the home side, who went on to beat Southampton, Portsmouth, Liverpool, Birmingham City and Everton to win their first FA Cup title in front of 100,000 fans at Wembley. You could forgive Neil Franklin for feeling a touch of bitterness at the manner of Colchester's cup exit, especially as their opponents went on to lift the trophy at Wembley, but you would never have found any.

Besides, there was no time for Colchester to feel sorry for themselves. Since Christmas, when attention had been firmly focused on the FA Cup, with the team seemingly locked in mid-table obscurity, the wheels had somewhat fallen off in the league. The club recorded six straight defeats as unexpected relegation concerns began to surface.

Centre-forward Jim Oliver had been brought in for £2,000 from Brighton in January, but he failed to score a single goal in the fifteen outings between his arrival and the end of the season. After the U's lost 5-1 to Scunthorpe United, one of the few teams who were below them by this point, and Mansfield Town won on 11 March, Franklin's slide slipped into the relegation places for the first time. They would never climb back out of it. In fact, they didn't even manage to win another game. Between Christmas Day 1967 and the season finishing in May 1968, which constituted twenty-three games (exactly half a season), Colchester won just one game. Such a disastrous run comfortably wiped out the breathing room they'd built up in the first half of the campaign, and the club finished four points from safety in 23rd place.

As mid table Peterborough United were docked 19 points for making irregular payments to players, 23rd would become 22nd. That saw the Posh finish in last place, despite having scored 10 goals more than the title winners, Oxford United. Peterborough's punishment saved Mansfield's skin, but it did little for Colchester, who remained four points from safety despite the reshuffle.

First-team regular Dennis Mochan struggled to put his finger on quite why things fell apart so rapidly. There were no major player departures, no dressing room bust-ups and no fall-outs between the manager and his players. The goals just dried up at one end, and Mochan and his teammates began shipping them more regularly at the other. At one stage, Neil's son Gary recalls that the U's board had told Neil they wanted to take over player selection, to which Neil said they could but he would want to make it public information. The club duly stepped back, but it's not unreasonable to suspect that this was probably the beginning of the end for Neil Franklin's managerial reign in charge of Colchester United.

The end came just three days after the final game of the season, a 5-1 defeat at home to the soon-to-be-relegated Peterborough United in front of only 2,483 spectators. Franklin's contract was 'mutually terminated' and the four-and-a-half-year association between manager and club came to an end.

Neil would never work as a professional football manager or coach again. After almost half a decade at Colchester, he didn't rush into applying for any new positions. The year that followed was a turbulent one for managers up and down the country, and it convinced Neil that football management was neither a safe nor shrewd career path for him.

Speaking a year after his departure from Layer Road, Neil declared that he would never return to full-time football, stating that, 'There is far too much tycoonery in soccer nowadays, some men coming into the game now have never had any experience of it before, yet as soon as they arrive, they seem to know everything. The sacking of football managers has become ridiculous, only the successful survive and there can only be a very few successful teams every season.'

That was Neil Franklin talking in 1969. Half a century on, he would no doubt despair at the state of English football in 2019.

CHAPTER 20

The Legend and the Licensee

There were two sides to Neil Franklin. There was the ever-confident, composed and unflappable Neil Franklin on a football pitch, and the Neil Franklin who was charming and personable yet reserved and typically rather awkward in the face of praise or recognition away from a football pitch.

It is the second of those two sides to Neil that is the focus of this chapter of the book, although, predictably, Franklin and football are often difficult to separate for too long. As well as there being two sides to him, there were also two professions that dominated his life. The first was professional football, and the second was working as a licensee at multiple public houses. The two had overlapped during the second half of Neil's career, you may recall. The first pub he took over was the Blue Bell Inn during his time playing for Hull City, followed by the Bell & Bear shortly after he left Hull to sign for Crewe. Both of those two were based in Shelton, where Neil was born, and both lasted a few years.

When in between pubs, Neil occasionally stood in for fellow licensees whilst they were out of town. After leaving Colchester, he quickly returned to Staffordshire and moved into a new home with his wife Beryl. Within a year, an opportunity arose to take over a pub known as the Thwaites Arms in Oswaldtwistle, Lancashire, which Neil duly did. A 1969 interview with Franklin featured this opening paragraph:

'The man contently pulling pints was once the toast of every football ground in the country. Physically Neil Franklin seems scarcely to have changed since those days 20 years ago when he was probably the most skilful centre-half England has ever known, but Franklin has changed and changed a lot. He has, he believes, achieved the great psychological feat of turning his back on the game that has given him "a very good life" for most of his 47 years.'

Although Neil had left the world of day-to-day playing or managing and taken over the Thwaites Arms, it was still pushing it to say he had left football behind. As soon as he returned to Staffordshire, he began attending Stoke City matches, and in February 1969, he joined the 'Pools Panel'. Far less popular today, the football pools date back to the 1920s, with entrants betting small stakes with extremely long odds and potentially enormous returns on the outcome of top-level football. You may recall the particularly hazardous winter of 1946–47, the season in which Stoke City came so close to winning the First Division title. Well, the winter of 1962–63 was even worse, officially Britain's worst winter since 1740. This caused havoc for the Football League, as two months passed with very little football being played. The three major football pools companies decided something had to be done, so they set up the 'Pools Panel' to decide upon the outcome of postponed matches.

The original panel of six included Neil's former England teammates Tommy Lawton and Tom Finney, although both had left by the time Neil joined the panel at the start of 1969. The only founding members still on the panel by that time were former Scotland centre-half George Young and the former international referee Arthur Edwards Ellis, who had officiated at the 1950, 1954 and 1958 World Cup tournaments. Alongside Arthur, George and Neil was the unforgettable Raich Carter, pre-and post-war England forward Frank Broome, Rangers legend Ian McColl and that brilliant inside-forward Jimmy Hagan who had spent twenty years starring for Sheffield United. Stan Mortensen and George Swindon would also later join the panel, and all were handsomely rewarded for their efforts.

Then there were the not-so-infrequent returns to the field. There can have been few retired professionals in the history of the game who have taken part so often and so keenly in benefit, charity and testimonial matches as Neil Franklin. His boots were rarely given chance to gather dust, since Neil wasn't one to pass up on an opportunity to get back out onto the pitch. He remained impeccably physically fit throughout the years, and occasionally turned out in the local leagues, that is when there wasn't a famous former pal having a testimonial or some worthy cause hosting a benefit game. From a Bobby Charlton all-star game in 1973 to a Macclesfield Town vs Stoke City All-Stars tie at Moss Rose in 1979, by which time Neil was fifty-seven, there was no game too big or too small for Neil Franklin. It wasn't just football either; Neil was also partial the occasional charity or benefit cricket match.

In his later years, Neil developed a particular fondness for bowls, where he regularly represented the 'Plume of Feathers' team. The Plume of Feathers was—and indeed still is—a pub in Barlaston, Stoke-on-Trent, and is now one of two pubs owned by the actor Neil Morrissey. As well as his continued sporting interests, Neil still enjoyed a flutter on the horses. Despite his fondness for the bookies, Gary doesn't remember Neil ever betting on football, only the horses.

Having bumbled around from pub to pub as a caretaker and stand-in for a while, Neil became the permanent licensee of the Dog & Doublet Inn in Sandon, Staffordshire in 1978. He and Beryl settled there, and it would become both his longest and last association with a pub. Patrons grew familiar with the friendly face of a footballer who they had previously watched with awe from the terraces. The pub walls reflected the illustriousness of the landlord's career, with various caps, medals and general sporting memorabilia on show.

This was in stark contrast to the unassuming nature of Neil himself, who was gradually becoming less and less recognisable, as the fleeting fame that football lends to even its most accomplished of exponents began to diminish. Neil was acutely aware and entirely at ease with this being the case; celebrity had never particularly suited him. Even during his playing days, Neil wrote the following:

> I knew that my past reputation would not help me one little bit, for the average sporting follower, or rather sporting follower, has an incredibly short memory. When you are on top you are his idol, he worships the ground you walk on, he writes to you, he cheers you, he greets you in the street.
>
> But once you are out of the game you are out of the limelight, and overnight you can be forgotten. That is not just a peculiar phenomenon of football. It applies to all sport and, indeed, all branches of the world of entertainment. There is nothing more 'ex' than an ex-entertainer.

Franklin was referring to his time in exile after returning from Bogotá, but it was even truer of a retired professional who hadn't played top-flight football for three decades. Of course, football fans of a sufficient vintage would still wax lyrical about Neil Franklin, but with many too young to have seen him play and with little surviving footage to substantiate the testaments of his ability, football was quickly moving on from Franklin, Carter and Lawton.

After all, every generation brings new greats, and British football had not been short of stars in that time. Moore, Charlton and Hurst had all achieved something the likes of Wright, Finney and Matthews never could—getting their hands on the World Cup, whilst Jimmy Greaves outscored (in terms of goals in a single season) any other post-war striker at the age of twenty-one. Then came the superstardom of George Best, who achieved a whole new level of fame and celebrity outside of the game. The 1970s heralded the arrival of Keegan and Dalglish, followed by Souness, Rush, Hoddle and Lineker in the 80s.

Add in the fact that there was so little surviving footage of the players from Matthews and Franklin's day and it's easy to see why their talents faded into footballing folklore more rapidly than those who followed. Neil wasn't totally banished to the footballing record books though. Fans, coaches and journalists from his era were always on hand to ensure that the legend of England's greatest defender was not fully forgotten. In 1972, the now defunct Saturday paper *Sports Argus* suggested that Jack Charlton and Roy McFarland were 'two of the most skilful pivots this country has produced since Neil Franklin.' In 1977, the *Liverpool Echo* described Anfield's latest centre-back signing Alan Hansen as 'a player in a similar mould' to Neil Franklin, adding that the Scot was 'a joy to watch'. Two years, one First Division title and one European Cup later, the same newspaper described Hansen as 'faultless', and drew comparisons with Franklin once again.

These would be the kind of sporadic mentions of Neil Franklin in newspapers from now on. No longer the toast of every club and pub the nation over, but instead a yardstick by which all current and future centre-halves would be measured for those old enough to have seen him play. It had started in the 1950s whilst Neil was still playing, when Ronnie Cope of Manchester United was compared to Neil in terms of his movement and interceptions by the *Daily Mirror*, first in 1958 and once again in 1960. That's the first recorded example I can find, but there were plenty more to come. In 1964, the *Coventry Evening Telegraph* described Sunderland legend Charlie Hurley as being 'on a par with Neil Franklin', who the writer described as the greatest centre-half he had previously witnessed. In 1968, it was Joe Mercer in the *Newcastle Evening Chronicle* claiming Tommy Booth was 'the best ball-playing centre-half since Neil Franklin and Stan Cullis'. A year later, it was Don Revie calling Roy McFarland the best footballing pivot since Franklin in the *Sports Argus*, and yet more comparisons with the Derby man were printed in the *Liverpool Echo* in 1971. We could go on . . .

ENGLAND'S GREATEST DEFENDER

Of all the records I have trawled through, there is no player who has been as frequently likened to Franklin as Roy McFarland. The comparisons were so plentiful that I thought it worthwhile to reach out to Roy, who now sits on the board of directors at Derby County. Roy told me he was aware of the comparisons, and that it had been picked up by the local press. Born in 1948, McFarland had never seen Franklin play, neither in the flesh nor on the television. Roy did meet Neil once though, having been introduced at a match during the two-time Division One winner's own managerial career. 'What a nice man he was,' Roy began, before going on. 'But, he was, well . . . He went off to Colombia, didn't he?' Almost seventy years on and the move still seemed slightly taboo, or at least the inflection in Roy's voice made it seem so.

After confirming that Neil had indeed left Stoke City to go to Colombia, and providing Roy with some context, he described Neil as 'a brave man'. There's certainly a case to be made for Franklin and the other Bogotá Bandits having greatly accelerated the abolition of the maximum wage and a footballer's right to greater self-determination. When John Charles left Leeds United to earn more money at Juventus just seven years after Neil signed for Santa Fe, few were outraged, and many more followed.

The aforementioned Don Revie, formerly a teammate of Neil's at Hull turned successful coach at Leeds United, was one of the biggest figures in football keeping the Franklin name alive. On Boxing Day 1971, Revie wrote a column in the *Aberdeen Evening Press* on his 'Great Britons XI', challenging readers to come up with an XI that could beat his dream team. With a blend of stars from Revie's playing days like Tommy Doherty and Tom Finney, to a couple of his Leeds United cohorts Billy Bremner and Johnny Giles, with even the great Dave Mackay from Leeds' rivals Derby County making the cut.

At centre-half, it was of course Neil Franklin, who Revie said, 'stands out as easily the most skilful pivot Britain has produced'.

THE LEGEND AND THE LICENSEE

These are the other occasions in which we see Neil Franklin cropping up in publications fairly sporadically up until the early 2000s. A limited edition book entitled *The Greats From The Golden Age of Soccer*, published by Endurance Limited, brilliantly compiled a list of 'Ultimate XIs' or 'Dream Teams' from Britain's finest footballers from the pre-war era up until the early 1970s.

The players asked to name their favourite XIs, of which Franklin is one, reads like a who's who of pre-1970 British greats. From Dixie Dean to Bobby Charlton, it's a pretty comprehensive collection, which ends with a best of the best 'Players' Selection', made up of the players in each position who received the most inclusions. Some of the stars who chose Franklin as their centre-half included Tom Finney, Jimmy Armfield, Billy Wright, Cliff Bastin, Peter Doherty, Johnny Carey, Stan Mortensen, Len Shackleton, Wilf Mannion, Billy Liddell, Nat Lofthouse, Tommy Lawton and Gordon Banks. That's right—Gordon Banks omitted his own England teammate and captain Bobby Moore in favour of Franklin! All that meant Neil took the number five shirt at centre-half in the overall players' XI, alongside Carey, Hapgood, Blanchflower, Mercer, Carter, Doherty, Matthews, Lawton and Finney, whilst it was a tie between Gordon Banks and Frank Swift for the goalkeeping position, and Bobby Charlton and John Charles as the lone reserve.

Neil retired for good when he left the Dog & Doublet after six years at the pub in 1984. He saw out the rest of his days with his wife Beryl, occasionally attending games at the Victoria Ground, particularly after Peter Coates became the club's majority shareholder in 1989. He continued to make sporadic appearances in veteran games until he absolutely had to call it a day, at which point bowls somewhat took the place of the sport that had dominated Franklin's life for half a century. He maintained his love of an occasional flutter on the horses, often heading down to the bookies with his old pal Dennis Herod to do just that.

Franklin died on 9 February 1996. In the last couple of years of his life, Neil—like so many former footballers, particularly of his generation—began to suffer from dementia. Most commonly the result of Alzheimer's disease, there is still a great deal we have to learn about the devastating neurodegenerative condition, and the understanding of the disease was far more rudimentary in the mid-1990s when it began to affect Neil.

One thing we do now know, following extensive research into the subject, is that the repeated heading of a football is likely to increase one's chances of suffering from what is now Britain's biggest killer, having recently overtaken heart disease. If modern balls can cause long-term damage to the human brain, it is little wonder that the balls used during Neil's career, which could become much heavier in wet conditions, resulted in Franklin and so many of his contemporaries suffering from serious mental health problems.

When Neil left for Bogotá, the world record transfer fee stood at £26,500, and the maximum wage was restricted to £12 a week. By the time he had hung up his boots, Luis Suárez had been transferred to Inter Milan for more than £150,000 and Johnny Haynes was earning £100 a week at Fulham. John Charles, Jimmy Greaves, Gerry Hitchens and Joe Baker could all earn even more than that with bonuses, having left the English game to play in Italy's more lucrative Serie A, and by 1996—the year of Neil's death—Alan Shearer joined Newcastle United for £15 million, signing a contract reportedly worth £34,000 a week.

In the time that I have been writing this book, the world record fee has risen from £89 million to £198 million, a teenager has been signed for £166 million and Liverpool have paid £75 million for a centre-back. There are now footballers earning more than £500,000 a week from their clubs. Between their playing salary, image rights and various endorsement deals, we are not far off the world's first £1 million a week footballer.

Neil's defection to Bogotá in 1950 had a detrimental effect on his career, but it had a hugely beneficial impact on the lives of footballers for generations to come. In a journey which started with Billy Meredith and ended, perhaps, with Jean-Marc Bosman, Neil Franklin played a significant role in freeing footballers from restrictions over their wages and movement.

Despite still having a reputation as poor travellers, there are now English footballers playing everywhere from the Philippines and Australia, to Norway and the United States. There is even one playing in Colombia.

ACKNOWLEDGEMENTS

This book would not have been possible, or at least it wouldn't have been very long, were it not for the invaluable help of a number of people. To those who were kind enough to lend their time and share their memories, and to those who put me in touch with people who were able to do so, I am eternally grateful. I must first thank Gary Franklin, Neil Franklin's son, and the rest of the Franklin family, without whom this book would never have got off the ground. Special thanks also go to Charles Owen Potts, Ashling Bowles, Pete Smith, Mike Clark, Keith Goalen, Dennis Mochan, Bert Mozley, Bernard Morgan, Peter Coates, Fraser Nicholson, Ian Brown, Marcus Heap, Ian Watts, Roy McFarland, Peter Morse, Anton Rippon, David Bernard, Dave Powell, Ken Roberts, David Instone, Sean Eratt, Mark Tattersall, Geoff Andrew, James Morgan, Geoff Bielby, the Hull City Supporters' Trust and all my family and friends. To anyone who has contributed in any way who I have missed off that list, I offer my sincere apologies.

I would also like to acknowledge and offer my thanks to previous publications that proved to be very useful resources in the writing of this book, such as *Bogota Bandit* (Richard Adamson, Mainstream Publishing), *Golden Boy* (Nick Varley, Aurum Press), *The Way It Was* (Stanley Matthews, Headline), *My Autobiography* (Tom Finney, Headline), *My Twenty Years of Soccer* (Tommy Lawton, Heirloom Modern World Library) and most notably of all, *Soccer At Home And Abroad* (Neil Franklin, Stanley Paul).